The Concept of Revelation in Judaism, Christianity and Islam

# Key Concepts in Interreligious Discourses

Edited by
Georg Tamer

In cooperation with
Katja Thörner

**Volume 1**

# The Concept of Revelation in Judaism, Christianity and Islam

Edited by Georges Tamer

DE GRUYTER

ISBN 978-3-11-042518-5
e-ISBN (PDF) 978-3-11-047605-7
e-ISBN (EPUB) 978-3-11-047479-4
ISSN 2513-1117

**Library of Congress Control Number: 2020932542**

**Bibliographic information published by the Deutsche Nationalbibliothek**
The Deutsche Nationalbibliothek lists this publication in the Deutsche Nationalbibliografie; detailed bibliographic data are available on the Internet at http://dnb.dnb.de


Printing and Binding: LSC Communications, United States

www.degruyter.com

# Preface

This is the first volume in the book series "Key Concepts in Interreligious Discourses" (KCID), which publishes the results of the conferences organized by the Research Unit of the same name established at the Friedrich-Alexander-University Erlangen-Nuremberg. The conference on the concept of revelation in Judaism, Christianity and Islam was held in Erlangen on July 21–22, 2016.

The Research Unit KCID offers an innovative approach for studying the development of the three interconnected religions: Judaism, Christianity and Islam. With this aim in mind, KCID analyzes the history of ideas in each of these three religions, always considering the tradition of interreligious exchange and appropriation of these very ideas. In doing so, KCID investigates the foundations of religious thought, thereby establishing an "archaeology of religious knowledge" in order to make manifest certain commonalities and differences between the three religions via dialogic study of their conceptual history. Thus, KCID intends to contribute to an intensive academic engagement with interreligious discourses in order to uncover mutually intelligible theoretical foundations and increase understanding between these different religious communities in the here and now. Moreover, KCID aims to highlight how each religion's self-understanding can contribute to mutual understanding and peace between the three religious communities in the world.

In order to explore key concepts in Judaism, Christianity and Islam, KCID organizes conferences individually dedicated to specific concepts. A renowned set of researchers from various disciplines explore these concepts from the viewpoints of each of the three religions. The results of each conference are published in a volume appearing in the abovementioned book series. Particularly salient selections from each volume are made available online in Arabic, English and German.

In this fashion, the Research Unit KCID fulfills its aspirations not only by reflecting on central religious ideas amongst a small group of academic specialists, but also by disseminating such ideas in a way that will appeal to the broader public. Academic research that puts itself at the service of society is vital in order to counteract powerful contemporary trends toward a form of segregation rooted in ignorance. Mutual respect and acceptance amongst religions is thereby strengthened. Such a result is guaranteed due to the methodology deployed by the research unit, namely the dialogic investigation of the history of concepts, as documented in the present volume on the concept of revelation.

https://doi.org/10.1515/9783110476057-001

I wish to thank Dr. Albrecht Döhnert, Dr. Sophie Wagenhofer and their assistants at the publishing house De Gruyter for their competent caretaking of this volume and the entire book series.

Georges Tamer
Erlangen, September 2019

# Table of Contents

Frederek Musall

# The Concept of Revelation in Judaism

*"She is a tree of life to them that lay hold upon her, and happy is everyone that holds her fast; her ways are ways of pleasantness, and all her paths are peace." (Proverbs 3:17–18)*[1]

### A Preliminary Note:

*While Jews and Christians share most of the biblical books, they fundamentally differ in questions of canon. A canon is not just an order of sequence, but also a theological construct, shaping the very understanding of how to approach and read texts; it represents a principle theological decision and conception.*

*The Jewish biblical canon is a tripart arrangement, comprising the Torah (Pentateuch) Nevi'im (Prophets) and Ketuvim (Writings) and commonly referred to by its acronym TaNa"Kh. Unlike the Christian biblical canon, the Jewish canon is not structured chronologically, but rather reflects three different stages of significance: At the core is the Torah, the immediate revelation given at Mount Sinai; next are the works of the prophets, which as mediated prophecies often recall the teachings of the Torah; finally come the Writings, which instead of representing prophecies express human reflections of the encounter with and experience of the Divine.*

*I deem it important to raise awareness of this, as our respective understanding of revelation is shaped by the canonic conceptions and connotations we have in mind – conceptions and connotations that might lead to misunderstandings when being under the impression that Jews and Christians basically read the same biblical texts.*

---

**1** Here in the reversed sequence of the verses, commonly sung in many Ashkenazi synagogues when the *Torah* scrolls are returned to the ark after their public reading. In Jewish tradition, the *Torah* has been compared to the "tree of life" (*etz chayyim*) in the Story of Creation (Gen. 2:9). For almost two years I lived on Shady Avenue in Squirrel Hill, Pittsburgh, right across from the Tree of Life – Or L'Simcha synagogue on Wilkins Avenue. While it was not the synagogue that I attended (as a popular Jewish saying/joke goes), many of my friends and neighbors did. But on some occasions, like for example the community-wide *Tiqqun Leyl Shavu'ot*, the night of learning on the holiday of Shavuot, even we students from the National Conference of Synagogue Youth (NCSY), the Orthodox youth movement, went there to celebrate the giving of the *Torah* at Mount Sinai by listening to *shi'urim* ("lectures") and enjoying *kosher* cheese cake. When the anti-Semitic hate-crime took place on October 27th 2018, the vile and senseless murder of eleven innocent people that peacefully attended Shabbat morning services that day, it really struck home. To their blessed memory, this essay is dedicated.

https://doi.org/10.1515/9783110476057-002

# 1 Remarks and Frameworks

## 1.1 Introductory Remarks

According to our modern way of understanding the order of things, said things have to fit into boxes, fall into categories, or apply to notions. Boxes, categories, and notions are necessary because they enable us to speak and relate to one another about how we perceive, process, comprehend, and interpret the world surrounding us. In other words: They allow for a basic orientation in a complex world. There appears to be, however, an epistemological drawback to this: All these boxes, categories, and notions we operate with, as well as the meanings and connotations we ascribe to them, tend to eventually become self-evident. Self-evidence often suggests that something speaks for itself, having a clear meaning, and that no further explanations are needed. Yet if we actually bother to take a closer look, we will eventually find out that this is where things start to get complicated...

Take for example 'religion': We all seem to have a more or less clear idea of what is meant by it; most of us even tend to have some kind of position towards it. Still, in our understanding of religion we often differ because, in fact, it very much depends on how we approach it, what experiences we have, and what knowledge we possess.[2] The study of religion as an academic discipline, for instance, offers a variety of etic approaches towards, and definitions of, religion – for example, discerning essential features (substantialist definition), asking about social functions (functionalist definition), or analyzing discursive formations (cultural studies' approach). However, the way one methodically approaches religion must by no means reflect how people who practice or identify with a certain religion understand their own religious beliefs and practices. Theology, on the other hand, as an emic scholarly endeavor, does not necessarily need to concern itself with the question of what religion is or how it can be objectively defined. Its task is rather to reflect upon its religious self-understanding and self-determination or to formulate its fundamental beliefs and doctrines. Accordingly, the study of religion and theology differ in their respective vantage points and methods. However, to simply call the former an objective method and the latter a subjective one would miss a crucial point: each respective approach does not only offer a particular perspective, but also tells a particular story. This is a narrative to which we can relate (one that in turn allows us to re-

---

2 Yandell, Keith E., *Philosophy of Religion. A Contemporary Introduction*, London/New York: Routledge, 1999, 16.

late to things); a narrative we both are actively and passively embedded in; and a narrative which enables us not only to relate to the past, but to shape the here and now.

I have to admit that these epistemological reflections and considerations are owed to my own philosophical views and poststructuralist dispositions. Nevertheless I am also certain that they apply to the very task at hand: A central problem often encountered in interreligious settings is that while people might share a common language, they tend to understand and relate to ideas, concepts, and definitions quite differently. This should not come as much of a surprise: Ideas, concepts, and definitions are, after all, not only constructed, but they also come with certain connotations and associations which imply that the meanings we ascribe to things are context-dependent. We all are embedded in certain historical, social, cultural, or religious frameworks. Frameworks that often intersect. Accordingly, the semantic fields we all operate with or within are produced and shaped by our respective knowledge and experiences. So when we encounter something that is different, foreign, or new to us, we tend to rely on ideas, concepts, and definitions that we are familiar with. Martin Buber (1878 – 1965) suggested in his *I and Thou* that in encountering the other we should refrain from using any presumptions, preconceptions, or images.[3] But that is often easier said than done. Maybe instead of trying to blank them out, we should rather attempt to critically scrutinize and re-examine them, based on and shaped by our encounter and experience with the 'other'. By doing so it should become clear that ideas, concepts, and definitions are discursively constructed. They are constantly negotiated; they are contextual and flexible, rather than fixed. Because our frameworks intersect with the frameworks of the 'other,' we – through the process of discourse and negotiation – can eventually arrive at a new understanding, a new understanding not only in relation to the 'other,' but also regarding ourselves.

I guess what I am trying to say is that the understanding of the concept of revelation in Judaism as conveyed in the following is not a definition but a narrative, one constructed and shaped by my personal and professional considerations and reflections, both as a Jew and as a scholar of Jewish Studies. It is an interaction of the within and the without – the emic and the etic – as different and differing as these vantage points might be. Moreover, these two also affect my understanding of the concept of 'revelation' as well as of what 'Judaism' is.

I therefore deem it important to problematize these notions and concepts in relation to the different narratives (ontological, public, conceptual, or meta-nar-

3 Buber, Martin, *I and Thou*, London: Continuum, 2004, 13 – 15.

rative)[4] at work. After all, they not only have an impact on how one perceives the world, but also on how one relates to it or acts within it. This might also explain why hereafter I am not intending to attempt any kind of systematic-theological inquiry, as this would a) imply ordering ideas and concepts hierarchically, and b) establish and represent an ideological position. Rather I would like to try to lend a voice to the discursive polyphony, trying to capture the multi-perspectivity and multi-narrativity that, in both my personal opinion and professional understanding, makes up Judaism. This flows not just out of an appreciation for the plurality of the religious tradition that I myself am embedded in, but out of my awareness that my understanding, as articulated here, will eventually also affect the understanding of others.

## 1.2 Some General Observations on the Concept of Revelation

Like the notion and concept of religion, 'revelation' can be approached from different perspectives, with various epistemological, metaphysical, aesthetical, ethical, and religious considerations and implications coming into play.

In a classic structuralist manner, concepts or notions can best be explained in relation to their respective antonyms, which in the case of 'revelation' is 'concealment.' Taking this into consideration, its semantic field resonates that 'that-which-is-(to-be)-revealed' must have been 'concealed' or 'hidden' beforehand, yet in its current state is somehow unperceivable or inaccessible to our senses or beyond cognition. Accordingly, the state of 'concealment' does not propose an absence of 'that-which-is-(to-be)-revealed'; on the contrary, it rather suggests the presence of 'that-which-is-concealed' and has *not yet* been discerned or disclosed.

In a religious context, the concept of revelation concerns the relationship between divine and concrete reality. It is an act through which the Divine makes itself or its will known and accessible, either through an act of self-revelation or through a medium or mediator disclosing the Divine. Accordingly, revelation allows human beings to relate to the Divine. It is a mode of discerning, knowing, and communicating. Communication can take place verbally and non-verbally; it can be one-way or two-way; it can be understood directly or is in need of processing, translation, or interpretation; it occurs between the Divine and an indi-

4 Somers, Margaret R./Gibson, *Gloria D.*, "*Reclaiming the Epistemological 'Other.' Narrative* and the Social Constitution of Identity," in: Craig Calhoun (ed.), *Social Theory and the Politics of Identity*, 1994, 37–99, Oxford/Cambridge, MA: Wiley-Blackwell.

vidual or a group of people. Revelation can be natural or supernatural in origin, with the latter sometimes viewed as a superior form of knowledge within certain epistemological frameworks. Furthermore, revelation encompasses various social functions as well; it can serve as the narrative framework for a community, defining its history, its values, and its norms. It provides orientation and guidance concerning how we encounter, relate to, and interpret the world.

## 1.3 Narratives

After this brief etic approach towards the concept of revelation, let us now attempt a first take on revelation in Judaism from an emic perspective. Revelation is generally considered a core principle of Judaism, even described by R. David Novak as the most important doctrine for Jewish theology, as, after all, Jewish theology is mainly concerned with interpretation of the divinely revealed text, the Torah.[5] But is it not – conceptually speaking – too narrow to simply confine revelation to a single text?

The German-Jewish philosopher and theologian Franz Rosenzweig (1886–1929) in his seminal work *The Star of Redemption* (1921) distinguished between a *general* and a *specific* meaning of revelation.[6] General revelation is that which allows the transcendent God to relate to the immanent world. This way of relating through revelation is reified in three moments in history, namely creation, revelation, and redemption, which for Rosenzweig are the main themes of the biblical narrative. However, this triadic process of creation–revelation–redemption is for him more than just a concept; it rather constitutes the foundational framework of reality itself. Rosenzweig's specific understanding of revelation, on the other hand, relates to the notion of 'Torah,' yet he often uses it in a rather indeterminate way, as it appears that he does not want to simply confine the notion of 'Torah' to the *Chumash* or *Pentateuch.*[7] Rather, the other books of the Hebrew Bible along with the classical works of rabbinical literature are all for him sources of revelation.

In other words, revelation is more than just *a* text. It can refer to a) said textual source, the Torah; b) the experience of receiving the Torah (popularly

5 Novak, David, "Revelation," in: Nicholas de Lange/Miri Freud-Kandel (eds), *Modern Judaism. An Oxford Guide*, 278–289, Oxford/New York: Oxford University Press, 2008, 278.

6 Rosenzweig, Franz, *The Star of Redemption*, transl. Barbara E. Galli, Madison, WI: University of Wisconsin Press, 2005, 169–220.

7 Benjamin, Mara H., *Rosenzweig's Bible. Reinventing Scripture for Jewish Modernity*, New York: Cambridge University Press, 2009, 142–143.

termed as the "standing at Mount Sinai (*ma'amad har Sinay*)" or the "giving of the *Torah* (*matan Torah*)"); and c) that which follows from the Torah, namely the interpretations and commentary literature. However, the Torah is more than just this: God reveals the Torah at Mount Sinai, but through the revelation of the Torah God reveals Himself and makes His will be known. The Torah gives the account of God's interaction with His creation and His acting in history, yet the Torah is also the medium through which God interacts with His creation and acts in history. It is therefore the object, content, and method of revelation.

In order to make these rather abstract assumptions more tangible, I would like to sketch out a short narrative approach to how the concept of revelation is commonly presented in 'Jewish tradition'[8] (a term I actually prefer to 'Judaism' when speaking about religious concepts and ideas, as it gives fuller expression to the relationship between foundational literary texts and historical experience). The biblical text itself presents various types of revelatory experiences: It starts off in the book of Genesis with God as the Creator revealing Himself to His creation and interacting with a few significant figures like Adam, Enoch, Noah, Abraham, Isaac, and Jacob, sometimes directly (Gen. 12:1–4; 17:1–21; 18:17–33; 22:1–2), sometimes through intermediaries (Gen. 16:7–8; 18:1–16; 22:11–12; 32:22–32), through visions (Gen. 15:1; Gen. 35:1–15), or dreams (Gen. 28:10–19). In the book of Exodus, however, revelation is taken to a whole new level, namely when God reveals himself not only to certain individuals, but to an entire group of people at and through the giving of the Torah at Mount Sinai (Exod. 19–24). It is here in the wilderness of Sinai where the covenant is made between God and the Israelites, who have been chosen by God to become "a kingdom of priests and a holy nation (*mamlekhet kohanim ve-goy kadosh*)" (Exod. 19:5–6). Due to the covenant, they are henceforth duty-bound to follow God's will, which is set down in the laws and practices revealed at Mount Sinai, and is according to rabbinic tradition transmitted in both "written (*bi-khtav*)" and "oral (*be-al-peh*)" form (*Pirqey Avot* 1:1; b. *Shabbat* 31a; *RaSH"Y* on Deut. 30:14).

But over the course of time, the Israelites more and more neglect these laws and practices and stray off the path God has destined them to walk. Once again, God reveals himself to chosen individuals, to prophets (*nevi'im*) whose task it is to act as intermediaries and convey God's messages to the Israelites, warning them that they need to change their ways or else face the consequences of their actions. The destruction of the First Temple in the year 586 BCE and the

8 On this matter, see Rotenstreich, Nathan, *Tradition and Reality. The Impact of History on Modern Jewish Thought*, New York/Toronto: Random House, 1972, particularly 7–18.

subsequent Babylonian Captivity mark a decisive turning point in Jewish history: While it is generally interpreted as a sign of God's punishment, it does not amount to Him forsaking His people. Rather, God remains with Israel in exile. In His revelations to the prophets during the exilic period, He strikes a new tone: Prophecies encouraging the Israelites to trust God in bringing about imminent redemption. Most prominently, the prophecies of Ezekiel and Isaiah speak of national and religious restoration with the return of the captives to the land of Israel and the ultimate rebuilding of the Temple in Jerusalem.

After the end of prophetic activity, which according to rabbinic tradition ceased to exist with the last prophets Haggai, Zechariah, and Malachi (t. *Sotah* 13:2–3; b. *Bava Batra* 14a; b. *Yoma* 21b; b. *Sanhedrin* 65b), the rabbis eventually took it upon themselves to act as legitimate successors of the prophets (b. *Bava Batra* 12a). In fact, according to rabbinic understanding the *talmidey chakhamim* (the Torah scholars), with their knowledge and understanding of the revealed text, are held in higher regard than a prophet (*Sifrey Numbers* § 112; b. *Horayot* 13a). Nevertheless, the rabbis were well aware that their own historical and social contexts differed from those of the Bible. Their complex discourses reflect their endeavors to relate the biblical tradition to their respective actual situations, thereby upholding and guaranteeing the continuity of a dynamic tradition commonly referred to as the "chain of tradition" (*shalshelet ha-qabbalah*) (*Pirqey Avot* 1:1–18, 2:8). The Torah hence has to be understood as a complex frame of reference, comprised not only of the *Written Torah* and the *Oral Torah*, both revealed at Mount Sinai, but furthermore of all the interpretations, contributions, and innovations made by the rabbis over the course of time as articulated in their diverse legal, theological, philosophical, or mystical writings. According to the rabbinic understanding, as a result the concept of Torah encompasses various generations with different religious needs, concerns, and sensibilities, who have faced different situations and challenges, coming up with different interpretations and decisions.[9] It allows for articulating the existing anew and to actualize that which is fundamentally given forever.

## 1.4 Categorizations: Judaism as a 'Revealed Religion'(?)

As we have seen so far, revelation (comprised of – according to rabbinic tradition – both the *Written Torah* and the *Oral Torah*) makes up the core of classical Jew-

9 Hartman, David, *Israelis and the Jewish Tradition. An Ancient People Debating Its Future*, New Haven, CN: Yale University Press, 2000, 161.

ish belief. But is it therefore objective to characterize and define Judaism as a 're-vealed religion,' as often referred to and portrayed in respective literature? In other words: Is Judaism solely based on revelation or only defined by it?

A closer examination shows that the very term 'revealed religion' is in itself not unproblematic; it resonates with much of the critical attitude of the Enlightenment towards the concept of supernatural revelation as well as any form of doctrinal dependence on it. That is not to say that there ever existed one unified position on this matter, as Enlightenment thought is in fact comprised of a variety of opinions and positions towards religion, ranging from deism to fideism to atheism. What, however, somehow brought together these different views was that they were challenging the truth-claims constitutional for certain religious beliefs and doctrines. Due to new scientific discoveries and developments, the classically defined relationship between reason and revelation as sources of knowledge and truth was up for a critical re-examination. While it had been a central subject of medieval philosophical-theological discourse – with thinkers like R. Saʿadiyah Gaon (882–942), R. Abraham ibn Daud (ca. 1110–ca. 1180), or R. Moses Maimonides (1138–1204) springing to mind – this relationship had in many instances been defined hierarchically, with philosophy as reason-based knowledge often ending up as the handmaiden of theology as revelation-based knowledge. Enlightenment thinkers set out to fundamentally change that by attempting to divide the two concepts from one another. Not only did they establish reason as an independent source of knowledge, but due to its ascribed universal accessibility they furthermore declared it as the superior form of knowledge as well. This subsequently led to a skeptical stance towards the very idea or belief in some form of supernatural revelation. In their engagement with religion, the deists elaborated on the idea of a 'natural religion', which is not dependent on any kind of supernatural revelation and solely based on man's faculty of reason. They thereby ultimately reduced religion to some core beliefs like the existence of God, moral duties and the immortality of the soul, while getting rid of all those elements which they considered irrational, supernatural, superstitious, or legalistic.

In its struggle for the fundamental principles of individual freedom and equality, the Enlightenment's attacks were first and foremost aimed at the validity and authority of Christianity's truth-claims as well as the Church as an institution of political power; yet it was Judaism that had to take the blow. After all, for many leading Enlightenment figures including Voltaire (1694–1778), Hermann Samuel Reimarus (1694–1768), Immanuel Kant (1724–1804), or Friedrich Schiller (1759–1805), Judaism was synonymous with the "Old Testament," embodying the very belief in supernatural revelation which they intellectually sought to overcome. The assumed superiority of universal reason over a particular and supernatural revelation often resulted in a reductionist view of Jewish beliefs and practices. In fact, Judaism eventually became the main representation of the 'other', serving as a categorical lens through which Enlightenment thinkers defined and classified 'other' forms of religious beliefs that in their opinion did not conform with European, Western, and Christian ideas and articulations.

Despite the initiatives of people like John Toland (1670 – 1772), Gotthold Ephraim Lessing (1729 – 1781), or Christian Wilhelm Dohm (1751 – 1820), the overall Enlightenment attitude towards Judaism and the Jews was rather quite paternalistic, condescending, and prejudiced. Nevertheless, its ideas of human equality and emancipation encouraged Jews to embrace and become engaged in its own project of social and cultural transformation. Attempting to reform Judaism on their own terms, prominent representatives of the *Haskalah*, the Jewish Enlightenment, like Moses Mendelssohn (1729 – 1786) or his associate Naphtali Herz (Hartwig) Wessely (1725 – 1804), were facing the challenge to articulate a new Jewish self-understanding that would allow them to remain committed to both their philosophical ideals and their Jewish religion. In his opus magnum *Jerusalem, or, On Religious Power and Judaism* (1783) Mendelssohn eventually argued that Judaism could and should not be defined as a 'revealed religion', but rather as a 'revealed legislation', which is legally binding solely to the Jewish people.[10] He furthermore expressed his belief that Judaism essentially combined both universal rational principles and particular revealed laws. Or to be more precise: it entails particular revealed laws, which in turn lead to universal rational principles. By doing so, he picked up on the conception of Baruch Spinoza (1632 – 1677) that the Bible, despite being primarily a particular political document, indeed contained universal truths. Yet unlike Spinoza and many Enlightenment thinkers in his wake, Mendelssohn did not consider the Jewish 'ceremonial laws' obsolete, but rather understood them as an educational medium to teach about principal moral and social norms.[11] In a similar fashion, Wessely distinguished in his *Divrey Shalom ve-Emet* ("Words of Peace and Truth"; 1782) between the universally accessible "Law of Man" (*Torat ha-adam*) and the "Law of God" (*Torat ha-Elokim*[12]) accessible through revealed knowledge, though he gave clear preference to the former as he actually deemed it being a prerequisite to the latter.

---

**10** Mendelssohn, Moses, *Jerusalem. Or, on Religious Power and Judaism*, Hanover: NH & London: University of New England Press, for Brandeis University Press, 1983, 97.

**11** Eisen, Arnold, "Divine Legislation as 'Ceremonial Script.' *Mendelssohn* on the Commandments," in: *AJS Review* 15, no. 2 (Fall 1990), 239 – 67.

**12** It is traditionally customary not to spell out the name of God, even a transliterated form, hence it is spelled here with a 'k' instead of 'h.'

The educational reforms promoted by *Haskalah* must be understood as a Jewish reaction to the challenge of modernity. They were first and foremost aimed at determining a new place for Jews within the intellectual parameters and social frameworks defined by secular Western-European societies. This not only fundamentally changed Jewish self-understanding in regard to the new social and cultural options that it had opened up, but it also brought conflicting priorities and loyalties to the surface, which eventually made it necessary to find and articulate new expressions of Judaism.

## 1.5 Crossroads

The Enlightenment – and in its wake the *Haskalah* – also had a profound impact on Jewish interpretations and understandings of revelation. Moses Mendelssohn still understood the 'revealed legislation' – and the respective *halakhic* (legal) system based upon it – as binding for Jews, yet to many of his co-religionists his overall stance towards Jewish tradition seemed inconsistent: The traditionalists feared that Mendelssohn's emphasis on the universal values would eventually give rise to a downplay of Jewish religious practices, whereas the more liberal voices who advocated a reform of Judaism ultimately criticized him for letting himself still be confined to the restrictive authoritative framework of traditional-normative Judaism.

Consequently, Mendelssohn's successors explored different options, which not only concerned their take on modernity and progress, but also their approach towards revelation as a source of Jewish self-understanding. R. Abraham Geiger (1810 – 1874) for example, one of the founding father of the Reform movement in Germany, was not so much concerned with the question of defining the relationship between reason and revelation, but was rather interested in what role revelation could play for the individual consciousness of a Jew. For him the idea of revelation was no longer tied to particular legal traditions, but rather found expression in the concept of a 'religious genius' of the Jewish people.[13] This 'religious genius' implied a consciousness of the God-idea shared by all Jews, which ultimately expressed itself not only as a special insight, but as a creativity aimed at aspiring to and achieving a greater good. In Geiger's understand-

13 Grözinger, Karl E., "Abraham Geigers theologische Wende vor dem Hintergrund der neuzeitlichen Debatte von Religion und Vernunft," in: Christian Wiese/Walter Homolka/Thomas Brechenmacher (eds), *Jüdische Existenz in der Moderne. Abraham Geiger und die Wissenschaft des Judentums*, 15 – 36, Berlin: De Gruyter, 2013, 34 – 35.

ing, revelation was a 'religious idea' with ethical implications rather than a legal tradition.

Counter to this view, Geiger's contemporary R. Shimshon Raphael Hirsch (1808–1888), the founding figure of so-called Neo-Orthodoxy, argued that "since the completion of the Written and Oral Law at Horeb, the determination of its content is not tied to prophetic inspiration from heaven".[14] In other words, the ultimate authority of Jewish law derives from its very divine origin, which furthermore accounts for its self-consistency, meaning that it does not depend on any kind of 'religious genius.' Hirsch furthermore distinguished between four general forms or sources of revelation, namely nature, history, law, and consciousness, all of which serve as enabling structures to allow for mankind's improvement and ultimate realization as God's partner in creation. For Hirsch, revelation is all about a consequent actualization of the revealed.

The main difference between Geiger and Hirsch – who are taken here illustratively for the simple reason that they are former friends turned rivals – is that, according to Geiger's understanding, actualization is not dependent on any kind of tradition, while for Hirsch any attempt of actualization must always be conscious of and therefore corresponding to tradition.

Yet despite their apparent differences, Geiger's and Hirsch's approaches can nevertheless both be characterized as optimistic, as they share the principal belief in the transformative process of actualization through revelation, which allows for the ultimate realization of human perfection.

However, this optimistic outlook of the 19th century came eventually to an abrupt end: The traumatic events and crisis during the end of the 19th and first half of the 20th century – from the fallout of the Dreyfus affair to the total collapse of Western civilization and its values through World War I and Word War II, and the systematic persecution and murder of 6 million Jews during the Shoah – deeply upset and distressed Jewish thinkers concerned with these questions. Consequential responses to these developments and experiences demanded conceptual shifts in Jewish theological thought. Particularly those commonly labeled as "Jewish existentialists" (comprising thinkers as diverse as Martin Buber, Franz Rosenzweig, R. Abraham Joshua Heschel (1907–1972), Emmanuel Lévinas (1906–1995), and R. Joseph B. Soloveitchik (1903–1993)) took it upon themselves to explore and articulate new directions in Jewish philosophical-theological thought, thereby putting a stronger emphasis on the human existential dimension and relevance of revelation.

---

**14** Hirsch, Samson Raphael, *Horeb. A Philosophy of Jewish Laws and Observances*, transl. Isidore Grunfeld, London: Soncino Press, 1962, 21.

Yet while these voices are presently still echoing, it appears that today the overall belief in revelation plays an even less important role within the broader framework of what Judaism is in modern times, as ethno-national, political, cultural, or even humanistic ideological articulations and positions have opened up new alternatives of Jewish self-understanding and self-determination. Moreover, it is the hybridity of these possible self-definitions that poses a challenge to understanding Judaism not only from without, but also from within. Today, to be a Jew can encompass many things – many of them even concurrently – as the quest for individuation is shifting more and more from the collective to the individual. With these developments typical for Western culture in mind, the main question – to pick upon the provocative book title of the Israeli historian of philosophy Menachem Kellner (b. 1946) – maybe has to be: Is a Jew still obligated to believe in anything?[15]

## 1.6 Summary

To briefly sum up for the moment: We have seen that the concept and corresponding understanding of revelation in Judaism is not a static one, but over the course of history underwent various (re-)interpretations and transformations, making it rather difficult to come up with something like a single precise definition. Yet apart from the contextualizations we need to make in order to discern its respective meanings and connotations, at the same time we must be aware that revelation can conceptually resonate and therefore represent many different things simultaneously: A relationship between divine and concrete reality, a medium of transmission, a process of transmission, a mode of knowing, an orientation, an act of uncovering.

It furthermore should have become clear that we have to carefully distinguish between the concept of revelation in Judaism and the concept of Judaism as a 'revealed religion', as the latter is for many reasons not unproblematic, despite some recent scholarly attempts to justify such conceptions.[16]

The dynamic, discursive, and non-dogmatic framework Judaism provides is nowadays challenged by needs for and expectations of a clear orientation in re-

15 Kellner, Menachem M., *Must a Jew Believe in Anything?*, Oxford/New York: The Littman Library of Jewish Civilization, ²2006.

16 See for example Fleischacker, Samuel, *Divine Teaching and the Way of the World. A Defense of Revealed Religion*, New York: Oxford University Press, 2011; see also the critique by Melamed, Yitzhak Y., "Review of Samuel Fleischacker, Divine Teaching and the Way of the World (Oxford University Press, 2011)," in: *Philosophical Review* 125 (1/2016), 151–154.

gard to a world that is perceived as having become more and more complex. Yet the need for clarity, often due to a loss of knowledge and an uncertainty about one's tradition, threatens the very tolerance of ambiguity that in my eyes makes up Judaism. Maybe that is why instead of offering definitions and classifications, as scholars usually do, I would rather like to sensitize the readers to the complexities of what Judaism was in the past, what is at present, and how it will eventually develop and articulate itself in the future. I do so because I not only think that clear-cut categories fall short of adequately capturing its multifacetedness, but because it seems more than odd and questionable to me to override the varieties of Jewish religious experiences and self-determination by trying to fit them into said categories.

I consider it important to raise awareness of these issues made above due to the discursive framework provided in this book. To create a sensitivity and appreciation for the key concepts in inter-religious dialogue, we are beforehand tasked to sincerely scrutinize and explicate out the very criteria that we apply to our respective identifications, assessments, and definitions.

# 2 Concepts and Ideas

## 2.1 Notions

It might prove interesting to some readers that there exists no word that would adequately translate as "revelation" in the Hebrew Bible. Rather, the three Hebrew verb roots *g-l-h* (גלה; "to uncover", "to reveal"), *r-'a-h* (ראה; "to see"), and *y-d-'a* (ידע; "to know") are frequently used (particularly in their reflexive *nif'al* forms) to describe the human encounter with and experience of the Divine, differing in their respective semantics and thus offering different connotations of how revelation might actually occur.

The verb *g-l-h* (גלה, "to uncover", "to reveal") generally refers to forms of sensory awareness and perception. For example as used in the phrase *galah ozen p'* (literally "to open up someone's ear," "to disclose something to somebody") in order to reveal something to someone (1Sam. 9:15; 20:2, 12, 13; 22:8, 17; Ruth 4:4). It is frequently used to describe the act of God revealing himself, either to a prophetic mediator (1Sam. 9:15; Isa. 22:14) or to an ordinary human being (Job 33:16; 36:10, 15). In other places, it represents God's way of bestowing prophecy (1Sam. 2:27; 3:7, 21; Amos 3:7; Dan. 10:1). While in the verses referred to above it often indicates an auditory experience of the Divine, it can also refer to visual experiences, as for example in Jacob's theophanic encounter at Bet El ("[B]ecause there God was revealed unto him (*ki sham niglu elav ha-Elo-*

*kim*)", Gen. 35:7, in reference to Gen. 28:10–22) or Balaam's vision of the angel ("And the Lord opened up Balaam's eyes (*va-yigal Hashem et-'einey Bil'am*)", Num. 22:31). In Isaiah, it is also used to describe God's acting in history ("And the glory of the Lord shall be revealed (*ve-niglah kevod Hashem*)", Isa. 40:5; 53:1; 56:1).

Regarding the divine law, an important onto-epistemological distinction is made between 'that-which-is-concealed' and 'that-which-is-revealed': "The concealed things (*ha-nistarot*) belong unto the Lord, our God; but the things that are revealed (*ha-niglot*) belong unto us and to our children forever, that we may do all the words of this law" (Deut. 29:28). Nevertheless, in other passages the hope is expressed that God will not withhold anything from His children (1 Sam. 20:2).

The verb *g-l-h* can take on a secondary meaning, referring to a "state of exile" (Ezek. 12:3; Isa. 24:11; Job 20:28) or "captivity" (Amos 1:5; Jer. 13:19; Ezek. 39:28). The nouns *golah* and *galut,* which both refer to a "state of exile" or a "community in exile", have themselves become central theological concepts in Judaism; and particularly in modern Jewish thought the etymological relatedness between *galut* ("exile") and *hitgalut* ("revelation") has furthermore developed into a central theme of theological speculation and discourse. (It is worth noting that the noun *hitgalut* ("revelation"), which eventually has become the Modern Hebrew word for "revelation", actually first appears in later rabbinic literature.)

While *g-l-h* allows for wide range of sensory experiences and cognition, the verb *r-'a-h* (ראה; "to see") puts a clear emphasis on the visual aspect of revelation. Its semantics suggest that which perceived is somehow visually perceivable and must possess some form of visual manifestation. This consequently implies that God must have some kind of visual manifestation, which is often called *mareh* ("appearance", "sight," "vision"). When Moses first encounters God at burning bush at Mount Horeb, what he actually perceives is the "appearance of the angel of the Lord (*va-yera malakh Hashem elav*)", which is also described as "the great appearance (*ha-mareh ha-gadol*)" (Exod. 3:2–3). God appears in a "pillar of cloud (*'amud anan*)" and in a "pillar of fire (*'amud esh*)," thus visually perceivable to guide the Israelites through the wilderness of Sinai by day and by night (Exod. 13:21–22; Num. 14:14; Deut. 1:33; Ps. 99:7; Neh. 9:12; 9:19; Ps. 99:7). Shortly before Moses' death on Mount Nebo, God once more "appeared [...] in a pillar of cloud" at the Tent of Meeting (Deut. 31:15) in order to teaching him a "song (*shir*)" as an instruction for Israelites in the time after Moses' passing (Deut. 32:16–18; 32:1–43). Another well-known example of a visual manifestation is the "visions of God (*mar'ot Elokim*)" of the prophet Ezekiel (Ezek. 1:1–28; 8:1–16).

All these "appearances" and "visions" suggest that the 'hidden' God is somehow discernable, mediated through certain phenomena. Nevertheless, there are also passages that seem to suggest that He can be visually perceived directly. For example, from the dramatic encounter of his wrestling with the 'angel of God'[17] at the river Jabbok, Jacob emerges a changed man, as 'Israel,' stating: "[F]or I have seen God face-to-face, and my life is preserved (*ki ra'iti Elokim panim el-panim va-tinatzel nafshi*)" (Gen. 32:31). In addition, Moses' special status as a prophet and law-giver is generally derived from his ability to relate to God directly: "[T]he Lord spoke to Moses face-to-face like a man speaks to his fellow man (*ve-dibber Hashem el-Mosheh panim el-panim ka-asher yedaber ish el-re'ehu*)" (Exod. 33:11). However, when Moses asks to actually see God's "glory (*kavod*)," which in the context of this passage is taken as synonymous for His countenance, God responds negatively, emphasizing the impossibility of Moses' request: "You cannot see My face, for no man shall see Me and live!" (Exod. 33:20). However, He allows him to glance at His "(back)side (*achoray*)", which later on becomes a central motif in Jewish theological exegesis.

That something is visually perceivable seems to attest to some kind of proof: When God reveals Himself to Moses at Mount Horeb, He refers to the patriarchs as reliable witnesses who have experienced God's presence beforehand: "I also appeared to Abraham, to Isaac, and to Jacob (*va-era el-Avraham el-Yitzchak ve-el-Ya'akov*)" (Exod. 6:3).

The noun *ro'eh* is sometimes used as an old-fashioned or alternative designation for a prophet (Isa. 30:10; 1 Sam. 9:9). Furthermore, there seems to exist some kind of relationship between God's appearance and God's speech. The phrase "And He appeared to him (*va-yera elav*)," which is found in many places throughout the Hebrew Bible, often serves as some kind introductory formulation to the divine speech which is about to follow (e.g. Gen. 18:1–15; 26:2–3; Judg. 6:12; 1Kings 3:5; 9:2).

While *g-l-h* and *r-'a-h* seem speak about a sensory perception, the verb *y-d-'a* (ידע; "to know," "to discover") refers to a mental cognition, processing, and eventual understanding of what is perceived. Unlike the former, it does not necessarily depend on or involve any kind of visual image or acoustic experience. Moreover, it articulates some kind an intuition or knowledge allowing an apprehension not necessarily what God is but rather what He wants (Exod. 33:13; Hosea 2:22; Eccles. 3:14) – an awareness of the divine will, which the wicked, on the other side, are lacking, ignoring, or rejecting (e.g. 1Sam. 2:12; Jer. 2:8;

17 While in Gen. 32:25 the scene is described that Jacob wrestled with a "man (*ish*)", in Hosea 12:5 this "man" is identified as an "angel (*malakh*)".

4:22; Job 18:21). This apprehension also implicates an acknowledgment of God's sovereignty: "Yet I am the Lord, your God, from the land of Egypt; but you know no God but me (*ve-Elokim zulati lo teda'*)" (Hosea 13:4). As the latter statement is not apprehended or accepted by the others nations and their leaders (Exod. 5:2), the prophets beseech God to act and reveal Himself by demonstrating His power and might in order "[t]o make Your name known to Your adversaries (*le-hodia' shimkha le-tzareykha*), that the nations might tremble at Your presence" (Isa. 64:1), going as far as to evoke drastic consequences for ignoring God's will and sovereignty: "Pour out your wrath upon the nations that do not know You (*shefokh chamatekha el ha-goyim asher lo-yeda'ukha*)" (Ps. 79:6). Their visions of divine wrath should, however, not be mistaken for a simple call to enact vengeance. They rather express the hope of the ultimate fulfillment of divine justice so that "the earth shall be filled with the knowledge of the glory of the Lord (*lada'at et kevod Hashem*)" (Hab. 2:14).

## 2.2 Revelation: Torah

Discerning biblical etymologies eventually reveals (pun intended!) a variety of different revelatory experiences. Yet for Judaism, none seems to be as determining and decisive as the revelation of the Torah at Mount Sinai. Moreover, both 'Torah' and 'Mount Sinai' have become somewhat synonymous with revelation.

As outlined before, the Torah not only acts as a mere medium of revelation, but is also a material manifestation of the divine will. It represents both a) an immediate revelatory experience (communicated directly by God to Moses, but at the same time also immediately witnessed by all Israelites present at Mount Sinai) as well as b) a mediate one (the Torah as a textual medium allows the generations following the events at Mount Sinai through its reading and study to take part in them). Analogously, the Torah a) stands for a momentary act of revelation (namely the revelation of the Ten Commandments at Mount Sinai in Exodus 19–20), but it also b) acts as a supratemporal medium, which guarantees the continuity of that which was the revealed (Deut. 5:27 ff.). Unlike the other books of the Hebrew Bible, the Torah does not simply convey a specific vision or prophecy revealed to a particular prophet in certain historical context; it extends beyond the mediatorship of Moses (Exod. 19–24), being addressed to all of Israel (Deut. 5).

## 2.3 Reception: The "Giving of the Torah" (*matan Torah*)

While there is no classical Hebrew word for "revelation", various concepts exist in Jewish tradition to express and label the act of revelation of the Torah at Mount Sinai: It is usually described as *matan Torah* (literally "giving of the Torah") or *qabbalat Torah* (literally "receiving of the Torah"), emphasizing the unique relationship and bond between God and the Israelites. Another commonly used expression is *ma'amad har Sinay* (literally "standing at Mount Sinai"), which is particularly found in medieval Jewish philosophical literature (e.g. Sa'adiyah Gaon, Moses Maimonides).

The Torah is conceptually considered a gift entrusted by God to Israel, symbolized in the two "tablets of stone" (*luchot ha-even/avanim*) as a materialized expression of the covenant made between them. Through the giving of the Torah, God not only reveals His will to Israel. In doing so, He also designates Israel as His chosen (people): "Now therefore, if you will listen to My voice indeed, and keep My covenant (*u-shem'artem et briti*), then you shall be My treasure (*segulah*) from among all peoples; for all the earth is Mine; and you shall be to Me a kingdom of priests and a holy nation (*mamlekhet kohanim ve-goy kadosh*)" (Exod. 19:5–6). This is indicated by His coming from His place, in order to encounter the Israelites:

> 'And Moses brought the people out of the camp to meet with God (*liqrat ha-Elokim*)' (Exod. 19:17). R. Yossi said: Yehudah would expound, and he said, 'The Lord came *from* Sinai (*mi-Sinay*)' *(Deut. 33:2)*. Do not read this (*al tiqre*), but rather: 'The Lord came *to* Sinai (*le-Sinay*)' – to give the Torah to Israel. Or perhaps you should not say this, but rather: 'The Lord came *from* Sinai (*mi-Sinay*)' – to receive Israel, like a bridegroom who goes out to meet his bride (*ke-chattan* [...] *liqrat kallah*)" (*Mekhilta de-Rabbi Yishma'el Ba-Chodesh, Yitro* 3).

What takes place at Mount Sinai is a metaphorical marriage between God and Israel – most importantly, a voluntary one. Not only does God choose Israel, but Israel chooses God as well, as is expressed in Moses bringing the Israelites towards Him:

> "[The Lord] Came from Sinai" – He went forth towards them when they were about to take their stand at the foot of the Mount, like a bridegroom who goes out to meet his bride, as it is said, "And Moses brought the people out of the camp to meet with God." (Exod. 19:17). This teaches us that He was Himself going out to face them. (*RaSH"Y* on Deut. 33:2)

God and Israel, bridegroom and bride, meet each other half-way, as it is customary in traditional Jewish weddings – with Moses taking on the role of the matchmaker. Correspondingly, based on the rabbinic interpretation of the verse "On the day of his wedding (*be-yom chaltunato*)" in Song of Songs 3:11, the revelation at Mount Sinai is described as a wedding day between God and Israel (b. *Ta'anit* 26b). As a matter of fact, standing under the *chuppah* (canopy), during a Jewish wedding ceremony is both symbolically and ritually understood as a kind of re-enactment of the events at Sinai.

In His giving the Torah, God expresses His unconditional love to Israel. Israel responds by unanimously accepting His Torah: "All the people answered in one voice (*qol echad*), saying, 'All that the Lord has spoken, we will do (*na'aseh*)!'" (Exod. 24:3). Israel accepts what the rabbis call the "yoke of the *Torah* (*'ol ha-Torah*)" (*Pirqey Avot* 3:5), meaning the sole sovereignty of God's will, both willingly and unconditionally. This is affirmed a few verses later with a noticeable amendment: "All that the Lord has spoken, we will do and we will hear (*na'aseh ve-nishm'a*)" (Exod. 24:7). In the rabbinical interpretation, the word *nishm'a* is often interpreted as referring to an understanding of the laws. That Israel gives 'doing' precedence over 'understanding' is an expression of their unconditional devotion love to God, for which Israel is praiseworthy (b. *Shabbat* 88a).

In another allusion to the wedding metaphor, the roles are slightly changed: Israel takes on the role of the bridegroom and the Torah becomes the intended bride: "'Moses commanded us the Torah, an inheritance (*morashah*) for the congregation of Jacob' (Deut. 33:4). Do not read it as inheritance (*morashah*); rather, read it as betrothed (*me'orasah*)." (b. *Pessachim* 49b).

While the relationship between God and Israel is an intimate one, it does not take place in secret. Through the giving of the Torah, it is displayed out in the open and for all to see. This actually finds a ritual expression during the synagogue prayer service when the open Torah scroll is lifted up (*hagbahah*) after the reading of the Torah: "And this is the Law which Moses set before the children of Israel" (Deut. 4:44). The Torah is a testimony of the relationship of God and Israel, which is ritually affirmed by those who bear witness during the prayer service (according to some customs emphasized by pointing the little finger at the Torah when saying "And *this* is the Torah (*ve-zot ha-Torah*) ...").

But like in any relationship, even an intimate and intense one, the danger of negligence and unreliability is always given, compelling God to constantly remind Israel to treat the gift of the Torah with utmost respect:

> R. Yehoshua ben Levy said: Each and every day a heavenly voice (*bat qol*) goes out from Mount Horeb, and announces and says: 'Woe to the creatures for disparaging the *Torah*'; for anyone who does not involve himself in the *Torah* is called 'rebuked' (*nazuf*), as it is said: 'A ring of gold in a swine's snout is a beautiful woman who turns from discretion.' (Prov. 11:22) (*Pirqey Avot* 6:2).

While Israel might have become somewhat insensitive to the admonitions of the "heavenly voice", it is the rabbis who take it upon themselves to remind their fellow Jews to apprehend and appreciate that what appears to be a "yoke" is instead the gift of true freedom:

> And it says: 'And the tablets (*luchot*) were the work of God, and the writing was the writing of God, graven (*charut*) upon the tablets', (Exod. 32:16) do not read (*al tiqre*) 'graven' (*charut*) but rather 'freedom' (*cherut*), for there is no free man except one that involves himself in *Torah* learning; And anyone who involves himself in *Torah* learning is elevated, as it is said: 'and from *Mattanah* (a place whose name literally means 'gift', and correspondingly can refer to the giving of the *Torah*) [to] *Nachaliel*; and from *Nachaliel* [to] *Bamot* (a place whose name literally meaning 'high places')' (Numbers 21:19)" (*Pirqey Avot* 6:2).

In other words: The *Torah*, as a gift given from a higher place, actually allows for true interpretative freedom, lifting oneself from the bounds and constrictions of the "yoke of government and the yoke of the way of the world (*'ol makhut ve-'ol derekh eretz*)" (*Pirqey Avot* 3:5); it enables one to elevate oneself to 'high(er) places,' in order to come and be near to God.

## 2.4 Experience: "Seeing voices"

"And it came to pass on the third day in the morning, that there were [thunderous] sounds and lightnings (*qolot u-verakim*), and a thick cloud upon the mountain and the sound of a horn (*qol shofar*) exceedingly loud, so that all the people in the camp trembled" (Exod. 19:16). The imminent encounter between God and His chosen people takes place in what is described as a dramatic and even terrifying atmosphere, accompanied by thunder and lightning, fire and smoke. It is a tangible experience, affecting and challenging all senses. In this built-up tension, God eventually reveals Himself to Israel: "And God spoke all these words, saying" (Exod. 20:1).

However, according to the classic rabbinic interpretation of the Ten Commandments, the Israelites were only able to hear the first two commandments:

> R. Simlay taught: There were 613 commandments (*mitzvot*) stated to Moses in the *Torah*, consisting of 365 prohibitions corresponding to the number of days in the solar year, and 248 positive commandments (*'aseh*) corresponding to the number of a person's limbs. Rav Chamnuna said: What is the verse [that alludes to this]? It is written: "Moses commanded to us the *Torah*, an inheritance" (Deuteronomy 33:4). The word *Torah*, in terms of its numerical value (*gimatriyya*) is 611. In addition, there are [two other commandments]: "I am (*anokhi*) [the Lord your God]" and: "You shall have no (*lo yehiyeh lekha*)

> [other gods]" (Exodus 20:2, 3), that we heard from the mouth of the Almighty, for a total of 613. (b. *Makkot* 23b–24a)

To illustrate this point, I would like to make use of the classical rabbinic hermeneutical method of *Gematria*, which has risen to popular prominence due to its use in the context of *Qabbalah* and other Jewish mystical traditions. In *Gematria*, every Hebrew letter is assigned a specific numerical value, and through the combination of letters and their respective numeric values one can construe numerical identities in certain words. In the case of the letters comprising the word *Torah*/תורה it is *tav* (400) + *vav* (6) + *resh* (200) + *he* (5) add up to 611. Correspondingly Rav Chamnuna concludes that Moses taught Israel 611 commandments and that the two additional commandments were received directly from God, namely the first two of the Ten Commandments, adding up to a total of 613 commandments (תרי"ג/*TaRY"aG ha-mitzvot*). This implies that, while Moses understands what follows from God's words clearly, the experience of God 'speaking' appears to completely overwhelm the visual and auditory senses of the Israelites: "And all the people saw the sounds/voice(s) (*ve-kol ha-'am ro'im et ha-qolot*), and the lightnings, and the sound of the horn, and the mountain smoking; and when the people saw it, they were shaken, and stood afar off." (Exod. 20:15). The immediateness of the God encounter appears to evoke a state of cognitive confusion, or else how can one possibly 'see' sounds or voices?

Two possible explanations with radically different outlooks can be taken from a famous disagreement (*makhloqet*) between R. Yishma'el and R. Aqiva:

> "And all the people saw the sounds, and the lightnings" (Exodus 20:15). "They saw what was visible and heard what was audible". These are the words of R. Yishma'el. R. Akiqa says: "They saw and heard what was audible. There was nothing that left the mouth of the Almighty (*mi-pi ha-Gevurah*) which was not engraved (*nechtzav*) on the tablets, as it is written: 'The voice of the Lord (*qol Hashem*) hews/engraves (*chotzev*) (with) flames of fire.' (Psalm 29:7). (*Mekhilta de-Rabbi Yishma'el, Ba-chodesh, Yitro* 9)

R. Yishma'el articulates a position that is commonly characterized as a 'naturalist' one by stating what cognitively makes sense. R. Aqiva, on the other hand, emphasizes the 'super-naturalist' aspects of the experience, suggesting that it is that very 'super-naturalism' which authenticates revelation.

The question of what was actually heard and seen at Sinai continued to puzzle medieval Jewish Bible commentators as well. In their interpretative endeavors they argumentatively followed in the respective footsteps of R. Yishma'el and R. Aqiva, developing them further. For example, the medieval Bible commentator R. Shlomoh Yitzchaki of Troyes (1040–1105), better known by his acronym *RaSH"Y*, interprets Exodus 20:15 as follows: "'They saw the sounds/

voice(s)' (*ro'im et ha-qolot*) – they saw that which should be heard, something which is impossible to see" (*RaSH"Y* on Exod. 20:15). In his opinion, the experience at Sinai proves incomprehensible to the Israelites. On the other hand, the Italian Bible commentator R. Ovadyah Sforno (ca. 1475–1550) concludes that the word

> "they saw/seeing (*ro'im*)" [is to be understood] like [the same word in] "and my heart saw (*ve-libi ra'ah*) [many things of wisdom and of knowledge]" (Ecclesiastes 1:16). [It means] that they understood the meaning of these sounds (*hitbonenu 'inyan ha-qolot*). (Sforno on Exodus 20:15)

For R. Sforno, *r-'-h* ("seeing") actually appears to be conceptually synonymous with *y-d-'* ("knowing") in these verses. A similar understanding appears to be expressed in the verse "The Lord spoke to you out of the fire; you heard the sound of the words but you perceived no shape – nothing but a voice" (Deut. 4:12), suggesting that what is implied here is the Israelites' inability to see God, for such an experience would prove fatal: "You cannot see My face, for man shall not see Me and live" (Exod. 33:20).

But what is furthermore peculiar in this context is the use of participial form of *r-'-h*, '*ro'im*', instead of the usual past tense. It could be translated as "they see", suggesting that their experience is, as a matter of fact, processual rather than momentary. So while in the end it remains unclear what the Israelites actually experienced at Mount Sinai, we can conclude that it proved both overpowering and transformative, resonating in them and the generations that followed.

## 2.5 Presence: "A Great Voice and It Did Not Cease" (*qol gadol ve-lo yasaf*)

A crucial question for the rabbis is their concern about the consequences of the Sinaitic experience: Is the Torah given a perfect entity? And if so, would that not suggest that the revelation at Sinai was just a one-time event? Or does it mark rather an ongoing endeavor, which allows humans to actively engage and creatively contribute to the process of ever-perfecting that which was revealed at Sinai?[18] At the core of their respective discussions is the interpretation of the following verse: "These things the Lord spoke to your entire assembly on the mountain, [...] a great voice and it did not cease (*qol gadol ve-lo yasaf*)" (Deut. 5:19).

**18** For a detailed discussion, see Silman, Yochanan, *Qol gadol ve-lo yasaf – Torat yisrael beyn shlemut le-hishtalmut*, Jerusalem: Magnes, 1999.

How can the cryptic phrase "and it did not cease" be understood? Does it simply mean that the volume of the divine voice that did not decrease, thus affecting anyone present at Sinai? Or does it imply that it continued to resonate beyond the actual concrete moment of revelation?

The Torah clearly states that *"You shall not add (lo tosifu) to that which I command you, and you shall not subtract (ve-lo tigreʿu) from it, to keep the commandments of the Lord, your God, which I command you" (Deut. 4:2), suggesting that everything what God intended to be revealed was actually revealed in the Torah. In other words: The Torah given at Sinai is perfect.* The rabbis consequently argued that future prophecies did not add anything to what was revealed at Mount Sinai; rather, the Sinaitic experience indeed contained all future prophecies: "And God said all of these things, saying" (Exod. 20:1). R. Yitzchak said:

> What the prophets were to prophesize in the future in each generation (*be-khol dor va-dor*), they received from Mount Sinai (*qiblu me-har Sinay*). As Moses said to Israel: "But with those here with us standing today and with those not here with us today." (Deut. 29:14). It does not say [at the end of the verse], "with us standing today (*ʿimmanu ʿomed ha-yom*)", but rather, "with us today (*ʿimmanu ha-yom*)"; these are the souls that will be created in the future, who do not have substance, about whom "standing" is not mentioned. [...] Isaiah said: "[F]rom the time it was, I was there." (Isa. 48:16). Isaiah (meant to say) "From the time the *Torah* was given at Sinai, 'I was there' and received this prophecy", "and now the Lord God did send me and His spirit" (Isa. 48:16), [meaning] until now, he was not given permission to prophesize. (*Exodus Rabbah* 28:6)

In other words: Isaiah's prophecy, though articulated for a particular time and circumstance, was already included in the revelation of Mount Sinai; however, it was not destined to be revealed until its designated time had come, making Isaiah somewhat like a prophetic 'sleeper agent.' Moreover, Isaiah "was there", anachronistically receiving his prophecy at Sinai. The Sinaitic revelation is not just a singular moment in history; as a matter of fact it transcends any defining local and temporal dimensions. For the rabbis, however, this extends well beyond the prophecies of the prophets; they actually equate the knowledge of the rabbinic sages with prophetic inspiration: "And it was not only of the prophets who receive their prophecy from Sinai, but also the sages who arise in each generation – each of them received what was his from Sinai. So it states: 'These things the Lord spoke to your entire assembly on the mountain, [...] a great voice and it did not cease.' (Deuteronomy 5:19)." (*Exodus Rabbah* 28:6).

The "great voice [that] did not cease" resonates in the opinions and decisions of the rabbis, which like the prophecies of the prophets are directly derived from Sinai, as both "were there". If we move beyond the literal reading of the *midrash*, we can conclude two things: a) the rabbis are on the same level as the prophets and are consequently the latter's legitimate successors as interpreters and conveyors of the divine will; and b) "being there" might suggest that the rabbis are claiming here that when they are engaged in their interpretative endeavors, they "are" at Sinai by relating the Sinaitic revelation to their actual circumstances, making the "great voice" present.

Another *midrash* develops this idea even further:

> Not only the prophets (*ha-nevi'im*) but also all the wise men (*kol ha-chakhamim*) who were there, and those who were destined to come [received their inspiration at Sinai], as it is said: 'These things the Lord spoke to your entire assembly on the mountain, [...] a great voice and it did not cease.' (Deut. 5:19). What is meant by a 'great voice and it did not cease'? Our sages said: The entire Ten Commandments (*aseret ha-dibrot kulan*) came forth from the mouth of the Almighty (*mi-pi ha-Gevurah*) in sound/voice (*be-qol*)" (*Midrash Tanchuma, Yitro* 11:2).

The *midrash* establishes a link between the divine voice and the giving of the Ten Commandments, suggesting that everything was already contained in the utterance of the Ten Commandments. While the Ten Commandments are not identical to the 613 commandments, they are indeed representative of them. To elucidate this, we again make use of some simple *gematric* calculations: As we have seen above, every Hebrew letter corresponds to a specific numerical value. We already know that the number 613 is written in Hebrew תרי"ג – *tav* (400) + *resh* (200) + *yud* (10) + *gimmel* (3). In simple *gematric* additions, the tens and hundreds can be dropped, making the equation 4 + 2 + 1 + 3 = 10. The number 10 corresponds to the numerical value of the letter י, the first letter of the "ineffable name of God" (*shem ha-meforash*). Through the letter/number י/10, God reveals Himself in a revelation that contains everything as represented by 613 commandments, even their interpretations:

> "And the Lord spoke to Moses on Mount Sinai, saying" (Lev. 25:1): Why is *shemitah* (the section on the Sabbatical year) juxtaposed with Mount Sinai? Were not all the commandments (*mitzvot*) given at Sinai? [The purpose of the juxtaposition is to indicate that] just as the general rules and specifications (*kelalutiah ve-diqduqiah*) [of *shemitah*] were enunciated at Sinai, so with the general rules and specifications of all [the commandments]. (*Sifra Be-Har* 1:1)

However, the discussion in *Exodus Rabbah* opens up an even broader perspective, as it expands not only what was revealed but to whom it was revealed as well: "R. Yochanan said, 'One voice was split into seven voices and they were divided into seventy languages'" (*Exodus Rabbah* 28:6). The seventy languages correspond to the seventy nations that descended from Noah (Gen. 10) – that is all of humankind. R. Yochanan thus stresses the universality of the Sinaitic revelation, as through the giving of the Ten Commandments, the "great voice" actually reached out to all of humanity. This, however, comes with a devastating effect:

> R. Yochanan said: "The voice would go out and divide into seventy voices for the seventy languages, so that all the nations would hear. And each and every nation would hear in the language of the nation (*bi-lshon ha-ummah*) and their souls would depart. But Israel would hear and they were not injured." How did the voice go out? R. Tanchuma said, "It would come and go with two faces; [one] would kill the idolaters who did not accept it, and [one] would give life to Israel that did accept it." This is what Moses stated to them at the end of the forty years. "For who is there of all flesh, that has heard the voice of the living God speaking out of the midst of the fire, as we have, and lived?" (Deut. 5:22). You would hear His voice and live, but the idolaters heard and died. (*Exodus Rabbah* 5:9)

Due to their unconditional acceptance of the Torah, finding a literary expression both in Exodus 24:3 and Exodus 24:7, the Israelites are collectively able to withstand the immense power of the divine voice unharmed. Moreover, the rabbis make an interesting differentiation concerning how the people experienced this moment of revelation:

> Come and see how the voice would go out among all of Israel, each and every one according to his strength (*lefi kocho*): The elders according to their strength; the young men according to their strength; the infants according to their strength; the sucklings according to their strength; the women according to their strength; and even Moses according to his strength, as it is stated: "Moses would speak and God would answer him with a voice (*be-qol*)" (Exodus 19:19), with a voice that He could withstand. And so [too,] it states: "The voice of the Lord is in strength (*ba-koach*)". (Psalm 29:4). It is not stated, "in His strength (*be-kocho*)", but rather "in strength (*ba-koach*)"; in the strength of each and every one, and even the pregnant women, according to their strength. (*Exodus Rabbah* 5:9)

Counter to the impression one could get from the dramatic built-up in Exodus 19:16 ff., the divine voice did not overpower the Israelites, but rather held back by conveying to each of them only what he or she was able comprehend and digest according to his or her respective mental and physical capacities. The *midrash* articulates a remarkable awareness of the individual experience within the collective experience at Sinai.

In the Jerusalem Talmud, we encounter yet another interesting aspect of characterizing the revelation at Mount Sinai as an overall 'transcending' event. The rabbinic discussion revolves around the status of the book of Esther (*megillat Esther*) as a canonical book. Analogously to what we have seen concerning the prophets and the rabbis, the latter make a striking argument that even the historical experience of the Jews was already included in the revelation at Sinai:

> Rav and R. Chaninah and R. Yochanan and Bar Kapara and R. Yehoshua ben Levy said, "This *megillah* was given to Moses from Sinai, however there is no [chronological sequence] in the *Torah*." R. Yochanan and R. Shimon ben Laqish (however disagreed about the following matter): R. Yochanan said, "The *Prophets* (*nevi'im*) and the *Writings* (*ketuvim*) will be nullified in the future, but the Five Books of the *Torah* will not be nullified in the future. What is the reason? (Because it is written:) 'a great voice and it did not cease' (Deuteronomy 5:19)" R. Shimon ben Laqish said, "Also the *megillah* of Esther and the laws (*halakhot*) will not be nullified in the future; it states here, 'a great voice and it did not cease' and it states later, 'and their memory did not cease (*ve-zikhram lo yasuf*)' (Esther 9:28); the Laws, [as it is written,] 'His ways (*halikhot*) are forever (*olam*) (Habakuk 3:6).'" (j. *Megillah* I 5 (7a)).

Through the words *yasaf* – *yasuf*, R. Shimon ben Laqish establishes an inter-textual connection between the Torah and the book of Esther – between a book that contains the revelation of God and a book wherein God's name is not even mentioned once (apart from the rabbinic interpretation of "from another place (*mi-makom acher*)" in Esther 4:14).

## 2.6 Content: What Was Revealed?

What exactly was revealed at Mount Sinai? From a close reading of the biblical text we can discern the following things: At the core of the revelation and transmission of the *Torah* at Mount Sinai are the two "tablets of stone" (*luchot ha-even/avanim*), also referred to as "the tablets of the covenant" (*luchot ha-brit*) (Exod. 34:1) or "tablets of the testimony" (*luchot ha-edut*)" (Exod. 31:18): "And the Lord said to Moses: 'Come up to Me unto the mountain and be there; and I will give you the tables of stone, and the law and the commandment (*ve-ha-torah ve-ha-mitzvah*), which I have written, that you may teach them'" (Exod. 24:12). In the context of the revelation at Mount Sinai "the law and the commandment" has been commonly interpreted as referring to the Ten Commandments (biblical *'aseret ha-devarim*; Mishnaic *'aseret ha-dibbrot*) that were written on the stone tablets. In the opinion of R. Chanina ben Gamliel, each tablet contained five commandments: "How were the Ten Commandments given? Five on one tablet and five on the other [...] (But) the sages say: Ten on one tablet and ten on the other" (*Mekhilta de-Rabbi Yishma'el, Ba-chodesh, Yitro* 8).

*RaSH"Y* concluded that the two stone tablets not only contained the Ten Commandments, but all of the 613 commandments (*RaSH"Y* on Exod. 24:12). It is, however, interesting to note that the Torah actually indicates that not everything was revealed at Mount Sinai: Rather, some laws and instructions were actually given beforehand (Exod. 12:24), while others followed after the events at Mount Sinai had transpired (Num. 36:13).

Nevertheless, some classical rabbinic sources go even further, concluding not only that the Torah given to Moses at Mount Sinai encompassed the Five Books of Moses, the *Chumash* or Pentateuch, but that God in fact taught Moses the following order: The Scriptures, the *Mishnah*, the *Talmud*, the *Tosefta*, and the *Aggadah* (*Exodus Rabbah* 47:1; j. *Peah* II:6 (17a)). In an explication of above mentioned verse from Exodus 24:12, the rabbis try to actually identify these works within the biblical text:

> R. Levy Bar Chama said that R. Shimon Ben Laqish said: Why does it say: "And I will give you the tables of stone and the law and the commandment (*ve-ha-torah ve-ha-mitzvah*), which I have written, that you may teach them." (Exodus 24:12). "The tablets" – these are the Ten Commandments. "*Torah*" – this is the Scriptures (*miqra*). And the commandment – this is the *Mishnah*. "That I have written" – these are the Prophets and the Writings. "[To] teach them" – this is the *Gemara*. This teaches you that all of them were given (*shekulam natnu*) to Moses on Sinai. (b. *Berakhot* 5a)

In other words: The Torah revealed at Mount Sinai already contained all its future potential interpretations. This implicit unity between the Torah and its commentaries, between text and interpretation, is characteristic for rabbinic Judaism. It conceptually distinguishes between "*Written Torah*" (*torah she-bi-khtav*) and "*Oral Torah*" (*torah she-be-al-peh*) which both were given at Mount Sinai, as the biblical text itself actually refers to the Torah in plural:

> These are the statues (*ha-chuqqim*) and the ordinances (*ha-mishpatim*) and the laws/*ha-Torot*" (Leviticus 26:46). "The statutes" – these are the *midrashic* interpretations (*ha-midrashot*); "and the ordinances" – these are the judgements (*ha-dinim*). "And the *Torot*" – this teaches that two *Torot* were given to Israel: One written (*bi-khtav*) and one oral (*be-'al-peh*). (*Sifra Be-Chuqqotai* 8:12)

Throughout *Mishnah* and *Talmud*, the idea of the two *Torot* (pl. of *Torah*) given at Mount Sinai is often an emphasized motif. For example, when a gentile asks Shammay, one of the central rabbinic authorities of his time, how many *Torot* Israel has, the latter answers: "Two: *Written Torah* and *Oral Torah*" (b. *Shabbat* 31a). The idea of the two *Torot*, of *Written* and *Oral Torah*, is fundamental for rabbinic self-understanding in the Pharisaic tradition; the rejection of the *Oral Torah* by rival groups like the Sadducees is legally classified as *minut* (heresy).

However, not all rabbinical authorities seem to share the idea of the two *Torot*. In a famous passage in *Sifra*, a *halakhic midrash* to Leviticus, R. Aqiva acts rather astonished by the suggestion that Israel has two *Torot:*

> Did Israel have only two *Torot?* Where not many *Torot* given to them? "This is the *Torah* of the burnt-offering" (Leviticus 6:2); "This is the *Torah* of the meal offering" (Leviticus 6:7);

> "This is the *Torah* of the guilt-offering" (Leviticus 7:1) [...] Moses merited becoming the messenger (*shaliach*) between Israel and their Father in heaven, "on Mount Sinai by the hand of Moses (*be-har Sinay be-yad Mosheh*)" (Leviticus 26:46). We are hereby taught that the (entire) *Torah* – (together with) its halakhot and its specifications and its interpretations (*halakhotiah ve-diqduqiah u-perushiah*) – was given to Moses at Mount Sinai. (*Sifra Be-Chuqqotai* 8:10; cf. b. *Nedarim* 25a)

What R. Aqiva essentially argues here is that, rather than conceptually being two *Torot*, there is actually only one Torah, which contains all its potential interpretations. I have to add here that R. Aqiva is not just 'another' rabbi who voices his opinion, but rather *the* leading legal authority of his time, best illustrated in the following rabbinic story: When Moses witnessed how God prepared the Torah by "tying crowns[19] on the letters" (*ve-qosher ketarim la-otiot*), he asks Him for the reason therefore. God answers that in the future a certain R. Aqiva will deduce laws from them. He even transports Moses into the future, into the study hall where R. Aqiva is expounding the Law and discussing it with his students. Moses, however, is unable to follow the discussion. Yet when one student asks R. Aqiva from where he derived his conclusions, he explains – much to Moses' relief – that this is a "law of Moses from Sinai (*halakhah le-Mosheh mi-Sinay*)" (b. *Menachot* 29b).

A similar opinion to the one of R. Aqiva about the 'all-inclusiveness' of the Torah is expressed in another *halakhic midrash:*[20]

> We are hereby taught that the Word (*ha-dibbur*) left the mouth of the Holy One, blessed is He, and Israel perceived it (*mistaklim bo*) and knew how many *midrashim* it contained, how many *halakhot* it contained, how many leniencies and stringencies (*qalim ve-chamurim*) it contained and how many verbal analogies (*gezeyrot shavot*) it contained." (*Sifrey Deuteronomy* § 313)

This, furthermore, underlines that the *Written Torah* and *Oral Torah*, according to rabbinic conceptions, indeed build a unity, comparable to a blueprint coming with its detailed instructions.

---

**19** A special scribal feature referred to *keter* (plural *keterim*) in Hebrew or *tag* (plural *tagin*) in Aramaic resembling little decorative crowns that can be found on certain Hebrew letters (*gimel, zayin, tet, nun, ayn, tzady* and *shin*).

**20** Langer, Gerhard, *Midrasch*, Tübingen: UTB (Mohr Siebeck), 2016, 42.

## 2.7 Authorship: The "Torah of Moses" (*Torat Moshe*)?

While the Torah is also commonly referred to as "Law of the Lord (*Torat Hashem)*" (Exod. 13:9; Ps. 19:8), indicating God's ownership of the Torah, in other books of the Hebrew Bible the phrase "Law of Moses (*Torat Mosheh*)" is found (Josh. 8:31; Mal. 3:22). The two phrases are apparently at odds with each other, as both could be understood as having competing claims of authorship and authority. Accordingly, the rabbis raise the question regarding what exact role Moses did play in the revelation at Mount Sinai. They seem particularly concerned with the question of how exactly God transmitted the Torah to Moses. As a matter of fact, not only one but various opinions are offered – for example, that God taught Moses the Torah (b. *Nedarim* 38a; b. *Menachot* 29a), Moses received a written copy (*Song of Songs Rabbah* 5:14; b. *Megillah* 19b; b. *Nedarim* 38a), or that God dictated the Torah to Moses and that the latter acted as a scribe and author: "And who wrote them [i.e. the books of the *TaNa"Kh*]? Moses wrote his own book (*sifro*) [i.e. the Torah] and the portion of Balaam and the book of Job" (b. *Bava Batra* 14b; cf. b. *Bava Batra* 15a; b. *Gittin* 60a; *Sifrey Deuteronomy* § 34).

In a somewhat apologetic, but decisive, undertone R. Yehoshuah ben Levy prominently stated that the designation "Torah of Moses" by no means implies any kind of original authorship on Moses' part (b. *Shabbat* 89a). However, to speak of the "Torah of Moses" is according to another *midrashic* interpretation quite legitimate, as it actually refers to the second set of stone tablets that were exclusively given to Moses (*Exodus Rabbah* 47:3).

## 2.8 Origins I: The "Torah (is) from Sinai" (*Torah mi-Sinay*)

Besides questions of how the act of revelation actually occurred and what exactly was revealed, the rabbinic tradition gives equal importance to where the revelation of the Torah took place. In the phrase "Moses received the Torah from Sinai (*Mosheh qibbel Torah mi-Sinay*)" (*Pirqey Avot* 1:1), the rabbis emphasize the significance of Sinai as the origin of both the *Written Torah* and the *Oral Torah*. Yet, why at Sinai? What makes this particular place so special?

A careful reader might have noted that I worded my translation as 'Sinai' instead of 'Mount Sinai.' While 'Sinai' in above quote from *Pirqey Avot* surly refers to Mount Sinai, the biblical text sets a more complex stage of where the revelation took place: Following their flight from Egypt, the Israelites eventually come into the "wilderness of Sinai (*midbar Sinay*)", where they set camp "before the mountain (*neged ha-har*)" (Exod. 19:1–2). Only several verses later this mountain is referred to as "Mount Sinai (*har Sinay*)" (Exod. 19:11) and henceforth designated as the site where the giving of the Torah will occur. So Sinai can actually refer to two places: The wilderness of Sinai and Mount Sinai.

Let us first take a closer look at the wilderness of Sinai: According to a famous *midrash*, the Torah was revealed in the wilderness of Sinai, because the wilderness is considered "ownerless (*hefker*)". Being ownerless seems to be the ontological default setting in order to be able to acquire something: "Unless one does make himself ownerless like the wilderness (*ke-midbar hefker*), he will be unable to acquire the wisdom and the Torah (*eyno yakhol liknot et ha-chokhmah ve-ha-torah*)." (*Numbers Rabbah* 1:7). In other words: True acceptance requires that one has to voluntarily accept something, meaning the Israelites have to shed and leave behind their slave mentality from Egypt in order to be able to voluntarily accept God as their new master – and, accordingly, to accept His will as expressed in the Torah.

But freedom of any bonds as a prerequisite for accepting the Torah has another important connotation to it: Because the Torah was given in a place that belongs to no one, no one people or nation can stake a claim to it. In other words, the Torah is not a national property. Moreover, had the Torah been revealed in the land of Israel, it would have been tied to that particular place, implying that it is valid only within its boundaries. Furthermore, the fact that the revelation takes place in the wilderness – a place not defined by any boundaries – underscores its universal validity. This finds its expression in a famous *midrash*, wherein God actually offers His Torah to other nations first, but one by one they reject it: The Romans (*Esav*) because they have a problem with the prohibition against murder; the Ammonites and Moabites because they have a problem with the prohibition against adultery; the Arabs (*Ishmael*) because they have a problem with the prohibition against stealing. (So much for prejudices and stereotypes.) After He asked all the other nations, who all find something unacceptable for themselves, God finally turns to the Israelites who "accepted the *Torah* with all its specifications and its interpretations (*kiblu et ha-torah be-diq duqeyah u-be-perusheyah*)" (*Sifrey Deuteronomy* § 343). However, according to another well-known rabbinic story, their acceptance is not as voluntary as thought: In a demonstration of His power and might, God lifts up the whole mountain and threatens Israel into accepting His Torah:

> "[A]nd they stood at the lowermost part of the mount" (Exodus 19:17). [...] This teaches that the Holy One, Blessed be He, overturned the mountain above (the Israelites) like a tub, and said to them: If you accept the *Torah*, excellent, and if not, there will be your burial! (b. *Shabbat* 88a)

Just as the surrounding wilderness is pretty much a no-man's-land, Mount Sinai is according to a *midrash* pretty much what can be called a no-name-place. Nevertheless, God disregarded all other mountains and hills for the lowliest and most insignificant of mountains, namely Mount Sinai, to rest His "divine presence" (*shekhinah*) upon it. "[A]nd He did not choose to raise Mount Sinai up" (b. *Sotah* 5a), meaning that God lowered Himself down to the level of the mountain. The way Mount Sinai is characterized here reminds one of the humbleness of Moses, who like Mount Sinai at first appears to be an unlikely candidate to act as God's chosen prophet –an outsider regarding his royal Egyptian upbringing, married to a Midianite wife, and impaired by a stutter. The analogy between the two is furthermore underscored, as in the same *sugiah* (Talmudic discussion) a reference to Moses' first encounter with God is made: "And He disregarded all of the beautiful trees and rested His divine presence on the bush" (ibd.). It is, therefore, not surprising that Mount Sinai is identified with Mount Horeb, the "mountain of God (*har ha-Elokim*)" and very site where the episode of the burning bush took place (Exod. 3:1; cf. Mal. 3:22; b. *Shabbat* 89a; *Pirqey de-Rabbi El-i'ezer* 51). In that respect, Mount Sinai marks the return to the very place from where the story of the Exodus began. Full circle. It is, however, noteworthy that while Mount Sinai plays of central role in the Pentateuch as well as in rabbinic literature, any mentions and references to it are relatively scarce in other books of the Hebrew Bible (Neh. 9:13; Mal. 3:22; Judg. 5:4–5; Ps. 68:9).

Still, one can also observe a change of attitude towards the significance of Mount Sinai within the different rabbinic generations: Particularly the rabbis of the Tannaitic period ($1^{st}$ – $3^{rd}$ century CE) appear to take a more critical stance in designating (Mount) Sinai as the origin of revelation,[21] as it is also the place of Israel's failing to recognize and worship God as its sole savior and sovereign in the episode of the so-called "golden calf (*'egel ha-zahav*)": "This is your god, O Israel, who brought you up out of the land of Egypt." (Ex. 32:4).[22]

---

**21** Halivni, David Weiss, *Revelation Restored. Divine Writ and Critical Responses*, Boulder, CL: Westview Press, 1997, 56–57.

**22** Mandelbaum, Irving J., "Tannatic Exegesis of the Golden Calf Episode," in: Philip R. Davies/ Richard T. White (eds), *A Tribute to Geza Vermes. Essays on Jewish and Christian Literature and History*, 207–223, Sheffield: Sheffield Academic Press, 1990; see also Marmorstein, Arthur, *Studies in Jewish Theology. The Marmorstein Memorial Volume*, ed. by Joseph Rabbinowitz/Meyer S. Lew, London: Oxford University Press, 1950, 198–206.

## 2.9 Origins II: The "*Torah* (is) from heaven" (*Torah min ha-shamayim*)

The rather negative attitude of the Tannaitic rabbis might have eventually led them to come up with a different origin story altogether. According to a prominent statement in *Mishnah Sanhedrin* 10:1, "[a]ll of Israel has a share in the world to come". There are, however, the usual exceptions to the rule: Among the Israelites who have no share in in the world to come are those who openly deny that the "*Torah* (is) from heaven (*Torah min ha-shamayim*)" (b. *Avodah Zarah* 18a). This is further explicated in the *Gemara*, the rabbinic commentary on the *Mishnah*, which points to a *baraita* or "outside" teaching:

> The sages have taught: "Because he has despised the word of the Lord and violated His commandment, that person shall be cut off" (Numbers 15:31) – this refers to one who says that the *Torah* (is) not from Heaven. [...] It has been taught in a *baraita* [dissenting opinion]: "Because he has despised the word of the Lord" – this refers to one who says that the *Torah* (is) not from Heaven, and even if he said that the entire *Torah* (is) from Heaven except for one verse which was not said by God but by Moses himself, it is said of him: "Because he has despised the word of the Lord". (b. *Sanhedrin* 99a; *Sifrey Numbers* § 112)

In other words: Even one verse attributed to Moses suggests a denial of the divine origin of the Torah.

The phrase "*Torah* (is) from Heaven" has a textual basis in the Torah, as refers to the verse: "I spoke to you from the Heavens" (Exod. 20:18).[23] But this concept it is not only concerned with divine origin and authorship; it moreover implies that every single verse, every single word, and even every single letter is indeed an articulation of God. While this claim sounds quite dogmatic and inflexible at first, there seems to be a profound rationale behind it: It not only allows but rather makes it necessary for the rabbis as interpreters of the divine articulation to discern its deeper meanings. In doing so, they need to move beyond the mere literality of the biblical text.

The concept that "*Torah* (is) from heaven" is, moreover, not only limited to the *Written Torah*, but extends to the *Oral Torah* as well. It comes to no surprise that the formulation "All of Israel has a share in the world to come" is also found at the beginning of *Pirqey Avot*, which, as mentioned earlier, is giving an account of the rightful process of the transmission of the *Oral Torah* through which the legitimacy of the rabbinic tradition is established. Accordingly, denying that

**23** Heschel, Abraham Joshua, *Heavenly Torah. As Refracted Through the Generations*, ed. and transl. by Gordon Tucker/Leonard Levin, New York: Continuum, 2006, 59.

the "*Torah* (is) from heaven" not only defies its divine origin, but doing so challenges the legitimacy of the rabbinic tradition as well.

Still it would be too narrow to reduce this concept to a mere question of authority and legitimacy. That the "*Torah* (is) from heaven" also has an epistemological dimension, as the divine knowledge convoyed in the giving of the Torah supposedly allows for a deeper insight into the nature of things. I would like to illustrate this with a rabbinic rationalization of why the Torah must be of divine origin: When discussing the camel, the hare, and the hyrax, whose features are difficult to discern regarding their classification as *kosher* or non-*kosher* animals, Rav Chanan bar Rava argues: "But was Moses our teacher a hunter or was he an archer? From here there is a refutation to those who say that the *Torah* (is) not from Heaven!" (b. Chullin 60b). In other words: How could Moses possibly have possessed such a complex knowledge about the nature of animals unless he had gained it from a superior source of knowledge – the 'Heavenly Torah'? As simple as Rav Chanan bar Rava's argument might sound at first, there is indeed a deeper logic behind it: Not only does the Torah teach that reality is structured, but it enables one to acquire an insight and an understanding of the structures of reality. This means not simply to perceive how things appear to us and then act upon it, but rather to cognize how they really are.

## 3 Aspects and Principles

The rabbinic tradition defines itself by approaching revelation through interpretation or by commenting on it, thereby revealing new facets and aspects to peruse and to pursue. This, however, makes it at the same time rather difficult to pick and choose from, considering the possible paths that one can explore. Based on some of the rabbinic ideas and concepts discussed above, I would like now to take a closer look at four aspects that have been eventually developed into fundamental concepts and principles themselves. They all concern a traditional Jewish understanding of revelation and how to live in accordance with it.

### 3.1 Decision-Making: "She Is Not In Heaven!"

The doctrine of the divine origin of the Torah establishes the authority and verity of God's authorship. Yet upholding it must eventually come into conflict with the authority and verity of human interpretation, posing a particular dilemma for rabbinic self-understanding. This is illustrated in the well-known and often cited story of the so-called "snake-oven" (*tanur shel akhnai*) in the Babylonian Talmud (b. *Bava Metzia* 59b). It tells about a dispute between R. Eli'ezer ben Hyrqanus, the leading legal scholar of his generation, and the majority of rabbis concerning the question whether said oven is to be considered fit for ritual purposes or not. In a heated exchange of arguments, R. Eli'ezer ben Hyrqanus is literally working wonders to emphasize his argument (for example, he causes a carob-tree to move), yet every time fails to convince his fellow rabbis. In an attempt of *ultima ratio*, he eventually calls upon the Divine to support his position – and see, the "heavenly voice (*bat qol*)" responds that R. Eli'ezer ben Hyrqanus is always right in matters of Jewish law! Whereupon R. Yehoshuah stand up and objects by quoting from the Torah itself, stating that "[s]he is not in heaven! (*lo be-shamayim hi'*)" (Deut. 30:12) – thereby ending the dispute. Afterwards it is added that God acknowledged his defeat: "My children have defeated me, my children have defeated me!"

The main idea communicated by the story of the "snake-oven" appears to be that according to the divine law, any legal decision has to be ruled according to the opinion of the majority (based on the rabbinic interpretation of Exodus 23:2, which leads them to conclude: "When there is a disagreement between an individual (*yachid*) and the many (*rabbim*), the *halakhah* is according to the many (*halakhah ke-rabbim*)" (b. *Berakhot* 9a)). Indeed, Eli'ezer ben Hyrqanus and God as represented by the heavenly voice are arithmetically in the minority and are consequently overruled by the majority of the rabbis. However, the irony of this story lies therein that God is not only defeated by His "children", but that, as a matter of fact, He is defeated by His own words as revealed in His Torah. For the rabbis, the issue raised here is not whether God lacks the power to overwrite His own will, but that He chooses not to do so, thus staying true to His own words. After all, God's will and His word are one, and it is upon the trustworthiness of His words that the covenant between Him and Israel is established. Whereas Israel is duty-bound to uphold the covenant, so is God obligated to guarantee its preservation.

Nevertheless, the story of the "snake-oven" raises a fundamental epistemological problem, as the main criterion in the process of decision-making is ultimately not the divinely revealed truth, but rather human considerations and interpretations (cf. Deut. 5:23, 27 ff.). This does not, by any means, suggest that the rabbis question the divine origin of the Torah. Rather they appear to emphasize it because the Torah is no longer hidden but revealed; divine revelation itself has henceforth become subject to human interpretation, as it is stated in Deuteronomy 29:28. Human interpretation, however, faces its limits in apprehending and permeating divine truths, despite one's best efforts that the interpreted is in accordance with those truths. Furthermore, human understanding is always conventional and context-dependent – and it has to be, as it is grounded in concrete reality and not in an ideal divine one. Consequently, b. *Bava Metzia* 59b makes a clear distinction between the ideal and the real, between theoretical *halakhic* knowledge and its subsequent practical application. The dialectical nature of rabbinic discourse can be understood as a methodical approach to carefully negotiate this dichotomist relationship. To make use of a Superman quote, the rabbis are aware that with the great power of interpretative freedom comes the great responsibility of considerate application – particularly in relation to divine truths. It is therefore not surprising that the story of the "snake-oven" is a central narrative of and for rabbinic self-understanding.

## 3.2 Pluralism: "These and Those" (*Elu va-elu*)

This conceptual distinction between theoretical knowledge and practical application not only affects the processes and principles of decision-making, but it also touches upon coming to terms with the dissenting – and sometimes even conflicting – explanations that the rabbinic tradition has to offer:

> R. Abba said that Shmuel said: "For three years, Beyt Shammay and Beyt Hillel disagreed." These said: The *halakhah* is in accordance with our opinion, and these said: The *halakhah* is in accordance with our opinion. Ultimately, a heavenly voice (*bat qol*) emerged and said: [Both] these and these are the words of the living God (*elu va-elu divrey Elokim chayyim*). However, the *halakhah* is in accordance with the opinion of Beyt Hillel. (b. *Eruvin* 13b; see also b. *Gittin* 6b)

Like in the story above about R. Eli'ezer ben Hyrqanus and the snake-oven, the heavenly voice once again intervenes in a rabbinic dispute, this time, however, not siding with one party but instead stating that despite their opposing viewpoints, both opinions are "in accordance" (*kemot*) with the divine will. But whereas b. *Bava Batra* 59b is mainly concerned in defining the necessary practical framework of decision-making, b. *Eruvin* 13b is often understood as making a case for the concept of *halakhic* pluralism, for which the phrase *elu va-elu divrey Elokim chayyim* has become somewhat of a tagline. But why, then, is it so important to accentuate that these conflicting opinions are both the "words of the living God"? The phrase *Elokim chayyim* is actually a biblical reference: "For who is there of all flesh, that has heard the voice of the living God (*qol Elokim chayyim*) speaking out of the midst of the fire, as we have, and lived?" (Deut. 5:22). After the dramatic encounter of God revealing the Ten Commandments, the Israelites urge Moses to be their emissary and: "You go near, and hear all that the Lord our God may say; and you shall speak unto us all that the Lord our God may speak to you; and we will hear it and do it (*ve-sham'anu ve-'asinu*)" (Deut. 5:23). A careful reader might notice that the initial order of "we will do and we will hear" (*na'aseh ve-nishm'a*) in Exodus 24:7 is reversed here; now, first comes hearing/understanding, then doing. Moreover, these passages are found within the same literary context as the verse about the "great voice and it did not cease (*qol gadol ve-lo yasaf*)" (Deut. 5:19), which – as we have already seen – according to the rabbinic interpretation suggests that every prophecy and every rabbinic explanation was previously conveyed at Sinai.

However, this holistic and pluralistic understanding of revelation might eventually lead to an epistemological crisis, as is expressed in another famous passage from the Talmud:

> Lest a person say: Now, how can I study the Torah? The verse states they are all "given from one shepherd (*me-ro'eh echad*)" (Ecclesiastes 12:11). One God (*Kel*[24] *echad*) gave them; one communal leader (*parnas echad*) [i.e., Moses] said them from the mouth of the Master of all creation, blessed be He, as it is written: "And God spoke all these words" (Exodus 20:1). (b. *Chagigah* 3b)

Corresponding to what we have seen above, the rabbis conclude that the use of the plural form "words" (*devarim*) indicates that in His giving of the Ten Commandments, God has conveyed all future interpretations with them. Consequently, the study of the Torah might lead to different and differing interpretations and explanations; and while these respectively even might result in varying applications and practices, they, after all, still represent the unity of revelation.

## 3.3 Authentication: Mass-Revelation and Authenticated Tradition

What sets the revelation of the Torah at Mount Sinai apart from other prophetic experiences is that it was revealed not only to a single prophet (e.g. Isaiah, Ezekiel or Amos, but also Jesus or Muḥammad), but rather to all Israelites above the age of twenty, amounting according to the biblical text to roughly 600,000 people (Num. 1:46). This point is particularly stressed by the Andalusian poet and philosopher Yehudah ha-Levy (1075–1142), who in his book *Sefer ha-Kuzary* ("The Book of the Khazar(-king)") argues against the competing truth-claims of Christianity and Islam that the validity and trustworthiness of the revelation of Mount Sinai is based on the fact that it was revealed to all Israelites and not

**24** See footnote 12.

just to Moses.[25] Moreover, this also becomes his argument when he is disputing the truth-claims of Aristotelian philosophy as well:

> [Aristotle] exerted his mind, because he had no tradition from any reliable source at his disposal. He meditated on the beginning and end of the world, but found as much difficulty in the theory of a beginning as in that of eternity. Finally, these abstract speculations which he made for eternity prevailed, and he found no reason to inquire into the chronology or derivation of those who lived before him. Had he lived among a people with well authenticated and generally acknowledged traditions, he would have applied his deductions and arguments to establish the theory of creation, however difficult, instead of eternity, which is even much more difficult to accept.[26]

In other words: True knowledge is only established when it is validated by a tradition, which in turn must be authenticated by a critical number of reliable witnesses. As Ha-Levy makes clear, 600,000 people cannot possibly err.

However, as stated before, the 600,000 people include only males over the age of 20 minus the tribe of Levy, which is exempted from the count. Also women and children are – according to the biblical text – not counted. But does it not say that *all* Israelites experience the "great voice"? And did we not learn above that the first two of the Ten Commandments were heard by "each and every one according to his strength (*lefi kocho*)" (*Exodus Rabbah* 5:9)? Unlike the *midrash*, the biblical text is actually quite ambivalent in this regard: Before the act of revelation, Moses ritually prepares the male Israelites by commanding them to "[b]e ready for the third day: do not come near a woman (*al-tigshu el-isha*)" (Exod. 19:15), which might give the impression that women are excluded as they are – for certain reasons not explicitly mentioned here – perceived to be ritually 'unclean' for men to be near them.[27]

In their *midrashic* interpretations, the rabbis, however, suggest a more inclusive reading and understanding of this verse: "So you shall say to the house of Jacob" (Exod. 19:3) – these are the women. God said to Moses, speak to them of the general matters (*yekholot*) that they are able to hear.

> And tell to the children/sons of Israel (*beney Yisrael*)" (Exod. 19:3) – these are the men. God said to Moses, say to them specifications of things (*diqduqey ha-devarim*) that they are able to hear. Another explanation: Why were the women first? Since they are keen to follow

25 ha-Levy, Yehudah, *Kitab al Khazari*, transl. Hartwig Hirschfeld, London: George Routledge and Sons, 1905, 1:83–87, 58–60; 1:97, 67.

26 Ibid., 1:65, 54.

27 Plaskow, Judith, "Contemporary Reflection on Parashat Yitro (Exodus) 18:1–20:23," in: Tamara Cohn Eskenazi/Andrea L. Weiss (eds), *The Torah. A Women's Commentary*, 423–4, New York: URJ Press, 2008.

> mitzvot (*mizdarzot be-mitzvot*). Another explanation: so that they could accustom their children to *Torah*. R. Tachlifa Deqeysarin [the "kingmaker"?] said, the Holy One, blessed is He, said "When I created the world, I commanded only the First Man (*adam ha-rishon*); and after that Eve was commanded, and she transgressed and corrupted the world. Now, if I do not call to the women first, they will nullify the *Torah* (*hen mevatlot et ha-Torah*) (*Exodus Rabbah* 28:2).

At first, the *midrash* carefully distinguishes between the "house of Jacob" and the "children/sons of Israel", thus allowing for a more inclusive reading concerning those present at the revelation at Sinai. It, however, also differentiates between what was actually revealed to both groups, as it suggests that God is attempting to grasp the attention of his respective audiences with different things so "that they are able to hear". Consequently, the so-called "general matters" (*yekholot*) are for the women and the "specifications of things" (*diqduqey ha-devarim*) – a notion we already encountered above concerning the special knowledge conveyed to the rabbis at Sinai – are for the men. Nevertheless, this could still be read as disparaging and discriminating towards women, as it suggests that women's intellectual capabilities are inferior to those of men. It is needless to remark here that the rabbis' conceptions of women's rights and roles differ much from our modern understanding. But what is remarkable in this passage is that they appear to considerately shift the issue from intellectual matters towards ascribed social roles by expressing appreciation for women's educational competences in initially teaching and accustoming children to the Torah. Still, it is a typical male viewpoint finding expression in this explanation.

Certainly, the most striking argument, however, is that God calls the women at Sinai first because of His bad consciousness for a mistake He made initially when creating 'man.' Their coming second in the creation process eventually led to envy and betrayal, so now – maybe in an attempt of righting an old wrong – God calls out to them first. Regardless of how this passage has to be understood correctly – as an expression of divine remorse or of divine justice – the rabbis make, in any event, a strong case for consequent inclusiveness of the Sinaitic experience, as God actually addressed it to all of Israel, to "each and every one according to her/his strength" (*Exodus Rabbah* 5:9).

## 3.4 Completeness: "This Whole Torah Which Is Found in Our Hands Today"

The concept of the "*Torah* (is) from Heaven" has also played an important role in the encounters with other religions like Christianity and Islam, with Jews having to face insinuations and accusations that they had distorted or abrogated the original Word (*dibbur*) of God. In this context, the famous dogmatic formulation commonly referred to as the "13 principles of faith" (*shaloshah 'asar 'iqqarim shel emunah*) by the medieval Jewish philosopher and legal scholar R. Moses Maimonides establishes a clear and decisive position.

However, this attempt of dogmatic positioning is not as typical and self-evident for rabbinic discourse as one might think. As a matter of fact, Maimonides' principles have been subject to wide critique and controversy throughout the centuries.[28] In a famous rebuke, Moses Mendelssohn stated that Judaism does not know any religious creeds, but it is rather defined by religious deeds (*mitzvot*). But one has to bear in mind the historical circumstances under which the principles were originally formulated: they were a response to the religious persecution under the Almohad dynasty in Al-Andalus and Northern Africa – a time of crisis, in which the possibility to simply fulfill religious deeds was challenged and consequently the possibilities to uphold Jewish religious identity were threatened. Maimonides' creed articulates a search for a Jewish religious identity beyond being defined by religious practice or 'orthopraxy,' paving the way for an 'orthodoxy' which establishes a framework of required belief. This, however, has normative consequences for the heterodox and deviant positions that stand or are perceived as standing outside this framework: As Maimonides makes clear, those who deny but one of the established principles of faith should no longer to be considered as Jews.

I must admit, Maimonides-scholars like myself sometimes have an apologetic tendency when it comes to offering an explanation of Maimonides more uncompromising views and positions; but for Maimonides there is much more at stake than just establishing a new basis for communal cohesion. Each of his principles also conveys a knowledge and respective understanding of God and how He relates to His creation. Any attempt to question any of these principles would question the very Maimonidean conception of God.

Concerning the question of revelation and whether the "*Torah* (is) from Heaven", the eighth and the ninth principles are of particular importance. The ninth principle, in short, states that the Torah will never be abrogated or changed, nor will there be another Torah given. On one side, this can and should be understood as a reaction towards Christianity and Islam, both believing that their respective revelations have superseded the Torah. But on the other side, truth cannot be subject to change. If the Torah is true, then its truth must be eter-

---

**28** *Kellner, Menachem M., Dogma in Mediaeval Jewish Thought. From Maimonides to Abravanel*, Oxford & New York: The Littman Library of Jewish Civilization, 1986.

nal. What can be understood as truth, can be concluded from the eighth principle.[29] It states

> [t]hat the *Torah* is from Heaven, and that is what we believe in, namely that this *Torah*, which is in our hands today, is the one given to Moses, our teacher, peace be upon him, and it is completely from the mouth of the Almighty; which is to say that it all came to him from God in a manner that is metaphorically called 'speech' (hebr. *dibbur*/arab. *kalām*). And no one knows how it came to him except Moses himself, peace be upon him, since it came to him. And we believe that he was like a scribe who is dictated to and writes down all of the events, the stories and the commandments. And therefore he is called the "engraver/lawgiver" (*mechoqeq*).[30]

The position Maimonides establishes here sounds like an attempted systematization of the various rabbinic opinions we have encountered above: God dictates the Torah and Moses acts as His scribe or "engraver". But Moses' special role as mediator between God and Israel is also epistemologically necessary due to Maimonides decisive oppositions to any anthropomorphic conceptions of God. As Maimonides lays out in the sixth and seventh principles, the uniqueness of Moses' prophecy derives from his superior intellectual faculties which allow him to know God's will; therefore he can act as "engraver/lawgiver", as a translator of divine knowledge into human language, of the ideal into the actual. Maimonides follows R. Yishma'el's famous dictum that "the Torah speaks in the language of 'men' (*dibrah Torah bi-lsehon beney adam*)" (*Sifrey Numbers* § 112). The epistemological problem, however, lies therein that the "language of 'men'" is conventional, it is context-dependent and subject to change. A consequent belief in the divine origin of the Torah therefore leads, according to Maimonides, to a radical epistemological consequence, namely that the divine knowledge conveyed in the Torah cannot be adequately comprehended by human understanding:

---

**29** As J. David Bleich has pointed out, the eighth principle can in principle be understood "as an affirmation of the authenticity of the Masoretic text," see Bleich, J. David, *With Perfect Faith. The Foundations of Jewish Belief*, New York: Ktav Publishing House, 1983, 365; for more detailed discussion of the problem of the Masoretic text in light of the Maimonidean principles, but also a critique of the modern day Orthodox conception of "Torah (is) from Heaven", see Shapiro, Marc B., *The Limits of Orthodox Theology. Maimonides' Thirteen Principles Reappraised*, Oxford/New York: The Littman Library of Jewish Civilization, 2011, 91 ff.

**30** Maimonides, Moses, "*Commentary on the Mishnah, Introduction to Pereq Ḥeleq*," in: *Haqdamot ha-RaMBaM la-Mishnah*, ed. by Isaac Shailat, Maaleh Adumim/Jerusalem: Mossad ha-Rav Kook, 5752 [1992], 144 (Hebr.); 372–373 (Arab.).

> And there is no difference between "And the sons of Cham were Kush and Mitzrayim" (Genesis 10:6), "and his wife's name was Meheytabel" (Genesis 36:39), "And Timnah was his concubine" (Genesis 36:12) and "I am the Lord, your God" (Exodus 20:2) and "Hear Israel" (Deuteronomy 6:4); since they are all from the mouth of the Almighty and it is all the *Torah* of God – complete, pure and holy truth. And anyone who says, "These type of verses or stories were written by Moses on his own", is for our sages and prophets a heretic (hebr. *kofer*/arab. *kāfir*) [...] since he thinks that there is a heart and a peel to the *Torah* and that these chronicles and stories do not have a point to them and that they are from Moses our teacher, peace be upon him.

In other words: Each verse and every word of the Torah is of equal importance, as they are all articulations of God, verbal manifestations of His divine will. Taken as a whole, the Torah reveals comprehensive insight into the true structures of reality – a divine master plan that cannot, however, be fully unraveled and comprehended by the human intellect. Distinguishing between "heart and peel", between core and surface, between what seems to be important and what appears to be less important, might be a human attempt to come to terms with its limitations by making sense through creating some kind of structure for basic orientation. But it should not be mistaken as an adequate understanding and true knowledge.

Consequently, to distinguish between divine and human knowledge is theologically important for upholding the principle of the divine origin of the Torah:

> And this matter of one who holds that the *Torah* (is) not from Heaven, the sages said about it,[31] that it is one who believes the whole *Torah* is from the mouth of the Almighty except for this one verse, which the Holy One, blessed be He, did not say, but rather it was from Moses himself. And this is "Because he has despised the word of the Lord" (Numbers 15:31). God, may He be exalted, is above the statements of the heretics. Rather every single word of the *Torah* contains wisdom and wonders for the one who understands it.

At first glance, it appears that Maimonides argues consequently in line with what we have seen before (e. g. b. *Shabbat* 89a). However, in the last sentence Maimonides moves beyond the implied apologetics. The phrase "the one who understands it" (hebr. *mi she-ha-mevino*/arab. *li-man fahima*) is noticeable, as similar formulations (hebr. *ha-mevin yavin*/arab. *yafham al-fahīm*) are frequently used in works of medieval Jewish thought, indicating that understanding of a certain matter requires a specific knowledge. To what Maimonides appears to somewhat cryptically allude are his personal philosophical-theological views, namely that true knowledge of God, like the one Moses possessed, can only be achieved

31 Cf. Sanhedrin 99a.

through the perfection of one's intellectual faculties. It cannot be acquired by simply adhering to popular beliefs based on inspired imagination.

# 4 Actualizations and Perspectives

The way fundamental concepts and principles are often presented suggests that they are indeed supratemporal articulations – or that is, at least, how they are commonly perceived. Yet in reality, the orientations, explanations, and meanings they provide only remain relevant to people as long as they relate to their actual and concrete historical experiences. This, of course, implies that counter to said suggestion these principles are never 'engraved' or static articulations, but must always be dynamically negotiated and actualized. Re-negotiation and re-actualization particularly matter in times of crisis, when established frameworks of traditional self-understanding and practice are fundamentally challenged. In many respects, modernity has posed such a challenge for Jews and Judaism as a whole, not just of the traditional normative kind. With the shift from a communal to an individual and private understanding of religion, with growing individual freedom vis-à-vis a growing feeling of rootlessness and existential alienation (*Entfremdung*), with the surfacing of new wants and needs which also necessitate the search for new meanings, these principles of traditional Jewish belief have themselves become subject of critical scrutiny.

## 4.1 New Thought(s)

Sensing abstract philosophical thought to be out of touch with real life, Franz Rosenzweig – whom we already have encountered above – deemed it necessary to articulate a 'new thought' (*Neues Denken*) – a 'philosophy of religion' (*Religionsphilosophie*) which is not aimed at an idealist understanding of the world through abstract concepts and principles, but is rather dedicated to discover meanings in concrete existence. He found a precursor in his former teacher, the neo-Kantian philosopher Hermann Cohen (1842–1918). Cohen, who himself ascertained that Immanuel Kant had not adequately investigated the question of religion within the system of philosophy, argued in his late work *Religion of Reason out of the Sources of Judaism* that revelation is a "creation of reason",[32]

32 Cohen, Hermann, *Religion der Vernunft aus den Quellen des Judentums*, Frankfurt a. M.: J. Kauffmann, $^{2}$1929, 84.

meaning an expression of moral reason enabling 'man' to become a moral being. Accordingly Cohen assesses that revelation should not to be simply understood as a one-time event that occurred at Mount Sinai. It rather represents an ongoing and continuous process working towards the end goal of the historic process, namely the ultimate realization of the moral perfection of humankind. Cohen's emphasis on the ethical dimension of revelation – the idea often referred to in a broader intellectual framework as 'ethical monotheism' – profoundly influenced many Jewish thinkers in his wake – for example, R. Leo Baeck (1873–1956), a leading figure of liberal Judaism in Germany and England, who, based on the Cohenian conception of 'ethical monotheism,' described revelation as a kind of religious 'revolution.'

Though Rosenzweig did not follow Cohen's definition of 'God' as a concept of universal ethical laws – as such radical abstraction actually implies both a depersonalization of God as well as a reduction of the divine agency – he shared the other's overall ethical outlook. Cohen's conception of correlation, the dialogical relationship between God and 'man,' had an impact on Rosenzweig's longtime friend and partner in translating the Hebrew Bible into German (*Verdeutschung der Schrift*), Martin Buber. Buber views revelation primarily not as a form of mediated experience, but as an actual experience that can only take place and realize itself in dialogical life, in the immediate subject–subject encounter and relationship of the 'I' and the 'Thou.' What is then meant by revelation is a subjective awareness of both the "Presence" (*Gegenwärtigkeit*) of the divine other and the actual "presence" (*Gegenwart*) of the relationship formed. What revelation is not, in Buber's opinion, is a source or medium of revealed content.

This dialogical-relational concept of revelation also plays an important part in the theological thought of Buber's successor at the *Jüdisches Lehrhaus* in Frankfurt am Main, R. Abraham Joshua Heschel (1907–1972). For Heschel, revelation is realized and finds expression in the dialogic encounter of God and humankind. As an actual experience, it has a living reality or presence that does not simply cease in the irretrievable fleetness and momentariness of a one-time event. Revelation is a communicative act that can be maintained and continued through mutual commitment and engagement. In Heschel's opinion, God deeply cares about His creation, is passionately 'in search of (hu)man (beings)'; He is affected by what happens in this world, is involved in history. This makes revelation a relational experience with regards to time, as the historical and meta-historical are indeed related to one another: "The prophet's task is to convey a divine view, yet as a person he is a point of view. He speaks from the perspective of God as perceived from his own situation."[33] Heschel furthermore argues that "Judaism is based on a minimum of revelation and a maximum of interpretation, upon the will of God and upon the understanding of Israel".[34] In other words, Judaism is less about the faithful and obedient fulfillment of the content revealed as expressed in the dictum *na'aseh ve-nishm'a* in Exod. 24:7, but actually calls for the critical but active engagement resonating in the *ve-sham'anu ve-'asinu* of Deut. 5:23.

Rosenzweig dedicated his philosophical investigations into Judaism to the question of the concrete and particular, voicing his concern that universal abstractions do not relate to actual human experience; Buber and Heschel on the other hand – in their own respective ways – both actually universalized the concept of revelation in Judaism. Yet despite their differing approaches and perspectives, R. Ignatz Maybaum (1897–1976), a German-British Reform rabbi and student of Franz Rosenzweig, characterized all of the above as modern representatives of what he calls "prophetic Judaism", that is, centered on the biblical faith of the prophets and the inherently moral messages of their prophecies. While Maybaum finds this "prophetic Judaism" also deeply resonating in classical rabbinic thought, he fervently wants to distinguish it from the "halakhic Judaism" of Orthodox Jewry, which due to its legalistic and doctrinal nature fails in his opinion to comprehend and implement the true meanings conveyed in revelation and prophecy.

However, Maybaum's somewhat polemic characterization of "halakhic Judaism" does not capture its inherent dynamics, which finds an expression, for example, in the dialectic theology of R. Joseph B. Soloveitchik (1903–1993). Based on Max Scheler's distinction between 'natural revelation' and 'positive revelation,' but also in accordance with the structuralist methodologies of the Lithuanian yeshivah world he came from, Soloveitchik articulates the idea of a dialectical consciousness of the religious personality: "The paramount principle is faith in His revelation to man, and the readiness to fulfill His will unconditionally. Man seeks God and is also a captive of God."[35] The typological '(hu)man' is existentially torn between opposing binary poles, never being able to fully overcome the dialectic tension. However, any dialectic tension also implies an established relation, enabling one to dynamically oscillate between the poles. Herein Soloveitchik senses the fundamental mechanic of the reality, finding an expres-

33 Heschel, Abraham Joshua, *The Prophets*, New York: Harper & Row, 1962, 2001, xxii.
34 Heschel, Abraham Joshua, *God in Search of Man. A Philosophy of Judaism*. New York: Jewish Publication Society of America, 1955, 275.
35 Soloveitchik, Joseph B., *And from There You Shall Seek*, Jersey City, NJ: Ktav Publishing House 2008, 41.

sion in the dialectic relation between transcendence and immanence, ideal and real, revelation and concealment.

While Soloveitchik's concern with the implementation of the ideal in the real world conveys a profoundly moral outlook – quite similar to what we have seen in Hermann Cohen – the Israeli religious philosopher Yeshayahu Leibowitz (1903–1994) assumes that religion and morality stand in stark contrast to one another. While the former is a heteronomic framework of laws and norms, the latter is autonomously based on human reasoning and is correspondingly intrinsically human-oriented. For Leibowitz, revelation as a religious experience cannot be related to or rooted in any kind of historical experience. Rather it finds its true religious realization in the moment of the intentional fulfillment of the divine commandments "for its own sake" (*li-shemah*), that is, "for the sake of heaven" (*le-shem shamayim*).

Counter to Leibowitz' one-sided concept of "for its own sake", R. David Hartman (1931–2013), a former student of R. Joseph B. Soloveitchik and founder of the Shalom Hartman Institute in Jerusalem, writes:

> Revelation, as I understand it, was not meant to be a source of absolute, eternal and transcendent truth. Rather, it is God's speaking to human beings within the limited framework of the human language and history. [...] Revelation is God's speaking to human beings for their own sake and not for the sake of uncovering the mysteries of the Divine Mind.[36]

Revelation is the infinite God's way of relating to concrete human existence and its historical particularity, finding an expression in the concrete moment.

Despite certain fundamental differences, the concepts and frameworks described so far can be characterized as 'theocentric' or as grounded in such a theological perspective. This notion is, however, fundamentally challenged by R. Mordecai Menahem Kaplan (1881–1983), the founder of Reconstructionist Judaism and a colleague of Heschel at the Jewish Theological Seminary of New York. Unlike most other Jewish theological thinkers, Kaplan absolutely rejects the notion of the Sinaitic revelation as a supernatural event: "Spiritual religion affirms that it is unnecessary to resort to supernatural revelation for experiencing the reality of God. Man's experience of God is as real as his experience of his own personality."[37]

In other words: The experience of God is grounded in the way in which humans experience and understand reality. Revelation is consequently that which enables them to live as a religious community. Unlike for Hermann Cohen, whose

36 Hartman, David, *Conflicting Visions*, New York: Schocken Books, 1990, 248.
37 Kaplan, Mordecai M., *The Future of the American Jew*, New York: Macmillan, 1948, 192.

basic ethical conceptions and concerns he shares, God is for Kaplan not a transcendent entity or transcending principle that exists beyond experienced reality. Rather the idea of God acts within experienced reality as a "power that makes for salvation".[38] Kaplan's radical critique of any type of supernatural revelation is profoundly influenced by the philosophical and sociological convictions of his time. By rejecting such conceptions, he offers a view of revelation as a creative act of self-revelation or self-liberation, as an expression of becoming.

Kaplan's concept of an evolving nature of revelation has lately been picked up and adapted by the Orthodox feminist philosopher Tamar Ross (b. 1938), as she therein finds similarities to the teachings of R. Abraham Isaac ha-Cohen Kook (1865–1935), for whom revelation is a cumulative and expanding process.[39] Both understandings of revelation eventually allow the incorporation and accommodation new voices and interpretations into the existing framework.

According to R. Louis Jacobs (1920–2006), a significant but controversial voice of Conservative Judaism in England, Judaism allows for such dynamic changes because, in the concept of revelation, the historical and meta-historical concur:

> Many of us have come to appreciate that the idea of God giving the Torah to Moses – call it "myth" if you will, since the connotation of this term in scholarship means truth expressed in non-historical terms – suggests that Judaism developed by using the God-to-Moses paradigm as a way of expressing the idea that Judaism is a developing and yet eternal faith.[40]

I pause here, but not out of lack of other potential voices. The ones presented above are what one could call the 'usual suspects,' meaning those who commonly appear and are mentioned within general works on modern Jewish thought. Although their ideas and positions have attained a certain prominence, influence, and representativeness within said discourse, they nevertheless should be rather read and understood as exemplary voices within a larger discursive framework dealing with the dynamic, dialogic, or dialectical relationship between God and human beings, between the universal abstract idea and the particular historical experience of revelation.

---

**38** See particularly chapter 2 of Kaplan's *The Meaning of God in Modern Jewish Religion*, New York: Behrman's Jewish Book House, 1937, which is entitled: "God as the power that makes for salvation."

**39** Ross, Tamar, *Expanding the Palace of Torah Orthodoxy and Feminism*, Lebanon, NH: Brandeis University Press, 2004.

**40** Jacobs, Louis, 'The Human Element in Divine Revelation,' under: https://louisjacobs.org/articles/the-human-element-in-divine-revelation/ (last accessed April 13, 2019).

## 4.2 Revelation and Reason, *Reloaded*

As discussed above (cf. 1.d.), the understanding of Judaism as a 'revealed religion' is for various reasons problematic, often overlooking or even dismissing the fact that Judaism is a flexible and dynamic religious tradition, influenced and shaped by ideas from within and without.

This dynamic can be best illustrated by taking a closer look at how the relationship between revelation and reason has been discussed within different contexts of Jewish thought. One of the central medieval discourses, for example, focuses on the question of the nature of religious laws. Based on the distinction between *mishpatim* (ordinances) and *chuqqim* (statutes), medieval Jewish thinkers attempted to discern and offer possible reasons for the commandments (*ta'amei ha-mitzvot*). Following the basic conception of the Mu'tazilite school of *Kalām* (Islamic systematic theology), R. Sa'adiyah Gaon established the difference between laws based of reason (*'aqliyyāt* in Arabic; *sikhliyot* in Hebrew) and revelational laws (*sam'iyyāt* in Arabic; *shim'iyot* in Hebrew), though he considered the latter to be epistemologically superior. Other medieval Jewish philosophical-theological thinkers like R. Yehudah ha-Levy, R. Abraham ibn Daud (1110–1180), R. Moses Maimonides or R. Chasday Qresqas (1340–1410/11) have offered similar or differing explanations of these categories shaped by their respective philosophical and religious dispositional beliefs; they will be taken up and reinterpreted by later thinkers like Baruch Spinoza, Moses Mendelssohn, or Hermann Cohen, who will adapt them to the discursive frameworks in which they are embedded.

However, the question of the relationship between revelation and reason is not solely about the possible results or conclusions to be drawn, nor is it an assessment of whether these are in conflict, complementary to each other, or even identical. From an exegetical standpoint, it is particularly the hermeneutics that matter in regard to how we methodologically approach the texts we intend to interpret. That is why I would like to point to two readings which have been the subject of recent discussion. The first reading concerns the Israeli political philosopher Yoram Hazony (b. 1964), known to a broader audience for his indeed controversial positions on the idea of nationhood. His book *The Philosophy of the Hebrew Scripture* is a fundamental critique of Western political thinkers like Leo Strauss (1899–1973),[41] whose influential model of Athens and Jerusalem presumes and establishes a dichotomic relationship between reason and revela-

41 Hazony, Yoram, *The Philosophy of the Hebrew Scriptures*, Cambridge: Cambridge University Press, 2012.

tion, doubt and faith. Consequently, Hazony is explicitly interested in the relationship between the universal/general and the particular in the Hebrew Bible. By carefully comparing Greek philosophers with the biblical prophets, and philosophical concepts with the biblical narrative, he works out similar questions, themes, and ideas. This eventually brings him to challenge the Straussian notion, concluding that the Hebrew Bible indeed contains and teaches about fundamental philosophical truths. Yet a close reading of Hazony's biblical close reading actually shows that he – more or less subtly – shifts the discussion about revelation and reason from the epistemological to the political. In doing so, it becomes quite evident that he conceptually operates within a modern political framework which defines how he reads the biblical text and narrative.

A somewhat different approach towards the questions at hand is articulated by Lord R. Jonathan Sacks (b. 1948), the former Chief Rabbi of the United Hebrew Congregations of Great Britain and currently one of the most prominent and influential Jewish voices in Europe. In the introduction to his *Covenant & Conversation: A Weekly Reading of the Jewish Bible*, in which he offers insights and commentaries to the weekly Torah portions, Sacks deems it important to point out the different approaches to truth that philosophy and the biblical narrative offer: "To put it at its simplest: philosophy is *truth as system*. Genesis is *truth as story*."[42] A philosophical system and a religious narrative not only differ in regard to their conceptions and considerations, but moreover they operate with different literary means and expressions. They come with specific presumptions which deeply affect the hermeneutical approach to the text as well as the respective exegesis. Herein lies the fundamental difference between Hazony's and R. Sacks' readings of the Bible: While the former reads the Bible as philosophy, the latter reads the biblical text philosophically.

The point that I am trying to make here is that the question of revelation and reason is not only about competing truth claims, but has much to do with the respective capabilities and experiences of how to cognitively approach reality in a broader sense. As my academic home is the discipline of philosophy, I consider it both epistemologically and ethically fundamental that we humans can share a universal understanding; but at the same time, I have to be aware of the limits of universal reason, consequently taking a skeptical stance towards any monolithic conceptions of truth. As a somewhat traditional Jew, I find orientation, meaning, and comfort in the words of the Torah, which have an impact on how I act in and interact with this world. Yet at the same time, I have to be aware

---

**42** Sacks, Jonathan, *Covenant & Conversation. A Weekly Reading of the Jewish Bible*, London/Jerusalem: Maggid, 2009, 6.

that this truth I believe in is always subject to human interpretation and understanding: "The Torah speaks in the language of 'men'". Lest to forget that "[s]he is not in heaven!"

Personally I find some comfort in the fact that I am not alone in facing these questions, that my intellectual heroes struggled with them as well: R. Moses Maimonides sought to achieve synthesis between philosophical knowledge and religious law, whereas Baruch Spinoza passionately argued for a consequent separation of the theological and the political for the sake of a greater common good; R. Abraham J. Heschel focused on the idea of transcendence, whereas R. Modercai M. Kaplan conceptually operated within the framework of immanent and concrete reality; R. Joseph B. Soloveitchik yearned to implement the halakhic ideal in the real world, whereas R. David Hartman challenged said halakhic ideal in defense of the human condition.

What I am trying to say is that the relationship between reason and revelation has – at least in my opinion – never been an either/or question, nor can it be answered in such fashion. Rather, the true challenge for every religious person lies in their dialectical relationship, confronting us with the paradox of how we come to terms with the different ways and means of how we experience and understand reality. This paradox is, in my opinion, summed up best by Franz Rosenzweig, who wrote about the biblical story of Balaam that all day one takes it to be some kind of fairy tale, but when one is eventually called to the Torah on Shabbat, it becomes "that which is communicated to me provided I am able to fulfill the commandment of the hour, namely to open my ears".[43]

Meaning cannot be found only through abstraction, but through concrete contextualization, by taking into account the respective particular contexts in which we experience and act. That is why in my opinion R. Jonathan Sacks' distinction of "Genesis is truth as story" matters: A narrative is not an abstract definition, but a framework that allows us to establish a connection and relation to that which is conveyed.

## 4.3 Dividing Lines

Origins generally account for one's beginnings, foundations, or points of departure; but moreover, they deeply affect one's very self-understanding. It makes a great difference to understand one's tradition as either having originated from a

43 Glatzer,Nahum N. (ed.), *Franz Rosenzweig. His Life and Thought*, New York: Jewish Publication Society of America, 1953, 246.

divine source or having been developed solely under specific historical circumstances.

Regarding the understanding and place of revelation in the broader framework of contemporary Judaism, the doctrine that "Torah (is) from Heaven" has become of increasing importance. Unlike in the Maimonidean context, wherein its main purpose is to apologetically define Jewish belief vis-à-vis the without, it is nowadays often used to establish theological-ideological boundaries within. Today, the belief in it serves as somewhat of a litmus test concerning where one stands or positions oneself along the spectrum of Jewish denominations. While these denominations provide a framework for association, they, of course, should not be viewed as monolithic or static entities. Like in most other religious movements and trends, they are rather fluid and dynamic in regard to the respective self-understandings they articulate; based on the various tendencies and leanings encountered within a certain denomination, the boundaries between these frameworks seem to be permeable rather than hermetical. Nevertheless, these denominations not only have a profound influence on the conceptual or ideological outlook and understanding of one's Judaism, but also practically affect the way in which one lives and acts as a Jew.

On one end of the denominational spectrum, we have traditional normative Judaism, commonly labeled as 'Orthodoxy.' For most of its various branches and movements, the Torah is the ultimate source of truth, but in a theoretical and in a practical way. The denial of the heavenly origin of the Torah is accordingly generally considered heretical, as those who deny it not only challenge its divine authorship and authority, but in doing so they also challenge rabbinic authority as well. Regarding this, Maimonides' eighth principle has become both a dogmatic cornerstone and bulwark for Orthodox Jewry. On the opposing end of that spectrum, we find the varieties of Reform/liberal/progressive Judaism, which hardly can be characterized as an overarching dogmatic movement at all, as for the most part it leaves matters of belief to the individual Jew. This appears to be a much more complex issue for Conservative Judaism in its coming to terms with both the belief that the Torah was revealed in a metaphorical sense and that the process of revelation continues, with its commandments and teachings correspondingly subject to historical development and change.

But the question of whether the "Torah (is) from Heaven" or not extends beyond the discourse of denominational positioning and beliefs. It, for example, also affects the question of how one should study Torah – or, to be more precise, how to position oneself to historical-critical approaches to the biblical text, like biblical criticism.

## 4.4 Concluding Remarks

I apologize in advance that in these concluding remarks I will here and there associatively bring in quotes from and references to pop culture. I am doing so because I feel that through these references and images my abstract overthinking might become more tangible and relatable.

All apologetics aside, I cannot shake off the feeling that in the end this essay feels somewhat like an episode from the 1990s TV-show *Seinfeld:* Like a great big musing about everything and nothing! Of course, the complexity and polyphony of Jewish tradition surely deserve way more than "6 seasons and a movie"[44] to scratch the surface, let alone to give a comprehensive understanding of the concept of revelation in Judaism. I can, therefore, only hope that what I have tried to convey in these lines might not prove too disappointing to some readers for missing out on a particular idea, text, or author that is important to them. But let me assure you that I am well aware of the many things I have not touched upon; for not having explored every possible angle. However, there are also reasons for this: For example, the rich Jewish mystical tradition I left out on purpose, as – in my opinion – it requires some pre-knowledge and historical context that I cannot presume or sufficiently cover here. Similarly, I have not dealt with Jewish perspectives on historical biblical criticism, as I am not really immersed in this matter. But I guess sometimes one needs to embrace one's flaws. The primary purpose of this essay is, after all, to serve as an introduction for those who are not yet familiar with the subject and the sources at hand. Consequently, all that I can eventually offer here is *a* and not *the* concept of revelation in Judaism; *a reflection on* and not *the great big book about* everything and nothing. But that it is *a* concept does not automatically suggest that the concept presented is solely and simply based on *my* own conceptions. Rather, it was important to me *not* to convey a particular message or conception shaped by my own personal, professional, or ideological defaults, prepositions, and preferences. However, as I am the one who is framing the narration, I am of course also the one responsible for steering the reader's attention in this or that direction. Maybe these reflections and considerations are indeed an act of overthinking concerning my own methods. But as I have stated in my introductory remarks, I wanted to approach the concept of revelation in Judaism through the multi-facetedness, multi-perspectivity and multi-narrativity of Jewish tradition, because a) I consider

---

44 This phrase originates in Dan Harmon's comedy TV-series *Community*, Episode 2.21 ("Paradigms of Human Memory"). Then after its cancellation, it became the fans' rallying cry to renew the show.

this very tradition our shared heritage, regardless of what we believe, where we position ourselves, or how we live as Jews; b) in sharing this tradition, we should refrain from staking any claims of interpretative exclusiveness; and c) as Judaism is an inherently plural tradition, we should take and treat its polyphony seriously by not confining Judaism to a single perspective, understanding, or trend.

On the other hand, it is this very polyphony which often appears to challenge us in our respective self-understandings. Nevertheless, in my opinion, the true challenge lies not in argumentatively defending and maintaining certain positions and beliefs, but in the choices we are facing and the decisions we eventually have to make and hold. And even though conceptually "all the pieces matter!" (to quote detective Lester Freamon from the HBO series *The Wire*), most of the time not everything can matter equally in a given situation or context.

Maybe these reflections of mine are somewhat redundant, but in 'interesting times' like these, when extreme or populist voices call for monolithic and exclusive views of the world, it somehow feels important to instead constantly remind oneself that the world, its phenomena, and yes, even one's own system of belief, are way more complex. In order to understand what Judaism actually is, one has to understand the Jews, as Judaism is shaped and defined by Jews, in each generation as well as from generation to generation, *le-dor va-dor.* It means to engage into the texts and traditions, to listen to voices, even if an understanding might at first prove difficult. Correspondingly, in order to understand the concept of revelation (in Judaism), one has to understand those who relate to and experience, interpret and re-interpret, struggle and live with it. And so while in the end the principal question – what the concept of revelation in Judaism is – might not have been tackled in its entirety, I do hope that it has become clear up till here that the understanding of revelation emerges out of Jews relating their tradition and their actual situation or circumstances to one another, out of relating texts and contexts.

For me as a Jew, the beauty of Jewish tradition lies therein – that it quite consciously deals with uncertainties, that it embraces the paradoxes of how we experience and relate to both divine and actual reality. Accordingly, the concept of revelation in Judaism cannot easily be defined as representing just one thing or idea; rather it echoes a dialectic unity of many opposites: Revealing the Divine as well as veiling it; being the origin and *telos*, the designation and purpose; marking a point of departure and a point of arrival, yet also encompassing the journey in between these two; a universal idea becoming tangible and relatable through a particular history.

Revelation is a communicative act and process between the Divine and human beings, an inter-subjective interaction through revealing and perceiving, speaking and hearing, giving and receiving. It is a call that can be answered or not; a gift that can be accepted or rejected; an invitation allowing one to agree or to disagree, to be in accord or at odds with the divine will. While it offers guidance and orientation, it also presents a constant challenge in coming to terms with the perspectives it provides. It determines the footsteps one should walk in, but also allows one to walk freely by choosing one's own path within the boundaries it defines.

In the end, revelation is about a special relationship, a coming together of radically different needs, interests, and expectations. Or as Abraham Joshua Heschel has so poetically phrased it: On one side we have "God in search of man" – of a partner in creation – on the other side we have "(a hu)man (being)" coming to a realization that she or he "is not alone" in her or his quest for meaning beyond the seeming absurdity of existence. Revelation is then about mutual sensitivities: In human beings it develops a sensitivity and appreciation of the Divine (voice) calling and reaching out to them, while the Divine enables human beings to explore the intricate complexities of reality by providing us the tools of understanding that "life, the universe and the everything"[45] else are not random. Yet by understanding this, human beings have to come to the realization that they, in turn, can only actually answer the divine call by accepting and fulfilling their designated responsibilities.

That is why in closing, I would like to associatively borrow a concept of one of the Jewish theologians, Michael Fishbane (b. 1943), a concept which he calls "sacred attunement."[46] It describes an act of becoming aware and a personal process of developing a sensitivity for the ineffable Divine. Ever since I had the pleasure to partake in a workshop when Michael Fishbane first introduced this idea, I imagine this 'attunement' functioning pretty much like amateur radio, trying to search for radio signals out there and tracing them back to their original sender. Maybe we are deliberately searching for a transmission on a particular frequency, or maybe we just accidently happen to stumble over one. But in any case, searching for a transmission requires us to carefully listen, focus, and push our senses through the static and other distracting noises of actual reality. At times, we often might feel out of sync, requiring us to constantly to make (re-)adjustments by taking into consideration how or from where we are actually searching.

However, I consider the sensitivity expressed in the concept of 'sacred attunement' important not only in regard to our personal search for the Divine,

---

45 Adams, Douglas, *Life, the Universe and Everything*, London: Pan Books, 1982.

46 Fishbane, Michael, *Sacred Attunement. A Jewish Theology*, Chicago/London: University of Chicago Press, 2010.

but also in regard to inter-religious encounters as well. Our sensitivity for a divine 'other' should correspondingly make us also sensitive in our approach and relationship towards anything or anyone 'other' than ourselves; it should enable us to see and appreciate the 'other' as our counterpart.

It might come somewhat as a surprise, but I personally do not think that, as it is often assumed and stated, we are actually listening in to the very same transmission or program (see the 'preliminary remarks' above) – but do we really have to? Moreover, would the fact that we do necessarily suggest that the other must be mistaken in his or her 'attunement'?[47] Contrary to what is often alleged, an acceptance and appreciation of the 'attunement' of the other does not, in my opinion, have to imply any relativization of what I myself am 'attuned' to. Rather, it might help us to hone and widen our own perceptions and susceptibilities, not only as a confrontation with or challenge towards our own respective self-understanding, but also as an appreciation of the diversity that makes up our shared reality.

Way too often we make ourselves dependent on our need for absolute clarity and absolute certainty concerning who we are, what we believe in, and how we see the world in order to be able to step out of our communal or personal comfort zones. In stepping out into a world not fully known or revealed to us, absolute certainty cannot and should never be taken for granted or considered to have absolute value itself. Indeed, we are vulnerable, but we may find comfort therein that we are not alone, as according to rabbinic tradition God is not an absolute being but a relational being, whose love finds ultimate expression the giving of the Torah. The covenantal relationship formed thereupon is realized in that the Torah invites and enables us to participate in the framework it offers. Participation is carried out through actively engaging in learning and interpretation of the Torah, not through a passive submission or blind acceptance. Moreover, in the Torah's call for participation resonates a special message, namely that it grants dignity to those it addresses by implying that the addressee indeed has a choice to participate. And this choice is always given, in the concept of *teshuvah*, "returning" or "repentance". But that is a key concept to be discussed another time.

---

**47** Hartman, David, *From Defender to Critic. The Search for a New Jewish Self*, Woodstock: Jewish Lights, 2012, 255.

# Bibliography

Adams, Douglas, *Life, the Universe and Everything*, London: Pan Books, 1982.

Benjamin, Mara H., *Rosenzweig's Bible. Reinventing Scripture for Jewish Modernity*, New York: Cambridge University Press, 2009.

Bleich, J. David, *With Perfect Faith. The Foundations of Jewish Belief*, New York: Ktav Publishing House, 1983

Buber, Martin, *I and Thou, London: Continuum*, 2004.

Cohen, Hermann, *Religion der Vernunft aus den Quellen des Judentums*, Frankfurt a.M.: J. Kauffmann, $^{2}$1929.

Eisen, Arnold, "Divine Legislation as 'Ceremonial Script.' *Mendelssohn* on the Commandments," in: *AJS Review* 15, no. 2 (Fall 1990), 239–67.

Fishbane, Michael, *Sacred Attunement. A Jewish Theology*, Chicago/London: University of Chicago Press, 2010.

Fleischacker, Samuel, *Divine Teaching and the Way of the World. A Defense of Revealed Religion*, New York: Oxford University Press, 2011.

Glatzer, Nahum N. (ed.), *Franz Rosenzweig. His Life and Thought*, New York: Jewish Publication Society of America, 1953.

Grözinger, Karl E., "Abraham Geigers theologische Wende vor dem Hintergrund der neuzeitlichen Debatte von Religion und Vernunft," in: Christian Wiese/Walter Homolka/Thomas Brechenmacher (eds), *Jüdische Existenz in der Moderne. Abraham Geiger und die Wissenschaft des Judentums*, 15–36, Berlin: De Gruyter, 2013.

ha-Levy, Yehudah, *Kitab al Khazari*, transl. Hartwig Hirschfeld, London: George Routledge and Sons, 1905.

Hartman, David, *Conflicting Visions*, New York: Schocken Books, 1990.

Hartman, David, *Israelis and the Jewish Tradition. An Ancient People Debating Its Future*, New Haven, CN: Yale University Press, 2000.

Hartman, David, *From Defender to Critic. The Search for a New Jewish Self*, Woodstock: Jewish Lights, 2012, 255.

Hazony, Yoram, *The Philosophy of the Hebrew Scriptures*, Cambridge: University Press, 2012.

Heschel, Abraham Joshua, *God in Search of Man. A Philosophy of Judaism*, New York: Jewish Publication Society of America, 1955.

Heschel, Abraham Joshua, *The Prophets*, New York: Harper & Row, 1962, 2001.

Heschel, Abraham Joshua, *Heavenly Torah. As Refracted Through the Generations*, ed. and transl. by Gordon Tucker/Leonard Levin, New York: Continuum, 2006.

Hirsch, Samson Raphael, *Horeb. A Philosophy of Jewish Laws and Observances*, transl. Isidore Grunfeld, London: Soncino Press, 1962.

Jacobs, Louis, 'The Human Element in Divine Revelation,' under: https://louisjacobs.org/articles/the-human-element-in-divine-revelation/ (last accessed April 13, 2019).

Kaplan, Mordecai M., *The Meaning of God in Modern Jewish Religion*, New York: Behrman's Jewish Book House, 1937.

Kaplan, Mordecai M., *The Future of the American Jew*, New York: Macmillan, 1948.

Kellner, Menachem M., *Dogma in Mediaeval Jewish Thought. From Maimonides to Abravanel*, Oxford/New York: The Littman Library of Jewish Civilization, 1986.

Kellner, Menachem M., *Must a Jew Believe in Anything?*, Oxford/New York: The Littman Library of Jewish Civilization, 2006[2].
Langer, Gerhard, *Midrasch*, Tübingen: UTB (Mohr Siebeck), 2016.
Maimonides, Moses, "*Commentary on the Mishnah, Introduction to Pereq Ḥeleq*," in: *Haqdamot ha-RaMBaM la-Mishnah*, ed. by Isaac Shailat, Maaleh Adumim/Jerusalem: Mossad ha-Rav Kook, 5752 [1992].
Mandelbaum, Irving J., "Tannatic Exegesis of the Golden Calf Episode," in: Philip R. Davies/Richard T. White (eds): *A Tribute to Geza Vermes. Essays on Jewish and Christian Literature and History*, 207–223, Sheffield: Sheffield Academic Press, 1990.
Marmorstein, Arthur, *Studies in Jewish Theology. The Marmorstein Memorial Volume*, ed. by Joseph Rabbinowitz/Meyer S. Lew, London: Oxford University Press, 1950.
Melamed, Yitzhak Y., "Review of Samuel Fleischacker, Divine Teaching and the Way of the World (Oxford University Press, 2011)," in: *Philosophical Review* 125 (1/2016), 151–154.
Mendelssohn, Moses, *Jerusalem. Or, on Religious Power and Judaism*, Hanover, NH/London: University of New England Press, for Brandeis University Press, 1983.
Novak, David, "Revelation," in: Nicholas de Lange/Miri Freud-Kandel (eds), *Modern Judaism. An Oxford Guide*, 278–289, Oxford/New York: Oxford University Press, 2008.
Plaskow, Judith, "Contemporary Reflection on Parashat Yitro (Exodus) 18:1–20:23," in: Tamara Cohn Eskenazi/Andrea L. Weiss (eds), *The Torah. A Women's Commentary*, 423–4, New York: URJ Press, 2008.
Rosenzweig, Franz, *The Star of Redemption*, transl. Barbara E. Galli, Madison, WI: University of Wisconsin Press, 2005.
Ross, Tamar, *Expanding the Palace of Torah Orthodoxy and Feminism*, Lebanon, NH: Brandeis University Press, 2004.
Rotenstreich, Nathan, *Tradition and Reality. The Impact of History on Modern Jewish Thought*, New York/Toronto: Random House, 1972.
Sacks, Jonathan, *Covenant & Conversation. A Weekly Reading of the Jewish Bible*, London/Jerusalem: Maggid, 2009.
Shapiro, Marc B., *The Limits of Orthodox Theology. Maimonides' Thirteen Principles Reappraised*, Oxford/New York: The Littman Library of Jewish Civilization, 2011.
Silman, Yochanan, *Qol gadol ve-lo yasaf – Torat yisrael beyn shlemut le-hishtalmut*, Jerusalem: Magnes, 1999.
Soloveitchik, Joseph B., *And from There You Shall Seek*, Jersey City, NJ: Ktav Publishing House 2008.
Somers, Margaret R./Gibson, *Gloria D., "Reclaiming the Epistemological 'Other.' Narrative* and the Social Constitution of Identity, in: Craig Calhoun (ed.), *Social Theory and the Politics of Identity*, 37–99, Oxford/Cambridge, MA: Wiley-Blackwell:, 1994.
Weiss Halivni, David, *Revelation Restored. Divine Writ and Critical Responses*, Boulder, CL: Westview Press, 1997.
Yandell, Keith E., *Philosophy of Religion. A Contemporary Introduction*, London/New York: Routledge, 1999.

## Suggestions for Further Reading

*Besides the quoted literature, the following works had a deep impact on my understanding of the concepts, ideas and themes discussed.*

Berger, Michael S., *Rabbinic Authority. The Authority of the Talmudic Sages*, Oxford/New York: Oxford University Press, 1998.

Halbertal, Moshe, *People of the Book. Canon, Meaning, and Authority*, London/Cambridge, MA: Harvard University Press, 1997.

Halbertal, Moshe/Margalit, Avishai, *Idolatry*, London/Cambridge, MA: Harvard University Press, 1992.

Hartman, David, *A Living Covenant. The Innovative Spirit in Traditional Judaism*, Woodstock: Jewish Lights, 1998.

Hartman, Donniel, *The Boundaries of Judaism*, London/New York: Continuum, 2007.

Kreisel, Howard (Haim), *Prophecy. The History of an Idea in Medieval Jewish Philosophy*, Dordrecht: Kluwer Academic Publishers, 2001.

Sagi, Avi, *The Open Canon. On the Meaning of Halakhic Discourse*, London/New York: Continuum, 2007.

Sommer, Benjamin, *Revelation and Authority. Sinai in Jewish Scripture and Tradition*, New Haven/London: Yale University Press, 2015.

Urbach, Ephraim, *The Sages. Their Concepts and Beliefs*, Cambridge, MA: Cambridge University Press, 1987 (reprint).

Christoph Schwöbel

# The Concept of Revelation in Christianity

## 1 Introduction: Contentious Foundations – the Debates on Revelation

The notion of revelation, the idea of God disclosing essential aspects of God's being, will and work to human beings, is of fundamental significance in the monotheistic religions. Everything in the practice and theoretical reflection of religion, in its life of worship and in the ethical orientation it offers, depends on God communicating with human creatures and granting them insight into God's identity and nature, into God's purpose and will for creation and specifically for human creatures. Revelation is the condition for being granted insight into the dynamic and faithfulness of God's actions in the world through which the creator actualizes the divine purpose for creation as it is grounded in God's own being. This is the presupposition for trusting in God, for doing God's will and so to be drawn into acting according to God's purposes. In this sense, every dimension of religious life in the monotheistic religions, their form, their content and the mode of their performance can be traced back to God's communication with the creatures.

One way to describe religions is to see them as multi-dimensional wholes in which every dimension is connected to the others.[1] By distinguishing these dimensions and by exploring their interrelationship, such an approach offers a way of grasping the particularities as well the holistic character of religions. The significance of the idea of revelation becomes immediately clear when one relates the different dimensions of religions to their foundational event, which in theistic religions is seen as a communicative disclosure event establishing a relation between God, humanity and the world which provides the basic orientation for humans who trust in the God who in this way relates to them.

For all monotheistic religions the *dimension of worship* is central. In all acts of worship, in turning to God in prayer, in thanksgiving, petition and praise, in listening to God's word as promise and guidance, it is presupposed that God has disclosed himself as the one who alone is to be worshipped because God is the creator, sustainer, judge and savior of creation. Monotheistic religions are char-

1 For such a multi-dimensional approach see Smart, Ninian, *Dimensions of the Sacred. An Anatomy of the World's Beliefs*, Berkeley/Los Angeles: University of California Press, 1999.

https://doi.org/10.1515/9783110476057-003

acterized in different ways by a *narrative dimension*, principally in their sacred scriptures, in which God is identified and predicated through narratives, recounting God as relating to humans in different modes of address and through God's mighty actions. The monotheistic religions are characterized by an *experiential dimension* where the whole of human experience is shaped and oriented to the revelation of the Divine in various ways. Although the modes of experience may vary from historical to mystical experience, it is always clear that the experience of God relating to humans and to the whole world is the framework for all other human experiences, for determining their significance and for judging their value by relating them to the foundational experience of the address of God in words and events. The way in which God relates to humans is seen in the monotheistic religions as the establishment of a *community*, as shaping its structures of sociality and prescribing its way of life. This community is understood as the exemplary form of sociality that displays the features of human being in relation on the basis of their communal and individual relationship to God. This community is characterized by a specific *ethos* that is grounded in God's relationship to humans. This ethos defines the orientation of human life, by determining the possibilities of action for created agents in relation to the creator and to other creatures, in setting goals that should be strived for, by defining goods which support that orientation, by displaying virtues, conforming to God's will for humans, and identifying vices that deviate from it, and by setting up norms for a human life lived in accordance with revelation. In the monotheistic religions, revelation shapes the *aesthetics* of religion, the way reality is perceived and aesthetically shaped to make its meaning apparent. The specific aesthetics that characterize Judaism, Christianity and Islam respectively trace their particularities back to the understanding of God that is disclosed in revelation and the understanding of what it means to be human that is implied in this disclosure. Every dimension of religious life is rooted in revelation and the specific constellations of these dimensions of religious life can be followed back to the specific content and mode of revelation. Looking at the way revelation is interwoven with the fabric of religion illustrates how revelation shapes the entire religious life and forms the basis for the way believers understand the whole of reality. In monotheistic religions revelation determines the whole understanding of reality. Since the author of revelation is believed as the ground, the meaning and the goal of all reality, so that everything has to be understood in its relation to God, the scope of revelation cannot be limited. Everything can become the means and vehicle of God's revelation.

In view of the foundational role of revelation it is not surprising that the Swiss Reformed theologian Emil Brunner states: "Wherever there is religion, there is the claim to revelation."[2] This should, however, not obscure the fact that there are characteristic differences between theistic, monotheistic and mystical religions, and also between the different monotheistic religions. In the Eastern religions, paradigmatically in Buddhism, the emphasis is on illumination, the granting of insight, *satori* as it is called in Japanese Zen Buddhism, an inexplicable, indescribable moment of Enlightenment, comparable to the intuitive experience of Gautama Buddha under the Bo-Tree, which cannot be grasped by ordinary logic, but constitutes a new ordering of the relationship to the whole of the universe of the one who undergoes this experience. This experience is not mediated by the senses. In fact, it occurs when the senses no longer affect the experience of the one who seeks illumination. In theistic religions this emphasis on the inner experience is characteristically combined with an emphasis on manifestation in the world of experience, mediated by the senses. In monotheistic religions such as Judaism, Christianity and Islam, this underlines that the God who discloses God's being, will and work is also the creator, the source of salvation and the ultimate judge of everything there is. Revelation, creation, salvation and consummation have the same author. The inner illumination of the recipient of revelation and the manifestation of God in external reality have the same ground and object, and so they are correlated in particular ways.

Because of its foundational character there have been extensive inner-religious discussions in the history of the monotheistic religions on the nature, form, content and effect of revelation.[3] Is revelation to be characterized as immediate or mediated disclosure of God? Should it be understood as direct or indirect communication? Does it occur primarily in the human person, in nature, or in history? Does revelation have the form of communicative actions in history and/or the effective communication of the divine word? What is the primary effect of revelation: Does it primarily grant insight or does it consist in offering guidance? Raising these questions already illustrates that the "or" in formulating these questions does not refer to an exclusive alternative, a complete disjunction, but rather to complementary aspects of revelation.

One of the most significant questions concerns the relationship between revelation and the witness to revelation, between the initial disclosure event and its appropriation in a history of interpretations. Is revelation an event in the past

---

2 Brunner, Emil, *Offenbarung und Vernunft*, Zürich: Theologischer Verlag Zürich, 1941, 2nd ed. Zürich: Zwingli Verlag, 1961; reprint: Wuppertal: TVG Brockhaus, 2007: "Wo immer Religion is, da ist Behauptung von Offenbarung.", 31.

3 For a perceptive overview of the issues in the discussion of revelation cf. Dalferth, Ingolf U., "Understanding Revelation", in: Ingolf U. Dalferth/Michael Ch. Rodgers (eds), *Revelation. Clarment Studies in Philosophy of Religion Conference 2012*, 1–25, Tübingen: Mohr Siebeck, 2014.

that needs to be appropriated in our respective present by interpretation and application? Does revelation refer to a present reality of experience that incorporates the past and opens up a particular view of the future? Or is revelation in the strict sense an eschatological event at the end of times so that what we have now are partial and fragmentary experiences of anticipatory disclosures? Even such a brief sketch illustrates the scope and the significance of the debates on the understanding of revelation. The foundational role of revelation in the religions is not only illustrated but also shaped by the way one responds to these questions.

In Judaism, Christianity and Islam an important cluster of questions focuses on the relationship between revelation and the sacred scriptures. Are the sacred scriptures themselves revelation? How is the relationship between the author, the medium and the effect of revelation to be assessed theologically, and how is scripture to be placed in that relationship? Is scripture to be seen as the divinely authorized witness to revelation or does scripture by itself carry divine authority? How is the relationship between scripture and tradition to be interpreted? Can the tradition of interpretation be regarded as being part of revelation? Or does scripture alone have divine authority? This question has considerable weight in all three monotheistic religions. While the view of the divine authority of scripture is mostly associated with Islam, Karaite Judaism also claims that the Tanakh alone has supreme authority. In Christianity, the Reformation and its principle "Scripture alone" and the subsequent development of a doctrine of verbal inspiration has been at the center of debates within the churches of the Reformation and with other Christian churches. The "inerrancy of scripture", in its variations of absolute, full or limited inerrancy, is one of the questions where the relationship between the understanding of revelation and scripture is passionately discussed. This question which is mostly discussed in Protestant churches, has a counterpart in the question of the infallibility of the teaching office of the church, mainly discussed in the Roman Catholic church. It is closely connected to the question of who has authority in interpreting scripture which presupposes a view on the understanding of who has the authority of interpreting revelation. Is that the prerogative of particular ministries or of all believers or must God himself be seen as the ultimate interpreter of revelation and so as the final authority in interpreting revelation?

In modern times the question of the relationship of revelation and scripture or tradition is hotly debated in connection with the question of "fundamentalism". This term has its origin as the self-description of Christian groups in the United States who claimed at the beginning of the 20$^{th}$ century that belief in the inerrancy of scripture is the first of "five fundamentals" that characterize true Christian faith.[4] In recent years the term has been used not only to characterize Christian groups but also, and predominantly so, strands within Islam and, to a lesser degree, in Judaism. The relationship between revelation and scripture which is at the center of these inner-religious debates and needs to be discussed theologically within each of the three monotheistic religions. Do the positions characterized as "fundamentalist" offer an authentic understanding of revelation or should they be seen as a case of "displaced foundations" since they invest scripture with an authority which only God can have as the only author, content and effect of revelation? Should the authority of Scripture be seen as strictly relative to the authority of revelation, a relation which then needs to be clarified theologically?

While these questions are at the center of *inner-religious* debates, interreligious conversations on revelation between Jews, Christians and Muslims have to take into account that in an important sense the scriptural traditions of the other form part of what is understood as revelation in one's own religion. How should Jews view the fact that the traditions of Tanakh are viewed by Christians, albeit in slightly different canonical form, as the Old Testament? How do they understand the written Tora, also claimed by Christians as an indispensable part of what constitutes the witness to revelation, in relation to the oral Torah which played a constitutive role in shaping rabbinical Judaism? And how should Christians deal with the fact that Jews see the Tanakh as their Hebrew Bible? How can both understand theologically that the Bible of Israel has two different and often conflicting histories of reception and of the use of Israel's Bible as scripture? Does this have significance for the understanding of revelation? Furthermore, how can Muslims deal with the fact that persons, events and traditions which are recorded in the Tanakh and in the Old Testament as well as in the New Testament are part of the Qur'ān, although, according to the testimony of the Qur'ān, in a form that is shaped by the sending down of the Qur'ān to the prophet Muḥammad as the ultimate revelation? Again, how should Jews and Christians relate to the fact that what they see as normative and, in a sense, ultimate revelation is seen as leading on to the ultimate revelation of the Qur'ān to Muḥammad? The interrelationships between the texts being claimed as a constitutive part of revelation for each of the three monotheistic religions complicates the view of revelation in the respective inner-religious debates.

It is important to note that we do not confront the situation of the interrelationship between the Bible of Israel, the Christian Bible and the Qur'ān as a new

4 Cf. Marty, Martin E./Appleby, R. Scott, *The Fundamentalism Project*, 5 vols., Chicago: University of Chicago Press, 1991–1995.

challenge. It has formed part of the critical, often polemical, but also constructive relationships between the three monotheistic religions over centuries. In medieval times, philosophy, whether of a Jewish, Muslim or Christian pedigree, was a partner in the debates, sometimes employed as a tool by each of the traditions, sometimes viewed as a relatively independent source of knowledge which has a problematical relationship to what the revelation discloses.[5] Contemporary interreligious dialogues can profit a great deal from recovering the history of the relations between the three religious and theological traditions of the monotheistic religions and their philosophical counterparts. Clarifying the differences and commonalities in the understanding of revelation is a significant part of that.

In the conversations with those outside the religious traditions, whether they describe themselves as sceptics, agnostics or as atheists, precisely the foundational character claimed for revelation is under dispute. The question of the relationship between revelation and reason accompanies the history of theological attempts at clarifying the notion of revelation. How is knowledge and insight that is constituted *for* human beings, as the religions claim, related to knowledge that is actively constituted *by* them? How are passivity and activity, receptivity and spontaneity related in human being, knowing and acting? Judaism, Christianity and Islam see human beings as capable of knowing and acting. However, they all emphasize in distinctive ways the fallibility of human knowing and the predicament of acting under conditions of deception, error and limited capacities, connected with created existence. As creatures, humans are oriented towards a truth that they have not ultimately defined for themselves. Therefore, they are as much in need of orientation as they are also capable of being misled and incapable of correcting themselves without divine help. Humans are dependent on insight that is granted to them, on knowledge that is disclosed to them and on guidance that is shown to them. The common denominator of all revelation is to provide humans with orientation which they could not find for themselves, of letting them understand the truth about the relationship in which they stand to the creator, to their fellow creatures and to themselves.

It is the very claim of revelation to show humans their right place in relation to God, to the world and to themselves and to set them on the right path in knowing and acting, that seems problematical for those outside the religious traditions. Are there any criteria by means of which claims to revelation can be judged? Or can revelation only be assessed by those who have received it? Is there a rational justification of claims to revelation? And can there be moral war-

---

5 Lutz-Bachmann, Matthias/Fidora, Alexander (eds): *Juden, Christen und Muslime. Religionsdialoge im Mittelalter*, Darmstadt: Wissenschaftliche Buchgesellschaft, 2004.

rants which could provide independent reasons by means of which one could assess whether the course of life oriented by divine revelation is the right one? Can the claims to revelation be publicly adjudicated in the court of reason?

The question of whether revelation is capable of or in need of rational warrants has accompanied the history of reflection on revelation from the beginning. Time and again, it has been claimed, most notably in the European Enlightenment, that all claims to revelation are in need of confirmation by the powers of reason. Again and again, the representatives of religious traditions have questioned whether the created and fallible intellect of humans can be able to adjudicate on what is given in divine revelation. In this context it is very important to clarify the relationship of revelation to other forms of human knowing. Is revelation an exception from the natural forms of knowing, one that would deserve to be called supernatural? Is revelation reserved for religious contents and situations? Or would it be more appropriate to see revelation as the normal and natural mode of gaining knowledge and receiving orientation, the foundation on which all other knowledge and all other forms of action rest?

Many of these epistemological questions, which are discussed in the conversations between those who are committed to religious traditions and those who would not recognize such a commitment, have been discussed under the heading of "foundationalism" in philosophy.[6] Are there clear and distinct universal criteria by means of which all epistemic claims can be assessed, or are such criteria internal to particular epistemic perspectives and its inherent internal criteria? If there are no independent external criteria for assessing claims to revelation, the only possibility to gain a view of the plausibility of claims to revelation is to seek clarification in dialogical exchanges, similar to those in inter-religious conversations. It belongs to the very character of revelation that persons who believe in revelation cannot provide a justification for the state of certainty which they see as the result of revelation, because it is constituted for them. They can, however, provide an account of the content of revelation. Respecting the other's basic certainties while at the same time inviting them to provide grounds for the content of revelation or the content of rival views not based on revelation, are the two basic requirements for helping to develop the situation of religious and ideological pluralism in which we live into one of dialogical pluralism. While respect for the basic certainties people confess – the principle of the freedom of conscience – is the foundation of the freedom of religion and of interreligious toleration, the willingness to give account of the basic content

6 Audi, Robert, *Epistemology. A Contemporary Introduction to the Theory of Knowledge*, London: Routledge, 2003.

of one's beliefs – the principle of dialogical accountability – should not be alien to the three religions in which the conviction that God alone knows the human heart is as central as the view that humans are responsible before God in a relationship of address and response.

## 2 Biblical Roots of the Concept of Revelation

The "revelation" (*revelatio*, *manifestatio*) became a technical term for the disclosure of God in the debates on the foundations of knowledge of God in the High Middle Ages. How is God's communication through external and internal means related to other means of gaining knowledge by rational inquiry (*scientia*) or through the initiation into a way of discerning the permanent order of the world in the changing circumstances of nature and history (*sapientia*)? The context of the formation of the concept of revelation is the establishment of European universities as institutions for the cultivation of knowledge in the different spheres of human interaction with reality. Religious knowledge as it is reflected in theology relates matters of temporal significance to eternal matters and orders the different areas of theoretical (philosophy) and practical knowledge (medicine, law).

The organization of the spheres of knowledge and a canon of the sciences presupposes a view of the human faculties and capacities for the cultivation of knowledge. Rational capacities in their different forms, generating theoretical, practical or empirical knowledge must be related to the human will and to the range of affections situated in the human heart. The concept of revelation was part of the attempt to determine the particular profile of knowledge of God, its foundations, content, methods and goals, and to relate it to knowledge of worldly temporal matters.

As institutions for the cultivation of knowledge, the universities, growing out of corporations of scholars, had to find their place in relation to the monastic schools, situated in convents and dedicated to the education and personal formation of clerics. Here the cultivation of theological knowledge was closely related to the life of worship, to maintaining a tradition of the transmission of religious knowledge by initiation. The sources of Christian theology, the Bible, the writings of the Fathers, the traditions of liturgy were transmitted through personal instruction, through building up and cultivating monastic libraries. Reference to revelation had its place both in the sources of the transmission of Christian knowledge as well as in the ordering of the Christian mind in connection with the formation of the person.

Both the monastic orders and the universities existed in a relationship, often characterized by significant tensions, to the institutional church and the teaching office practiced by the bishops and priests. The teaching authority of the church was seen to be based in many ways on the divine authority: by the authority of Scripture, by the authority passed on from the Apostles to those following them in office, and by the authority of dogma, formally agreed by the councils of the Church, and informally part of the tradition of the church. The appeal to divine authority bound these different sources of instruction, Scripture, tradition, dogma and apostolic teaching office together.

For the appeal to divine authority in its various forms reference to Scripture was constitutive. The plurality of ways in which the Hebrew Scriptures and the New Testament speak of God communicating with God's human creature, identifying himself through his name, offering guidance, pronouncing judgment or salvation is in the Middle Ages, as it were, condensed in the technical concept of "revelation". While the use of revelation as a technical term, a second order concept, summarizing and structuring the various ways of divine communication, is particularly useful for relating revelation to reason and the will, and for relating arguments from reason and appeals to the authority of Scripture, tradition and ecclesial office, it does not obliterate the plurality and variety of divine communication in Scripture. The first order expressions of divine communication in epiphanies, forms of address, and events always provided the foundation for re-adjusting the interpretation of the technical concept of revelation.

## 2.1 Divine Disclosure and Communication in the Hebrew Scriptures

The Hebrew Scriptures do not have a concept of revelation.[7] Divine self-disclosure is in almost all cases expressed in verbal form. A variety of verbal forms, derived from non-religious usage is employed to express forms of divine communication: *gālāh*, disclose or reveal, e. g. Gen. 35:7 God reveals himself to Jacob in Bethel; *jād'*, proclaim, making known, e. g. Exod. 25:22 God announces that he will meet with Moses and give his commandments to Israel; also with regard to God's actions which disclose his identity: Exod. 20:1; *nāgād*, report or commu-

7 A very helpful summary of the Biblical material is provided by Dunn, James D. G., "Biblical Concepts of Revelation," in: Paul Avis (ed.), *Divine Revelation*, 1–22, London: Darton, Longman & Todd, 1997. A detailed overview of the vocabulary employed in describing revelatory experiences can be found in Preuß, Horst Dietrich, "Offenbarung II. Altes Testament," in: Gerhard Müller (ed.), *Theologische Realenzyklopädie*, vol. XXV, 117–128, Berlin/New York, 1995.

nicate, e. g. Gen. 41:25 God announces to Pharaoh what he is about to do, *dābār*, speak, e. g. Gen. 28:13 where God introduces himself to Jacob with his name and promises him the land on which he lies. In these (and many other) examples the self-communication of God occurs in the context of a narrative. God's self-communication discloses the point of the narrative and becomes the context in which all of God's actions now have to be understood. God's self-communication turns God's actions into self-communicating actions. God's self-communication identifies him as the ultimate agent in everything that happens and so distinguishes God from all other finite agents and forces. If one surveys the means of God's self-communication in the Hebrew Bible one is struck by the scope and variety of means of God's communication. The "angel of JHWH" can be a means of God's own self-disclosure, of God's presence with his people, as one through whom God guides Israel on its way through the desert and turns to the people even after they have turned away from him. God discloses his glory (*kābōd*) perhaps at first in the temple, but after its destruction God discloses his glory which has left the temple (Ezek. 11:22) to individual prophets (Ezek. 1:18) and promises the return to a new temple (Ezek. 43:1). According to Second Isaiah God will demonstrate his glory for all nations as the sovereign power over nature and history (Isa. 40:5; Ps. 115:1).

The fact that God speaks (*dābār* occurs almost 400 times with JHWH as the subject of speaking) is expressed as God addressing humans in the 1$^{st}$ person and enabling humans to address god in the 2$^{nd}$ person as "you/thou". This is the predominant form in which God establishes God's relationship with the people, announces judgment, offers guidance and promises rescue. The verbal character of God's self-communication should not be contrasted to God's mighty actions. God's speaking effects what it says and God's actions communicate what God intends. As the presence of God's self-communication the words of JHWH can be seen as well as heard. In most cases God talks through the words of a prophet, but God addresses God's people as well as individuals also without prophetic mediation. God's word is the medium of his presence, it constitutes the presence of those who are addressed by God. God's self-communicating acts distinguish God from idols. Idols remain silent.

With his self-communication God intends to establish and to shape community with the chosen people, judges and corrects them where they deny and contradicts God's will to be in communion with his people. It is often emphasized that in the Hebrew Scriptures God's self-communication should not be interpreted as a way in which "the self" of God is disclosed. To know God fully from face to face is, at best, an expression of eschatological hope. Divine self-communication in its various forms and in its diverse mediations is a real encounter with God in that it brings the ones so addressed in a real relationship with God and not only with means of communication external to God's own being. This is sufficient for divine self-communication to establish a real community between God and his human creatures. In this community more and more will be known about God as and when the people become obedient to God's call and guidance. However, in the various strands of the traditions of the Hebrew Bible the dynamic of God's self-communication has not yet reached its goal. Only then will God be fully known and only then in the perfect communion with God's redeemed creation will creatures reach their fulfilment. There are different views in which this goal is envisaged: the rising of the glory (*kābōd*) of God over Israel so that the nations will come as pilgrims to Zion in order to be in Israel's light (Isa. 60). This can be connected with the vision of the Spirit-empowered redeemer who will preach good news to the poor, bind up the broken-hearted, proclaim freedom for the captives and release the prisoners from darkness (Isa. 61:1–2). It can have the form of the Lord assuming his rule over Zion so that the daughter of Zion shouts aloud and rejoices (Zeph. 3:14). It may be the vision of the judgment of God making peace between the nations so that swords are beaten into ploughshares (Mic. 4:3). This goal can be described as God taking his dwelling among his people, establishing a community where there will be no more death and every tear wiped from the eyes of the mourning (cf. Isa. 25:8; 35:10; Ezek. 37:27). God himself will answer the question that God puts the prophet when he shows him the valley of the dry bones: "Son of man, can these bones live?" (Ezek. 37:3). The vision of the last day, the "Day of the Lord" includes the expectation of a comprehensive enablement of all generations and of people of every social standing by God's Spirit to disclose the ultimate destiny for all nations and people:

> I will pour out my Spirit on all people. Your sons and daughters will prophesy, your old men will dream dreams, your young men will see visions. Even on my servants, both men and women, I will pour out my Spirit in those days. (Joel 2:28–29)

After the dreadful events preceding the final revelation, salvation will be realized: "And everyone who calls on the name of the Lord will be saved; for on Mount Zion and in Jerusalem there will be deliverance, as the Lord has said." (Joel 2:32)

## 2.2 God's Self-Communication in Jesus and the Early Christian Communities

In the New Testament there is a similar variety of linguistic expressions to talk of God's self-communication as in the Hebrew Bible. Verbs from the roots expressing visual communication *apokalýp-* reveal, *phanér-* show, *epiphaí* appear, but also expressions referring to auditory communication *legō* say, *akouō* hear and wider communicative terms *gnōrízō* know, making known, *dēlóō* lay open and, in the passive voice, *phaínoō* becoming apparent and *horáō* making seen etc., are all pressed into service to talk about God's self-communication and disclosure. The history of God's communications in word and act in Israel is presupposed so that the texts of the traditions of the Hebrew Bible are read as the means of God's continued self-communication. God's deeds are understood as part of a story that is not yet concluded and God's word is the beginning of a dynamic process of communication in which the last word has not yet been spoken. The decisive change in the writings of the New Testament is that all witnesses to divine self-communication are seen as pointing to Jesus whose message deeds and destiny are interpreted as God's ultimate self-communication, the one which has eschatological validity.[8] All communication from God after Jesus, often associated with the operation of the Holy Spirit, is concerned with actualizing, explicating and fulfilling all that is already contained in him as God's final act and ultimate word. The work of the Holy Spirit is seen as both enabling people to understand what has occurred in Jesus as anticipating and fulfilling God's comprehensive, eschatic revelation. This will complete the actualization of God's will to be in communion with creation which is from the beginning the purpose of creation. All these elements are present in the opening sentences of the Letter to the Hebrews which draws on the traditions of the Bible to present Jesus as effulgence of God's glory (*kābōd, dóxa*) and the speaker of God's word (dābār, lógos). He has this singular status as God's Son because he has overcome all obstacles for knowing God as he wants to be known, the deception of sin, of human contradiction against God's will and of turning away from his guidance.

> In the past God spoke to our forefathers through the prophets at many times and in various ways, but in these last days he has spoken to us by his Son, whom he appointed heir of all things, and through whom he made the universe. The Son is the radiance of God's glory and the exact representation of his being, sustaining all things by his powerful word. After he has provided purification for sins, he sat down at the right hand of the Majesty in heaven. So he became as much superior to the angels as the name ["the Son", cf. Ps. 2:7 and 2Sam. 7:14] he has inherited is superior to theirs. (Heb. 1:1–2)

8 Cf. A helpful synopsis of the exegetical and systematic problems is offered by Bauckham, Richard, "Jesus the Revelation of God," in: Paul Avis (ed.), *Divine Revelation*, 174–200, London: Darton, Longman & Todd, 1997.

The diversity of the ways of talking about divine self-disclosure is focused in a unique way on Jesus. In the synoptic gospels Jesus is portrayed as the one who in his words, deeds and suffering inaugurates the Kingdom of God, the ultimate end of God's ways with the world (Mark 1:15; Luke 14:17–21). Reference to Jesus appears as a decisive re-focusing of ways of speaking about God's communicative action in the Hebrew Scriptures. The salvation of God's people is brought about in Jesus through God's "finger" (Luke 11:20; Exod. 8:19) as "God's Immanuel ...God with us" (Matt. 1:23; cf. Isa. 7:14), a turn in history that amounts to a new exodus. Jesus' message, his "new teaching" (Mark 1:17) discloses the "mysteries of the Kingdom of God" (Mark 4:11), the final turn in history where all resistance to the actualization of God's will is overcome. This is associated with Jesus' own vision that the reign of Satan is already overcome in heaven so that his defeat on earth is decided but not yet disclosed: "I saw Satan fall from heaven like lightning." (Luke 10:18) For Jesus followers this means: "nothing will harm you." (Luke 10:19)

The unique status of Jesus as the focus of God's self-communication which is shared by all writings of the New Testament is depicted in Luke's Gospel as rooted in a unique Father-Son relationship. Knowledge of God is bound to the self-disclosure of the Father through the Son who communicates this filled with the Holy Spirit. Jesus, as the means of revelation of the Father, becomes the agent of God's self-disclosure, so that he becomes a unique means of access to knowledge of God which is not at the disposal of the wise and learned:

> At that time Jesus, full of joy through the Holy Spirit, said, "I praise you, Father, Lord of heaven and earth, because you have hidden these things from the wise and learned, and revealed them to little children. Yes, Father, for this was your good pleasure. All things have been committed to me by my Father. No-one knows the Son except the Father, and no-one knows the Father except the Son and those to whom the Son chooses to reveal him." (Luke 10:21–22)

For Paul, the mystery of God's justice as creative justice makes believers just in faith, by trusting in God and his justice alone, as it is revealed in the cross and resurrection of Christ. This self-disclosure establishes the perspective from which the believers can understand God's self-communication in Scripture (Rom. 1:2; 1Cor. 4:6 and 10:11) and in the world of creation (Rom. 1:19–20). God's word continues to be efficacious in Scripture and in the apostolic preaching. Paul can therefore describe the apostolic proclamation as a power from God (Rom. 1:17; 2Cor. 2:14). The revelation in Christ removes the veil which covers the face of Moses which Paul interprets in 2Cor. 3:13–15 with reference to Num. 4:4–6 as a reference to the understanding of the Torah, when it is not understood from the perspective of Christ. The removal of the veil through the revelation of Christ opens up a new understanding of God's self-communication through the Spirit. This disclosure of God's glory – the theme of *kābōd/dóxa* is again taken up – established freedom in the presence of God. Knowledge of God's glory is enabled by God, who created the light at the beginning of creation and who makes his light to shine into believer's hearts, so that they recognize the glory of God in the face of Christ.

> For God who said, "Let light shine out of darkness" made his light shine in our hearts to give us the light of knowledge of the glory of God in the face of Christ. (2Cor. 4:6)

Revelation thus allows believers to see the continuity from the initial act of creation to the disclosure of glory in the face of the resurrected crucified one. This is for Paul a form of embodied knowledge that displays both, being "given over to death" and being sustained by the hope that "the one who raised the Lord Jesus from the dead will also raise us with Jesus" (2Cor. 4:14). Paul says of himself as a paradigm of the believer's existence that "we always carry in our body the death of Jesus so that the life of Jesus may also be revealed in our body." (2Cor. 4:10) It is the certain hope of being raised with Jesus by God that constitutes freedom, a freedom that cannot be destroyed by death. The knowledge God gives to those who participate through baptism and in faith in the pattern of Christ's death and resurrection assures believers that there is no condemnation from God (Rom. 8:1–2) and so grants the freedom of the Spirit. In a striking passage which documents the interweaving of the understanding of the self-disclosure of God through Christ in the Spirit with the emerging proto-Trinitarian grammar of discourse about God Paul asserts:

> ...if the Spirit of him who raised Jesus from the dead is living in you, he who raised Christ from the dead will also give life to your mortal bodies through his Spirit, who lives in you. (Rom. 8:11)

The participation of believers in the eternal life of God is the content of the final revelation of the glory of God. The eschatological vision of Paul's understanding of revelation correlates the anthropological and the cosmological dimension of the liberation of the cosmos from the bondage to frustration and decay.

> I consider that our present sufferings are not worth comparing with the glory that will be revealed in us. The creation waits in eager expectation for the sons of God to be revealed. For the creation was subjected to frustration, not by its own choice, but by the will of the one who subjected it, in hope that the creation itself will be liberated from its bondage to decay and brought into the glorious freedom of the children of God. (Rom. 8:18–20)

For the Gospel of John the incarnation of the eternal Word of God (John 1:14) who is one with God in Jesus and his exaltation on the cross is the only self-disclosure of the invisible God (John 14:6–9), God's exegesis (*exegésis*, John 1:18) in the world of experience through the medium of created means of communication. The revelation of God is promised to those who love Jesus and receive his Spirit. This revelation has for John the form of mutual indwelling and love:

> I am in my Father, and you are in me and I am in you. Whoever has my commands and obeys them, he is the one who loves me. He who loves me will be loved by my Father, and I too will love Him and show myself to him. (John 14:20–21)

The witness of the Son (John 3:31–34) and the testimony of the Father disclose one and the same truth. It is this truth into which the Spirit leads believers: "...when he, the Spirit of truth comes, he will guide you into all truth." (John 16:13)

# 3 The Formation of the Understanding of Revelation in the History of Christian Doctrine

## 3.1 The Debates of the Early Church: Securing the Relationship between Author, Content and Actuality of Revelation

The understanding of revelation which is rooted in the Biblical witnesses to God's revelation had to be explicated and developed in distinction from pagan religions, in critical conversation with Judaism as the sister religion of Christianity and in critical engagement with the philosophical interpretations of reality. This provided the basis for the self-explication of Christian teaching over against misconstruals of the Christian message within the Christian communities themselves or on the margins of these communities. These different groups can be distinguished but cannot be tidily divided. Important strands of Judaism at the time were already engaged with philosophical schools and tried to demonstrate the superiority of the Jewish way of following the commandments of God over against philosophical orientations of the time.

The work of Philo of Alexandria (c. 20 BCE–50 CE) is a striking example of this, especially in the development of a theological hermeneutic that proved to be a major inspiration for Christian theology.[9] The philosophical schools could exist in connection with pagan religiosities in spite of the powerful philosophical criticism of religious practice and belief by the classical philosophers. However, they should not be interpreted as theoretical constructions of reality, but rather as initiation into a way of life, trying to reach the fulfilment of human life through philosophical engagement.[10] This made the philosophical schools natural rivals for Christian theology and very important partners in critical engagement. The main task of critical reflections on what was seen as a deviation from the truth within the Christian communities called for a way to elaborate the connections between the author, the content and the mode of occurrence of revelation. Since a second-order concept of revelation developed only in the Middle Ages, these discussions had to engage the main substantive teachings of the Christian church. In this way the discussions in the Early Church provided the background for reflection of a terminologically clarified concept of revelation. Clarifying the Christian understanding of God in a Trinitarian view of God, as it was elaborated in the Eastern Church, proved to be the most important foundation for later, and more technical discussions on revelation. Perhaps the most crucial factor is the critical engagement with what was regarded as misinterpretations of the Christian message by groups within or on the margins of the Christian communities who had the capacity for dividing the community, the so-called heretics. The engagement with the heretics, all of whom of course attempted to present the true exposition of Christian doctrine, showed most clearly that these questions were not confined to the definition of doctrinal truth.[11] All the issues that were discussed in the debates of the Early Church concerned just

**9** Cf. Runia, David T., *Philo in Early Christian Literature*, Assen: van Gorcum, 1993.

**10** Cf. Hadot, Pierre, *Philosophy as a Way of Life. Spiritual Exercises from Socrates to Foucault*, Oxford: Wiley-Blackwell, 1995 and the comprehensive reinterpretation of ancient philosophy in id., *What is Ancient Philosophy?* Cambridge, MA: Harvard University Press, 2004.

**11** Cf. for a rich documentation of the history of theological reflection cf. Helmut Hoping/Gerhard Kardinal Müller (eds), *Handbuch der Dogmengeschichte*, vol. 1, facicle 1a: Michael Seybold, *Offenbarung: Von der Schrift bis zum Ausgang der Scholastik*, Freiburg: Herder, 2014 and facicle 1b: Leo Schffczyk/Hans Waldenfels, *Offenbarung: Von der Reformation bis zur Gegenwart*, Freiburg: Herder 2011. – The most comprehensive and concise overview of the reflection on revelation in the history of Western theology and philosophy is Herms, Eilert, "Offenbarung V. Theologiegeschichte und Dogmatik," in: Gerhard Müller (ed.), *Theologische Realenzyklopädie*, vol. XXV, 146–210, Berlin/New York: De Gruyter, 1995. – For a concentrated account of the most important steps in the history of doctrine of the Early Church, cf. Hall, Stuart G., *Doctrine and Practice in the Early Church*, London: SPCK, $^{2}$2005. Mark Edwards has provided a spirited defense and ample material for the contribution of the so-called heretics to the formation of catholic doctrine: Edwards, Mark, *Catholicity and Heresy in the Early Church*, Farnham, Surrey: Ashgate, 2009.

as much the identity and integrity of the Christian Church, its forms of community organization, its ethos and, perhaps most importantly, its worship.

What were the main issues that had to be resolved in these debates in order to develop an understanding of divine self-communication that was appropriate to the witness of the biblical writings of the Hebrew Bible and the New Testament? A view of revelation that reflected the way in which divine self-communication was presupposed in the practices of Christian worship and that provided the basis of an understanding of God as creator, redeemer and consummator of the world. Such an understanding of revelation had to offer a view of the world as God's creation and the created stage for the drama of salvation. Finally such a view had to initiate Christians into a Christian way of life that was in accordance with was perceived as the disclosure of divine truth.

One of the most decisive steps was taken by Justin Martyr, who, born a pagan, became the most influential Christian apologist of the 2nd century. Born in 100 he was martyred some time between 64 and 68 CE. Intent to present the Christian faith as the true philosophy (*vera philosophia*) he identified Jesus Christ with the Logos of God, who is generated by God's will before all creatures and is the rational mediator of creation who then is the mediator of God's knowledge and will in the incarnation. His *Dialogue with Trypho* illustrates the complex triangle addressed by early Christian apologetics. Justin who travelled about, donning the dress of a philosopher, recounts his early philosophical training and engages in a dialogue with the Jew Trypho, trying to persuade him to join the Christian faith he himself had just converted to. The striking identification of Jesus Christ with the Logos of God serves as the foundation on which Christ's teaching, life and death can be understood as the communication of the truth of God in human, created form. However, this move also bequeathed to later theology the distinction between the *Logos asarkos*, the Logos without the flesh, before, and after the incarnation, and the *Logos ensarkos*, the Logos in the flesh.[12] The result of this argument for the understanding is immediately obvious: The truth disclosed in Jesus in time is the eternal truth of God by means of which the Logos is the mediator of creation and the instrument for its salvation and consummation.

Once Christ is seen as the Logos incarnate, the problem arises, in which sense and how, if at all the Logos of God can become incarnate. On a view like that of Philo of Alexandria who operates with a sharp distinction between

12 Cf. Jenson, Robert W., "Once More on the *Logos asarkos* (2011)," in: Robert W. Jenson, *Theology as Revisionary Metaphysics. Essays on God and Creation*, ed. by Stephen John Wright, Eugene, OR: Cascade Books, 2014.

the rational world and the world of sense experience the Logos has to remain discarnate. Could one then say that the Logos only appeared to be an embodied being? This so-called docetic view applies a dualist view of reality into the interpretation of Christian faith. It was a common denominator of many so-called gnostic teachings. Such a view undermines the integrity of Christian faith: It challenges the reality of the incarnation, but also the unity of reality if Jesus is seen as a spark of light, appearing on earth in order to lead those he instructs with the truth out of the bondage to the world of matter. The danger of a view of the Christ event which is focused on liberation from the world of matter is to drive a wedge between the creator who appears as an incompetent demiurge and the redeemer who liberates from the world the creator has so inexpertly cobbled together. Furthermore, once the Gospel is only about liberation from the world and no longer about the reconciliation of the world, the Hebrew Bible is no longer regarded as the record of authentic divine self-communication and must be discarded as authoritative Scripture, as Marcion proposed.

The whole bundle of teachings we regard as gnostic (although that might be a problematical simplification) was effectively criticized by Irenaeus of Lyon (c130–c202 CE).[13] He can be seen as one of the two first systematic theologians of Christianity, Origen being the other. Irenaeus construes the whole of the divine economy as one narrative in which everything is effected by God through his "two hands", the Son and the Spirit. The unity of reality is safeguarded by the one differentiated narrative of God's agency in creation, preservation, salvation and consummation. Working with a systematic typology of Adam and Christ, Irenaeus depicts Christ as the reversal of Adam's contradiction against God, as the *recapitulation* of the whole of history of humankind. The revelation of Christ discloses the whole of reality as one narrative ordered through the Trinitarian action of God. The authenticity of revelation is safeguarded through the witness of Scripture which reliably recounts the revelatory events, as if they were spoken by the Word of God and the Spirit (*haer* II,28,2: "*Quippe a Verbo Dei et Spiritu eius dictae*"). They preserve the truth of the revelation in Christ forever young and are the foundation for the "canon of truth" (*haer* III,24,1). They therefore support the work of the bishops as the successors of the Apostles in the authentic transmission of the testimony of God's revelation in Christ. Irenaeus is the first theologian who reflects in the question of how divine self-communication

---

**13** Cf. the short study of Nielsen, Jan T., *Adam and Christ in the Theology of Irenaeus of Lyons. An Examination of the Function of the Adam-Christ Typology in the Adversus Haereses of Ireaneus, against the Background of the Gnosticism of His Time*, Assen: van Gorkum, 1968. The ecclesial ramifications of Irenaeus' theology are well brought out by Farrow, Douglas, "St. Irenaeus of Lyons. The Church and the World," *Pro Ecclesia* 4,3 (1995), 333–355.

can be handed on in processes of transmission through human witnesses and nevertheless maintains its divine origin, content and mode of effectiveness.

While Irenaeus presents a quasi-linear integration of the whole of reality as comprised within one narrative of the divine economy, Origen (ca. 184 – ca. 253) developed a Christian view of the unity of reality as a vertical hierarchical system of ontological orders in *On first Principles*.[14] Origen's Christian metaphysics and his extensive work on the *Hexapla* as well as his exegetical writings must be seen as two sides of one project. He tried to show that God's revelation in Christ opens up a comprehensive understanding of reality, focusing on the conditions for the possibility of the divine self-manifestation in history as the ground for the process of *pronoia* (providence) and *paideusis* (pedagogy) by means of which the Logos reunites created reality with its origin in God. This understanding of reality is authentically testified in Scripture which therefore contains all truth. Scripture appears, if we may borrow this formula from J.A. Möhler, as "the extension of the Incarnation".[15] Origen is careful not to ascribe a quasi independent divine status to Scripture. Scripture is like every moment of the divine process of providence and the education of humankind rooted in the eternal being of God, communicated by the Logos through the Spirit. The *theopneustia* (inspiration) of Scripture relates it back to God's eternal being and will and does not establish an independent inerrancy.

The debates which were fought with passion and polemics in the Early Church concerned the way in which the author, the content and the process of divine self-communication can be thought of as one, although they are obviously differentiated. In order to clarify this question which eventually leads to the Trinitarian dogma, the status of the incarnate Son must first be elucidated. If Jesus Christ is a creature then he cannot in his person be the reality of divine self-communication but only a created pointer to the divine truth. If, however, he is of one being with God the Father, then the creaturely mode of divine self-communication does not falsify the claims made for its author and content. The problem, as it presented itself at the beginning of the 4th century was that the onto-

---

**14** Cf. Trigg, Joseph Wilson, *Origen*, New York: Routledge, 1998. A new translation: Origen, *On First Principles*, ed. by John Behr, Oxford Early Christian Texts, Oxford: Oxford University Press, 2017.

**15** Möhler writes: "So ist denn die sichtbare Kirche … der unter den Menschen in menschlicher Form fortwährend erscheinende, stets sich erneuernde, ewig sich verjüngende Sohn Gottes, die andauernde Fleischwerdung desselben, so wie den auch die Gläubigen in der heiligen Schrift der Leib Christi genannt werden." (Möhler, Johann Adam, *Symbolik, oder Darstellung der dogmatischen Gegensätze der Katholiken und der Protestanten nach ihren öffentlichen Bekenntnisschriften*, § 36, Frankfurt a.M.: Minerva, [6]1895, 332f.)

logical status of the Logos had not been defined clearly. When the divine status of the Logos had to be emphasized in stating that he really is the agent of God's self-communication, he could be brought close to God. When his involvement in history was emphasized he seemed to belong more to the creaturely realm. The controversy could be traced back to the writings of Origen. Although he clearly taught that the Logos is eternally generated (*aéi gennãtai*), he also taught that the Logos was subordinate to the Father, and the Spirit subordinate to the Logos. Arius basically triggered a debate on the question on which side of the dividing line between the uncreated eternal being of God and the created being of creation the Logos should be placed.[16] Arius suggested that the radical transcendence of God the Father could not be compromised and therefore taught that the Logos is the highest creature, created before the creation of the world, but nevertheless created.

The decision of the council of Nicaea of 325 CE that the Son is *homousios*, of one essence with the Father, was at the time quite contentious. Could the being of the Incarnate Lord be described with a phrase that did not have scriptural authority? And how should one accommodate two identities, the Father and the Son, in the one divine essence? Only around the middle of the 4th century the pro-Nicene party had consolidated and developed a view of the coessentiality of the Son with the Father. This, however, left the question how the status of the Spirit should be decided. Is the evidence of subordination to the Father not even stronger in the case of the Spirit? The so-called Spirit-fighters (*pneumatomáchoi*) who were also called Macedonians after the bishop Macedonius who had been installed in Constantinople through Constantius denied the full deity of the Spirit. Here it was the fourth Cappadocian Amphilochius of Iconium who persistently urged a rejection of this view and persuaded Basil of Caesarea to write his famous treatise *On the Holy Spirit*.

What was at stake for the understanding of revelation? The *homousios* (consubstantiality) of Christ was intended to secure that Christ is not just a pointer to God, a moral example that we should follow, but that in him believers encounter the true reality of God. The question of the consubstantiality of the Spirit raised the question whether the appropriation of the revelation of Christ was really part of the revelation of Christ or whether the revelation had to be made effective by some kind of human cooperation. Could the same Spirit be seen as the giver of faith to the individual believer and as the one who consummates the work of God in Christ, the true "first fruits" (Rom. 8:23) of the future perfection of God's

---

**16** Cf. Williams, Rowan, *Arius. Heresy and Tradition*, revised edition, London: SCM Press, 2009.

plan to be in communion with his reconciled and perfected creation, the Spirit who sets creation free?[17]

The famous Cappadocian solution to distinguish between *ousia* and *hypostasis* and to use one term (*ousia*) for the essence of God, the other for the personal identity of Father, Son and Spirit who coequally share in the divine essence is the correlate of Basil's view of God's Trinitarian action wherein each divine act the Father is the uncaused cause, the Son the causing cause and the Spirit the perfecting cause. For the understanding of revelation this implied that all revelation is rooted in the Father, occurs through the Son, the incarnation of the Creator Logos and is completed in the work of the Spirit who is coequally God with Father and Son. The implication of this view is that the whole of the divine economy is to be seen as a Trinitarian history of salvation. The important ecclesiological point that follows from this is that the activity of the Church is enveloped in the activity of the Trinitarian God. It does not have any independent agency, but is the creature and instrument of God's creative and perfecting agency. Positively, this means that the divine economy of revelation extends to the activity of the Church, enabling it to be an instrument for the actualization of God's revelation, both in the inspiration of the believer and through the sacramental life of the church.

The resolution of the debates on the ontological status of the Logos/Son and the Holy Spirit in relation to the being of the Father at the Council of Constantinople (381 CE) that was later cast in the formula *mía ousía – treĩs hypostáseis* indirectly had a decisive effect on the understanding of revelation: It must be understood as the self-presentation of the Father through the Son in the Spirit. However, how this solution, worked out in the debates in the East, was then received in the West is still a matter of debate. Did Augustine's work *De Trinitate*, the defining work of Western Trinitarian theology until today, reflect the solution reached in the East or is Augustine's legacy entirely problematical? Is Augustine's view on the reality of sin and actuality of grace the working out of the solution reached in the debates preceding the Council of Constantinople? It is perhaps more important that the "Cappadocian" Trinitarian theology is still present in the worship of Christian churches East and West when they use the Nicene (Constantinopolitan) Creed.

---

**17** Cf. on this cosmological dimension Bergmann, Sigurd, *Creation Set Free. The Spirit as Liberator of Nature*, Grand Rapids: Eerdman, 2005.

## 3.2 Reason and Revelation: Contours of the Medieval Debate

In the Middle Ages the indirect and largely implicit discussion of the concept of revelation through the reflection on the contents of Christian faith and the mode how they are given in the Early Church makes way for the direct and explicit reflection on revelation and its relationship to reason. Many factors contribute to the necessity to make the Christian revelation an explicit topic of theological reflection and to elaborate an explicit concept of revelation. There are, first of all, the tensions between different theological and philosophical traditions and the ways of approaching the topic from their respective perspectives. Secondly, there are also different modes of theological reflection, depending on whether theology is mainly pursued in a monastic or a scholastic context. Thirdly, there is the influence of other religious and theological traditions, engaging in many ways with similar challenges. These factors can be distinguished, but not separated. They form a bundle of influences with frequent interferences.

The Middle Ages are the time of the most intense interaction between Judaism, Christianity and Islam, occasioned through political and cultural encounters which were primarily due to the spread and clash of spheres of influence between Christianity and Islam. In connection with these political and economic relationships there is a far-reaching cross-fertilization of influences which pertain to all cultural spheres and intellectual pursuits, including theology and philosophy. Judaism had to survive and nurture its own culture as a minority in Muslim or Christian territories, and is therefore often characterized by the engagement with both traditions in order to maintain its distinctive identity. The world-wide encounter of religious and theological traditions in the second half of the 20$^{th}$ and the beginning of the 21$^{st}$ century has created a new sensibility and awareness for their interaction in previous centuries. What was formerly a specialist interest on the margins of theological teaching and research has become a major concern at the center of theological attention. The consequence of the recognition of a complex and interesting history of interaction has led to the acknowledgement that the history of Christian theology, of Islamic theology and Jewish thought in the Middle Ages cannot be written in separation from one another. It can only be fruitfully approached with the expectation that tracing the lines of interaction and the channels of mutual influence will provide us with a richer and more plausible picture of the history of each tradition and of the history of their exchanges. The history of Christian theology in the Middle Ages can no longer be written as a history that is independent of the parallel histories of Islamic and Jewish thought. The diachronic logic of development that was usually applied must now be supplemented by a synchronic logic of interaction, influencing the development in each of the three traditions. This new perspective is still in the process of being established. We can here merely give a few hints how the picture might change once we have a fuller view of those parts of the field that have so far been neglected. Engaging in this work, means for each of the three traditions discovering aspects of their own histories that cannot be understood apart from the relationship to the respective other. This discovery means that the identity of the other, approached as alterity from one's own standpoint, offers important insights into the making of one's own identity in the process of assimilating or rejecting, adapting or distancing the influences of the other. Making these processes transparent contains the promise that the discovery of these processes of exchange in the past provides us with resources for our present encounter in interfaith work and collaborative theological reflection.

The one problem that Judaism, Christianity and Islam had in common in the Middle Ages is the problem of the relationship of revelation and reason. This question is the framework in which all the other debates within each tradition and between the different traditions is discussed. The problem acquired this dominant character by the renewed relevance and attractiveness by the resurgence of philosophy in its new forms through the rediscovery of the sources from Aristotle reaching its full impact in the reception of Aristotelian writings by the Islamic philosophers and theologians of the Mu'tazilite school.[18] The importance of the influence of this school cannot be overemphasized. It defined the paradigm within which classical Dominican philosophy like that of Thomas Aquinas worked.

The second factor is the transmission of classic Neoplatonist philosophy through Christian theologians from the East to West so that classics of Neoplatonist Christian spirituality like the works of Pseudo-Dionysius became accessible in the metaphysical system of John Scotus Eriugena. One of the determining factors of how the revelation is understood in the medieval period depends on the philosophical view that is adopted and appropriated by Christian theologians. The critical engagement with 'the philosophers,' especially with regard to the interpretation of the meaning, scope and significance of revelation, is a central focus of classical forms of Jewish thought, like Yehuda ha-Levi's *Sefer ha-Kusari* (*The Kuzari*)[19] and Moses Maimonides' *Dalālat al-ḥā'irīn* (*The Guide*

---

**18** For a concise and magisterial overview cf. Ess, Josef van, *The Flowering of Islamic Theology*, Cambridge, MA: Harvard University Press, 2006.

**19** Halevi, Yehuda, *The Kuzari*, with an introduction by Henry Slonimsky, New York: Schocken Books, 1966.

*of the Perplexed*),[20] of Christian theology, like Thomas Aquinas' *Summa contra Gentiles* and the *Summa theologiae*, and of al-Ghazālī's *Tahāfut al-Falāsifa* (The Incoherence of the Philosophers).[21]

John Scotus Eriugena (c. 815 – c. 877 CE), the Irish monk, Neoplatonist philosopher, translator and commentator of the *Corpus Dionysiacum*, in many ways the bridge between ancient philosophy set the ball rolling with the bold thesis: "Authority is the source of knowledge, but our own reason remains the authority by which all authority must be judged."[22] This thesis introduced a sharp separation between faith and knowledge and gave to reason the role of being the final arbiter by sitting in judgment over all knowledge claims. This rationalist view presupposed a view of reality where revelation is understood as the transparency of creation in its graded divisions for its transcendent ground. The double movement, constitutive for Dionysius, of God transcending God's being in the *ekstasis* of descent in revelation to created being, and created being, in turn, transcending its finite boundaries in mystical ascent is reduced to one movement of theoretical ascent. This rationalist trajectory is continued by Peter Abelard (1079 – 1142), now within the framework of an Aristotelian logic, who emphasized the sufficiency of reason in all matters of religious knowing based on the investigation of the created world, because faith can only anticipate in a form estimation the more complete disclosure of truth in the hereafter.[23] The emphasis on the power of reason over against historical revelation rests on a view that knowledge of creation is sufficient for knowledge of God. Once creation is understood as natural, the priority of natural reason is affirmed.

By no means inferior to the logical sophistication of Abelard's dialectics, Anselm of Canterbury (1033 – 1109) devised a scheme in which the eternal word of God, understood as utterance (*locutio*) existed before everything is created by means of it and it can be known on the basis of the likeness of the created mind to the divine spirit as it makes itself known in time. The possibility of knowing God is rooted in the being of the supreme essence as self-communica-

---

**20** Maimonides, Moses, *The Guide of the Perplexed*, trans. with an introduction and notes by Shlomo Pines, with an Introductory Essay by Leo Strauss, 2 vols., Chicago/London: University of Chicago Press, 1963.

**21** Al-Ghazālī, *The Incoherence of the Philosophers*, A Parallel English-Arabic Text, trans., introduced and annotated by Michael E. Marmura, Provo UT: Brigham Young University Press, 1997/2000.

**22** Quoted in Freemantle, Ann, *The Age of Belief. The Medieval* Philosophers, selected with introduction and interpretive commentary, Boston: Houghton and Mifflin, 1955, 80.

**23** An impressive survey of Abelard's achievements is Marenbom, John, *The Philosophy of Peter Abelard*, Cambridge: Cambridge University Press, 1997.

tion which communicates itself in order to be known by finite beings. The Trinitarian constitution of God's being is in this way the condition for the possibility of God's self-manifestation not only in the order of creation but also in historical time through the witness of the church:

> ... it would seem possible that such a verbalization (*locutio*) exists in the supreme substance, and that it existed before its objects, in order for things to be created through it, and which exists now, in order that through it created things may be known.[24]

Therefore, faith is not relegated from the sphere of knowing as in Eriugena, but rather becomes foundational for understanding: *fides quaerens intellectum.* The *Proslogion* therefore starts with the petition: "Come then, Lord my God, teach my heart where and how to seek You, where and how to find you."[25] Finding God is the fulfilment of the human creature's purpose ("I was made in order to see You."). Nevertheless, even the seeking of God must be granted by divine revelation: "I can neither seek You if You do not teach me how, nor find You unless you reveal yourself. Let me seek you in desiring You; let me desire You in seeking You; let me find You in loving You."[26] The image of the Trinitarian God who is remembering (*memoria*), thinking (*intellectus*) and love (*amor*) in humans must be renewed in faith so that it is able to understand.

> I acknowledge, Lord, and I give thanks that You have created Your image in me, so that I remember You, think of you, love You. But this image is so effaced and worn away by vice, so darkened by the smoke of sin, that it cannot do what it was made to do unless You renew it and reform it.[27]

Therefore faith, based on the renewal of the image of God through Christ and in participation in the worship of the church, explicitly expressed in the form of the *Proslogion* as address to God in prayer, is the condition on which understanding rests – not the other way around: "For I do not seek to understand so that I may believe; but I believe so that I may understand. For I believe this also, that 'unless I believe, I shall not understand' [Isa. 7:9]."[28]

By means of his Trinitarian understanding of God reflected in the human mind, Anselm holds together God's revelation in creation, in Christ and through

---

**24** Anselm of Canterbury, *Monologion* 10, Anselm of Canterbury, *The Major Works*, ed. with an introduction by Brian Davies and G.R. Evans, Oxford: Oxford University Press 1998/2008.

**25** Anselm of Canterbury, *Proslogion* 1, *op.cit.* 84–5.

**26** *Op. cit.*, 86–87.

**27** *Op. cit.*, 87.

**28** Ibid.

the life of worship in the church. The fault-lines of the conflict become clear: Is the function of reason that of constituting knowledge of God or is its function the explication of faith which contains the knowledge of God that constitutes for humans in his revelation.

The orientation of revelation towards the experiential interiorization of the Word of God through the Spirit, active in Scripture and its liturgical use in the church, is the hallmark of medieval monastic theology. Its opposition with the rationalist interpretation of knowledge of God has become famous in the conflict between Bernard of Clairvaux (1090–1153 CE) and Abelard. For Bernard love is the striving for the communion with God which will only be fully realized in the beatific vision. The striving of the soul for communion with the Word (*anima quaerens verbum*) becomes the context for the understanding of revelation. This is not a mystical revelation apart from the disclosure of God in Christ and through the Word of Scripture transmitted through the worship of the Church, but rather the experiential focusing of the unity of God's Trinitarian self-disclosure.

The experiential focus of the understanding of revelation must not be interpreted reductively, but rather comprehensively as the focusing of God's self-disclosure which through the guidance of Scripture makes the whole of creation again readable as God's self-communication. This most clearly developed in the two major works of the great theologian of the Franciscan tradition: the *Breviloquium* and the *Itinerarium* of Bonaventure. While the *Breviloquium* offers a comprehensive account of Christian teaching, based on Scripture, the *Itinerarium* describes the journey of the soul to God. The *Breviloquium* demonstrates that all Christian teaching, from the doctrine of Trinity to the Last Judgment, indeed all knowledge "insofar as this knowledge serves the purpose of salvation" must be based on Scripture because, as the "Prologue" argues, it has its origin, development and end in the self-communication of the Triune God in words and deeds. Bonaventure offers this account of the Triune God as the source of revelation in Scripture, emphasizing the unity of God's communication in word and action:

> God, through Christ and the Holy Spirit speaking by the mouth of the prophets and of the others who committed its doctrine to writing. Now, God speaks not with words alone, but also with deeds, for with Him saying is doing and doing is saying; moreover, all creatures are the effects of God's action, and, as such, point to their Cause. Therefore, in Scripture, which is received from God, both words and deeds are meaningful. – Again, Christ the Teacher, lowly as He was in the flesh, remained lofty in His divinity. It was fitting, therefore, that He and His teachings should be humble in word and profound in meaning: even as the Infant Christ was wrapped in swaddling clothes, so God's wisdom is wrapped in humble images. (Prol 4.5)

This account, which Bonaventure supplements with a description of the breadth, length, height and depth of Scripture, is supplemented with a description of the method of Scripture and a short treatise on the interpretation of Scripture. This presents Scripture as the book of the world which makes everything in the world readable as an expression of the divine meaning invested in it. This, necessarily, involves an understanding of philosophy, where philosophy in everything it achieves, remains an instrument for the explication of the truth of Scripture. It treats the natural knowledge of philosophy as a mirror for reflecting things divine. Philosophy in this way becomes a subservient means for divine revelation:

> Now, philosophy is concerned with things as they exist in their nature, or again, as they exist in the soul by innate or empirical knowledge; but theology, being a science both based on faith and revealed by the Holy Spirit, is concerned with grace and glory and Eternal Wisdom. It uses philosophical knowledge as its servant, borrowing from the natural order what it needs to make a mirror for the representation of things divine; erecting, as it were, a ladder, whose foot rests upon the earth but whose top reaches heaven. And all this is done through the one Hierarch, Jesus Christ, who is Hierarch not only in the hierarchy of the Church by reason of the human nature He assumed, but also in the angelical hierarchy, and again, as the Second Person sharing the supercelestial hierarchy of the most blessed Trinity. Through Him, the grace of unction runs down from the supreme Head, God, not only upon the beard, but even to the skirt of His garment: not only upon the heavenly Jerusalem, but even to the Church Militant. (Breviloqu. Prol 3.2)

The true Jacob's ladder, however, is not philosophy, but the ascent of the soul to God which is described in the *Itinerarium.*[29] The external aspect of revelation is here correlated to the internal aspect of the soul's journey to achieve fulfilment in communion with the triune God. By relating the soul's powers of remembering, knowing and loving on the third step of the ladder to Father, Son and Spirit, he finds the source of the soul's structure and capacity in the Trinity who is Father, Word and Love, "non essentialiter, non accidentaliter, ergo personaliter" (It III.5). The next step then relates these capacities, as they are rooted in the Trinity to the divisions of philosophy, so that natural philosophy corresponds to the Father, rational philosophy to the Word and moral philosophy to Love. Bonaventure can then extend Anselm's ontological argument, on the sixth step, to a demonstration that the highest being ("*optimum quod simpliciter est quo nihil melius cogitari potest*" (It IV.2) necessarily must be thought of as superabundance (*bonum diffusium*) which is diffused perfectly and completely in the manner of the processions of generation and spiration. Having climbed the six steps, the

**29** Cf. the excellent interpretation of the *Itinerarium* in Harmless, William S.J., "Mystic as Cartographer," in: id., *Mystics*, 79–105, Oxford/New York: Oxford University Press, 2007.

soul finally finds its rest in communion with the Triune God. This is by no means a treatise on the knowledge of the Trinity by the powers of natural reason alone. Rather, it presents the internal correlate of the knowledge of God in Scripture, as it is developed in the *Breviloquium.* True knowledge of God is grounded in the correlation of the external aspect of God's self-communication in Scripture, summarizing the whole of his words and deeds, and of the internal aspects, the ascent of the soul to its origin in the Triune God. Philosophy seems to be consistently enveloped within the theological knowledge of revelation in both its external and internal aspects.

Thomas Aquinas (1225–1274 CE), the Dominican counter-part to the role Bonaventure played for the Franciscans, argues in the *Summa theologiae* that a sacred doctrine (*sacra doctrina*) is necessary if humans want to achieve the aim of their existence. Humans are as God's creatures oriented towards their end in God. This ultimate end transcends the discursive understanding of natural reason. Therefore, it is necessary for salvation that humans know their destiny through divine revelation.

> Therefore, in order that the salvation of men might be brought about more fitly and more surely, it was necessary that they should be taught divine truths by divine revelation. It was therefore necessary that beside philosophical science built up by reason there should be a sacred science learned through revelation. (STh I qu.1 a 1 resp.) [1]

Now, there are two kinds of sciences. Some proceed from principles known by natural reason because they are self-evident. Some proceed from principles established by the light of a higher science, as music works on the basis of the principles of arithmetic. Thomas continues:

> So it is that sacred doctrine proceeds from principles established by the light of a higher science, namely, the science of God and the blessed. Hence, just as the musician accepts on authority the principles taught him by the mathematician, so science is established on principles revealed by God. (Sth I qu.1 a 2[2])

This view entails a strict self-limitation of natural reason which is rooted in the fact human existence has a supernatural end. Knowledge of this end, communion with God, can only be revealed by God. What can be known of the end of human existence must therefore be revealed. Theology in its practice as a science is therefore a *scientia subalternata,* a subordinate form of science, wholly dependent on the science of God and the blessed, the self-knowledge of God in which the blessed share in the beatific vision. This knowledge, God's knowledge which is disclosed in revelation, must be taught by authority. If every science is defined by the nature of its object, how can theology be the science of

God, if the essence of God is inaccessible to natural human reason? What if John of Damascus is right, that the essence of God cannot be defined?[30] Thomas replies that just as in some philosophical sciences we demonstrate something about the cause from its effects, we must also proceed in theology. "Although we cannot know in what consists the essence of God, nevertheless we make use of His effects, either in nature or in grace, in place of a definition, in regard to whatever is treated of in this science."[31] If we look at the effects of God "in place of a definition" we are directed to revelation as the basis of all knowledge of God as long as we have not yet achieved the beatific vision. What follows from this for the use of reason? Thomas states: "Although arguments from human reason cannot avail to prove what must be received on faith, nevertheless this doctrine argues from articles of faith to other truths."[32] This anti-rationalist point of Thomas' argument could not be expressed more clearly: Human reason cannot prove by way of logical demonstration the truth of Christian faith, because it can only function properly if it accepts its self-limitation. Natural reason cannot offer grounds for accepting the truth of faith. Conversely, we can argue from the truths of faith to other truths. Natural reason must find a place in a framework of faith based on revelation, disclosed through the effects of God. The role of reason is not the rational justification of faith, but the explication of the truths of faith disclosed in revelation and their application to other fields of knowledge.

Thomas' own exposition of this programmatic statement, however, raises quite a number of questions. How does the authority of doctrine in the teaching of the Church create certainty with regard to the author, content and the effect of revelation? How can revelation in its authority be transmitted in the teaching of the Church? Such questions are dealt with in Thomas' account of three stages of public revelation: before the law (Abraham), under the Law (Moses) and under grace (Christ).[33] In explicating this three-stage process Thomas can develop a full Aristotelian psychology of revelatory experience. The great variety of means of God's self-disclosure through historical events, visions, dreams and intellectual intuitions must be assessed and adjudicated by the mind as it is empowered by the divine truth.[34] There remains an ambiguity here since it is not entirely clear to what extent the certainty as the effect of revelation is dependent on the judgement of reason on the credibility of the witnesses to revelation and on the rational demonstration of the necessity of relying on supernatural revela-

**30** STh I qu.1 a 7 obj. quoting John of Damascus *De fide orthodoxa* I, 4.
**31** STh I Qu 1 a 7 sed contr. [5].
**32** STh I qu 1 a 8 resp. [8].
**33** Cf. STh II-II q. 174, a.6.
**34** Cf. STh II-II, q. 173.

tion. This proved to be a tension in Thomas' account of revelation which opened up the on-going debates about the relationship of nature and grace, natural and supernatural knowledge with underlies the discussions within the Thomistic and neo-Thomistic schools and with the Thomists of all ages.

In view of Thomas' sharp distinction between natural knowledge and knowledge given in revelation, it is perhaps not surprising that the debate about the relationship between reason and revelation continues with opposing emphases. Whereas some theologians emphasize that divine revelation surpasses all capacities of natural reason so that Christian teaching must find its orientation in revelation alone, others, like the Catalan missionary Ramon Lull devise subtle schemes for proving the mysteries of faith by necessary reasons.

## 3.3 The Threefold Self-Giving of God and the Internal Testimony of the Spirit: Martin Luther and John Calvin

This ambiguity forms the background of the Reformers' new vision of revelation as a process of divine self-giving.[35] This new understanding combines the claims and questions from scholastic theology with the personal insight of monastic experience. The guiding question of the justice of God leads to a new view of the relationship of God's action and human action. Is it judicial justice, God's judgment over the actions of humans so that humans must appear just before God in order to receive God's grace, or is creative justice by which God himself makes sinners just by creating the conditions for accepting God's grace?[36] To be able to distinguish and relate them correctly is for Luther one half of what it means to be Christian, the other half is to trust that God does nothing contingently, in the sense of merely reacting to the activity of created agencies. The question of the capacities and incapacities of human nature and of the potentiality and actuality of grace is transformed into the relationship between law and Gospel. By the law God confronts humans with the demand of what he wants them to do to fulfil his will and so to reach their own fulfilment in communion with God. Confronted with the law humans have to recognize that they cannot do anything on the basis of their own powers to do the will of God. They must take refuge to

35 Cf. the detailed discussion in: Schwöbel, Christoph, "Offenbarung, Glaube und Gewissheit in der reformatorischen Theologie," in: E. Herms/L. Žak (eds), *Grund und Gegenstand des Glaubens nach römisch-katholischer und evangelisch-lutherischer Lehre*, 119–155, Tübingen: Mohr Siebeck, 2008.

36 Cf. Schwöbel, Christoph, "Justice and Freedom. The Continuing Promise of the Reformation," *Neue Zeitschrift für Systematische Theologie* 59 (2017), 595–614.

the Gospel which proclaims to them what God does in order to enable humans to do the will of God. The law discloses the soteriological impotence of humans to do God's will and so be acceptable before God. On the basis of their own powers they can do nothing to meet the demands of the law. The gospel proclaims that Christ has done everything to fulfil the law and so enables humans in faith to do the will of God joyfully. This insight leads to the transformation of the human affections. The disclosure of God's self-presentation transforms the human capacities and incapacities, reorganizes the "inner person" to live in the light of God's truth and to do the will of God in all dimensions of its embodied existence.

The triune author of God's self-communication, its content and its effect is comprised in the understanding of God's Trinitarian self-giving. In the summary of this process, the Apostles' Creed, we see "how God gives himself completely to us, with all his gifts and power, to help us keep the Ten Commandments: the Father gives us all creation, Christ all his works, the Holy Spirit all his gifts."[37] The divine self-giving has at its content the depths of God's fatherly love and the true purpose of human existence, to be sanctified in communion with the triune God, so that the divine self-giving brings humans into community with God. Luther writes about the Apostles' Creed:

> For in all three articles God himself has revealed and opened to us the most profound depths of his fatherly heart and his pure, unutterable love. For this very purpose he created us, so that he might redeem and sanctify us and make us holy, and moreover, having granted and bestowed upon us everything in heaven and on earth, he has also given us his Son and his Holy Spirit, through whom he brings us to himself. For ... we could never come to recognize the Father's favour and grace were it not for the Lord Christ, who is a mirror of the Father's heart. Apart from him we see nothing but an angry and terrible judge. But neither could we know anything of Christ, had it not been revealed by the Holy Spirit.[38]

Revelation which Luther refers to with a whole range of expressions, comprising all means of communication, speech, ostension, disclosing acts, and all forms of reception, audition, vision, being instructed, sensibility and experience, proceeds from the Father through the Son and the Holy Spirit. Its content is God's own triune being, God's will and God's heart. The *ratio essendi*, the order of being proceeds from the Father to the Son and the Spirit. The *ratio cognoscendi*, the order of knowing, begins with the work of the Holy Spirit who brings believers to Christ, personally and as persons-in-communion, so that in Christ they

---

**37** Luther, Martin, *The Large Catechism*, in: Robert Kolb/Timothy J. Wengert (eds), *The Book of Concord. The Confessions of the Evangelical Lutheran Church*, trans. Charles Arand [et al.], Minneapolis, MN: Fortress Press, 2000, 440.
**38** *Book of Concord*, 439–440.

have communion with God the Father. The description of the operation of the Holy Spirit also comprises all human capacities, reason, will and the affections of the heart.

> I believe that by my own understanding or strength I cannot believe in Jesus Christ my Lord or come to him, but instead the Holy Spirit has called me through the gospel, enlightened me with his gifts, made me holy and kept me in the true faith, just as he calls, gathers, enlightens, and makes holy the whole Christian church on earth and keeps it with Jesus Christ in the one common, Christian faith.[39]

These statements, written for catechetical instruction, show very clearly that for Luther, the communal dimension, the Church, and the individual dimension belong intrinsically together. The constitution of faith that is in this way described *is* the constitution of the community of faith.

This has far-reaching implications also for the conceptuality in which revelation is developed. The prime category of Aristotelian metaphysics, substance, is replaced by the biblical category of God's creative "word". The paradigm of causality, explaining divine action in terms of cause and effect, is replaced by the hermeneutical paradigm of address and response, which now includes the causality of efficacious speaking and reception. Revelation is consistently described as a communicative act, bound to the self-communication of God's word in the proclamation of the Gospel, made certain by God the Spirit in creating certainty in the human heart. The heart, understood as a communicative organ, in the true sense a "hearing heart" (1Kings 3:9) becomes the center of human orientation in its rational, voluntative and affective dimensions. The transformation of the human capacity to act is described as a reorientation of the affections which is summarized in the understanding of faith as trust. In this communicative paradigm the whole of the church's witness and service can be understood as the instrument which God employs in order to create certainty of faith and so build the church as a community of believers. Similarly, the revelation in Christ can also be described as a communicative act, a transposition in which Christ takes the place of sinners and sinners are invited to Christ's place as sons of God. This transposition, vividly described in Luther's *On the Freedom of a Christian*, includes the communication of all human sins to Christ who bears them and so destroys them and the communication of all Christ's goods to the believers. The nuptial imagery of mystical union employed here is reinterpreted as communion. The revelation of Christ interpreted as the calling of believers into communion with Christ lets the whole of creation be seen as a

39 *Book of Concord, Small Catechism,* loc. cit., 355–356.

divine communication in which everything that is has meaning. The act of creation is interpreted as a divine speech-act and the work of creation, the world, is understood as God's vocabulary ordered by the rules of grammar by God's speech.[40]

The language of divine self-giving makes revelation an act of divine self-communication in a precise sense, since the economic Trinity communicates in the different aspects of the one act of divine self-communication in the Spirit, in Christ and in God the Father the communicative being which God is. Luther can describe in many places God as a conversation between the Father and the Son in which the Holy Spirit listens in and communicates what he hears in this way to believers.[41]

This new interpretation of revelation which consistently interprets revelation as the self-disclosure of God's Trinitarian being rests on a pronounced view of the means of God's self-communication which can be grasped in Luther's use of Scripture. With poignant criticism of the claim of the medieval church to teach with authority where the teaching of Scripture seems opaque, Luther posits Scripture as the first principle of theological teaching through which God himself is "the teacher in our midst". God is seen as the first author of Scripture by employing the biblical authors to communicate divine truth in human means of communication which continuities the mode of communication of the incarnation. This constitutes the external clarity of Scripture and the privileging of the literal sense in Biblical interpretation. Scripture means what it says. When there seem to be opaque passages, one must turn to Scripture first. Scripture is its own interpreter in inter-textual exegesis. However, God is also the ultimate interpreter of Scripture since God the Holy Spirit appropriates the truth of the Biblical message to the reader of the Bible or to the listener when the Bible is preached. This way of interpreting the "Scripture alone" makes Scripture theologically relative to God's self-communication. It authorizes the use of Scripture as the primary authority for a Christian, but at the same time it relativizes this

---

**40** Cf. Schwöbel, Christoph, "'We Are All God's Vocabulary.' The Idea of Creation as a Speech-Act of the Trinitarian God and Its Significance for the Dialogue Between Theology and Sciences," in: A. B. Torrance/T. H. McCall (eds), *Knowing Creation. Perspectives from Theology, Philosophy, and Science*, vol. 1, 47–68, Grand Rapids, MI: Zondervan, 2018.

**41** Cf. Schwöbel, Christoph, "God as Conversation. Reflections on a Theological Ontology of Communicative Relations," in: J. Haers (ed.), *Theology of Conversation. Towards a Relational Theology*, BEThL 172, 43–67, Leuven [et al.]: Peeters, 2003. For the references in the different literary genres of Luther's writings cf. Schwöbel, Christoph, "Martin Luther and the Trinity," in: *Oxford Research Encyclopedia on Martin Luther*, Oxford, 2017, http://religion.oxfordre.com (last accessed Nov 4, 2019).

authority to the self-communication of the triune God. The content of Scripture must be understood from the self-communication of its first author. The other exclusive particles "through Christ alone", "by grace alone" and "in faith alone" make a similar point. God's personal self-communication through the incarnation of the eternal divine Word in Jesus makes God's self-communication in Christ the "vanishing" point in the interpretation of Scripture, the point external to Scripture in whom all perspectives of interpretation converge.[42] *Sola gratia*, by grace alone, is not an additional principle to Christ alone. It emphasizes that Christ is God's grace in person and makes it quite clear that human salvation is not the result of the cooperation of divine and human agency, or the joint product of the co-causality of nature and grace. "By grace alone", subsumes everything under God's initiative to bring about his communion with his reconciled creation. Ingolf Dalferth has pointed out that the different aspects underlined in the exclusive particles all point to "God alone" as the core of the Reformation as a "spiritual revolution."[43] God alone in his Trinitarian self-communication is therefore the key to understanding the point of the Re-conceptualization of revelation in Reformation theology.

In the *Institutes of the Christian Religion*, John Calvin, with regard to these questions Luther's true disciple, has developed this view into a systematic account of revelation in Book I. In developing the structure of the "connection between our knowledge of God and our knowledge of ourselves" (Chapters 1–4) and in considering "the knowledge of God displayed in the fabric and constant government of the universe" (chapter 5), Calvin first points to Scripture as the glasses which help humans whose sight has been distorted by the Fall see the true God clearly.[44] In the next step, Calvin argues that in order to understand Scripture as the truthful witness to revelation we cannot rely on external proof or arguments. "Hence, the highest proof of Scripture is uniformly taken from the character of him whose word it is." Since the prophets and apostles always reform to God as the source of their truthful witness. Therefore, Calvin argues, "the truth of Scripture must be derived from a higher source than human conjec-

**42** Dalferth, Ingolf U., "Die Mitte ist außen. Anmerkungen zum Wirklichkeitsbezug evangelischer Schriftauslegung," in: Christoph Landmesser/Hans-Joachim Eckstein/Hermann Lichtenberger (eds), *Jesus Christus als die Mitte der Schrift. Studien zur Hermeneutik des Evangeliums*, 173–198, Berlin/New York: De Gruyter, 1997.

**43** Dalferth, Ingolf U., "Creative Grace. The Spiritual Revolution of the Reformation," in: *Neue Zeitschrift für Systematische Theologie* 59 (2017), 548–571.

**44** Cf. Calvin, John, *Institutes of the Christian Religion* (1559), trans. Henry Beveridge, Grand Rapids, MI: Eerdmanns, 1989, bk I, ch VI,1; 64.

tures, judgements, or reasons; namely the secret testimony of the Spirit."[45] For Calvin, the superiority of the testimony of the Spirit is rooted in the fact that in the internal testimony of the Spirit God makes his own words, spoken through the instrumentality of human witnesses, certain in the hearts of believers.

> For as God alone can properly bear witness to his own words, so these words will not obtain full credit in the hearts of men, until they are sealed by the inward testimony of the Spirit. The same Spirit, therefore who spoke by the mouth of the prophets, must penetrate our hearts, in order to convince us that they faithfully delivered the message with which they were entrusted.[46]

This argument which secures the connection between the external word and the internal testimony of the Spirit and thereby rejects both a literalism, connected with later notions of verbal inspiration, and a spiritualism, which makes the testimonies of the Spirit independent of the word of Scripture, is made much stronger by the fact that Calvin regarded the Spirit of God as the only fountain of truth, effective also in pagan philosophers and the believers of other religions. "If we reflect that the Spirit of God is the only fountain of truth, we will be careful, as we would avoid offering insult to him, not to reject or condemn truth wherever it appears. In despising the gifts, we insult the Giver."[47]

When John Calvin developed his theory of the internal testimony of the Holy Spirit the Council of Trent had already been convened and promulgated in its fourth session on the 8th of April 1546 a decree that was intended to respond to the Protestant views of revelation. The Council of Trent can be seen as the beginning of Roman Catholicism, the reformation of the Catholic Church after the crisis triggered by the "spiritual revolution" of the Protestant Reformation in its different forms in Wittenberg, Strasbourg and Geneva. The Council did not use the concept of revelation, but instead spoke of the Gospel as "the source of all saving doctrine and moral discipline" (DH 1501). The Council was keen to establish the authority of the Church which had been challenged in the Reformation by seeing it as rooted in divine revelation and as continuing its authority in the present. In this sense it states that the Gospel which was "promised of old through the prophets of sacred Scriptures" is authoritatively promulgated by "our Lord Jesus Christ, Son of God, then through his apostles to whom he gave the charge 'to preach it to every creature' (Mark 16:15)" (DH 1501). This offers the ground for the authority of the Church as standing in the succession of the

**45** *Institutes* bk I, ch VII, 4; 71.
**46** *Institutes* bk I, ch VII, 4; 72.
**47** *Institutes* bk II, ch. II.15; 236.

Apostles. This is further strengthened by the assertion that the Gospel is transmitted in written scriptures and in unwritten traditions (*libris scriptis et sine scripto traditionibus*) "which have come down to us, having been received by the apostles from the mouth of Christ himself, or from the apostles themselves, by the dictation of the Holy Spirit, have been transmitted, as it were from hand to hand" (DH 1501). The complex of these teachings, Scripture and tradition "having been preserved by continual succession in the Catholic Church", are to be received as having the same authority as Holy Scripture. Consequently, the Council threatens to anathematize all those who contort the meaning of Holy Scripture according to their own taste (*sacram Scripturam ad suos sensus contorquens*, DH 1507).

The aftermath of the Protestant Reformation presents a picture of thoroughgoing pluralization in the understanding of revelation. Whereas the theology of Roman Catholic scholasticism in the 16$^{th}$ and 17$^{th}$ century attempts to clarify the relationship between mediate and immediate revelation, an attempt that is necessary if one wants to exclude that immediate revelation could contradict the mediate revelation and in this way challenge the authority of the church as the institution of the authoritative tradition of revelation. In the different Protestant schools the attempt was made to consolidate the authority of Scripture as the authoritative communication of revelation. The background of this attempt has to be seen in the close connection between the so-called Scripture principle and the priesthood of all believers which is constitutive for the different forms of church order in Protestantism. Only if Scripture is the clear, sufficient and normative witness to God's revelation, accessible to all, can Protestant forms of church order be justified. The insistence of both Luther and Calvin to keep the external word of Scripture (and the external signs of the sacraments) and the internal word of the Holy Spirit, creating certainty of faith with regard to the truth of the Gospel, together, because they have the same author, was challenged from two sides in the 17$^{th}$ century. On the one hand, theories of the verbal inspiration of Scripture developed which identified the word of Scripture with God's revelation. On the other hand, new spiritualist religious groups formed around leaders like George Fox (1624–1691) who rejected, often on the basis of the study of Scripture, all externals in religion and claimed that the inner light was sufficient for illumination with divine truth so that during meetings of the "Society of Friends" that came together around the middle of the 17$^{th}$ century silent waiting until one of the members was moved by the Spirit became a regular feature. Like so many other movements of the times the Quakers claimed that they had recaptured the spirit of the original Christian movement. The emergence of new spiritualist movements points to an unsolved problem in the understanding of revelation. Can the personal disclosure of truth here and now be convincingly related to the disclosure in the history and destiny of Christ? What happens if past, present and future are no longer enveloped by one continuous narrative, as it is narrated in the world book of the Bible? Can one still assume that human history is structurally isomorphic, displaying the same structural characteristics?

Similarly, the tension in the understanding of revelation between the universal revelation in creation and the special revelation in Christ was by no means resolved. In the age of emergent confessionalism the teachings based on special historical revelation seemed to be at the center of debate and of, sometimes violent, confrontation. It seems tragic that the understanding of God's communion with his human creatures in the practice and interpretation of Holy Communion was one of the main points of conflict and strife. If the doctrinal implications of understanding of God's revelation in Christ seem to be so controversial, it seems *prima facie* unlikely that it can provide the key to the understanding of God's revelation in creation. Should the relationship between God's revelation in creation and God's self-disclosure in Christ be approached from God's revelation in creation, the revelation that seems to be a common ground for the understanding of nature of the world and also appears to have a common basis in human nature? The implications of the question for interfaith relations is obvious.

The crucial questions that exercised debates on the understanding of the concept of revelation since the Early Church seem to be at the heart of the radical critique of revelation in the Enlightenment and of its rediscovery in the context of post-Enlightenment philosophy. The internal tensions of the long history of debates on revelation seem to be at least one factor in the radical critique of the concept of enlightenment and its reconstruction in the philosophy of idealism.

## 3.4 The Enlightenment Critique of Revelation and Its Rediscovery as a Philosophical Concept

The interpretation of the Enlightenment is a contentious theme of current debates in intellectual history, philosophy and public debates. The controversial issues of these debates have far-reaching consequences for interreligious relations and their intra-religious corollaries. The name of this particular epoch already points to its origins in a particular constellation of theological problems connected with the debates on revelation. The metaphor of light, evoked by the description of the epoch as *les lumière*, *illuminismo* or *Aufklärung*, betrays the theological roots of what is equally called by its defenders and its detractors the "project of the Enlightenment". While the jury is still out in finding the ultimate verdict in the assessment of the Enlightenment, one can at least establish some common problems to the diverse strands of the Enlightenment which differ considerably with regard to their cultural and religious context. Although one of the characteristics of the Enlightenment seems to be the emancipation of the different spheres of culture and of interaction in society from the tutelage of the church, it seems clear that the grounds for this liberation still betray their origin in theological disputes on revelation. First of all, a common feature is the claim that revelation in creation is sufficient for providing reliable orientation for humans in their relations to God, the world and with one another. When this is called "natural religion" or the "religion of nature", it is clear that for the justification of these truths no recourse to supernatural revelations is needed. The thesis is tersely expressed by John Locke (1632–1704) in his *Essay Concerning Human Understanding* (1700):

> Reason is natural revelation, whereby the Eternal Father of Light and Fountain of all knowledge, communicates to mankind that portion of the truth which he has laid within the reach of their natural faculties. Revelation is natural reason enlarged by a new set of discoveries communicated by God immediately, which reason vouches the truth of by the testimony and proofs it gives that they come from God.[48]

Revelation, interpreted as an "enlargement" of natural reason is seen here no longer as self-authenticating because of its divine author. Rather, that God is the divine author must be established by reason. While for earlier times the divine origin was the proof of the rationality of revelation, now the divine origin must be established by proofs of reason. On this presupposition it is not difficult to show *The Reasonableness of Christianity as Delivered in the Scriptures* (1695), as Locke did in the work of that title, ostensibly to refute Deists. The reasonableness of Christianity consists in its consonance with rational revelation which is demonstrated by reason, and this is shown from a most detailed scriptural exegesis. Locke's main argument that revelation speeded up and made accessible to the "vulgar masses" in a short time what would have taken much longer to discover by the processes of reason alone, became a standard feature of the discussions. John Toland's Work *Christianity Not Mysterious* (1696) plays on the notion that revelation means the drawing back of a veil, so that the understanding of revelation can be employed as a justification for demonstrating the "not mysterious" character of Christianity, i.e. that it is fully compatible, if not identical, with natural reason.[49] A similar thought is present in Matthew Tindal's (1657–

**48** Locke, John, *An Essay Concerning Human Understanding*, bk 4, ch. 19, no 4, New York: Dover Publications, 1959, 340.

**49** This did not convince the Irish Parliamentarians who called for Toland, as a citizen of the Kingdom of Ireland, to be burned at the stake. Fortunately, only copies of his book were publicly burnt by the hangman in Dublin.

1733) work *Christianity as Old as the Creation or the Gospel as a Republication of the Religion of Nature* (1730) who argued that the moral guidance of Christianity could be supported from natural reason.

Through translations, such as the one of Tindal's work as early as 1741, the thought of the English deists quickly spread to Germany. H. S. Reimarus *Vornehmste Wahrheiten der natürlichen Religion* (The most noble truths of natural religion) (1754) is based to a large extent on John Leland's criticism of deism.[50] Gotthold Ephraim Lessing had a much more positive view of revealed religion than Reimarus since he claimed that "what education is to the individual man, revelation is to the whole human race."[51] The critique of revealed religion moved into a different, and possibly more treacherous, terrain when he claimed that "accidental truths of history can never become the proof of necessary truths of reason."[52] The witness to God's self-disclosure had become accidental truths of history which are to be seen as entirely unreliable. History is no longer conceived within the framework of God's self-disclosure, therefore it loses its trustworthiness. If history is conceived within this framework, the very fact that the testimonies of God's self-disclosure are contingent and can only be known *a posteriori* points to the fact that they are rooted in God's will and action. This is the ground for their reliability. In contrast, the necessary truths of human reason become problematical, because they can only depend on God's self-determination and are therefore by no means necessary, but dependent on the freedom of God's self-determination which is the only necessity for a created world, including the human knowers in it. A similar observation can be made with regard to Lessing's powerful metaphor of the "ugly broad ditch" of history that separates us from the events of Jesus' life and death of which we only know through the testimonies of others. If we start from the human perception of time as the framework of history that might indeed be the case. Establishing continuity becomes a serious problem and it seems inevitable to give our own experience in the here and now, the present "inner truth" of the Christian message priority over the external truth reported by others. However, if we do not try to establish continuity from the standpoint of human observers of history, but see any continuity in history rooted in the continuity of divine self-communication which connects the past of the first beginning and the ultimate end and so locates humans and the discontinuities of human history within this one history, from Alpha to Omega, relating the

---

**50** The relevant texts are conveniently collected in Gay, Peter (ed.), *Deism. An Anthology*, Princeton, NJ [et al.]: van Nostrand, 1968.

**51** Chadwick, Henry (ed.), *Lessing's Theological Writings*, Stanford: Stanford University Press, 1957, 105.

**52** *Op. cit.*, 53.

external and internal dimensions, the "ugly broad ditch" has already been bridged in the continuity of God's self-communication. From such a standpoint it seems one can evade the Enlightenment antinomy between tradition and present experience, between the communication from others and the autonomy of our own judgement. Discarding the framework of divine revelation, Enlightenment thought was trapped in the dualisms between the tradition and one's own experience, between the contingent and the necessary, between the rationalism of innate ideas and the empiricism of impressions as the true source of knowledge, between the knowledge of the world and the knowledge of God.

There were, of course, thinkers who recognized the problematical character of these implications of Enlightenment thought. One who deserves particular attention in the attempt at sketching the role of the concept of revelation is Johann Georg Hamann (1730–1788), friend, interlocutor and opponent of Immanuel Kant who subjected the critical idea of pure reason to a perceptive meta-criticism. Hamann takes up the potential of Luther's view of the interaction of the "external" and the "internal" word and construes the image of God as an author who addresses his human creatures through the book of creation and enables them through the book of the Bible to reach an understanding of God, themselves and the world, inspired by the internal word of God's Spirit. Hamann rediscovers the role of revelation for reason and so views the way in which human reason is contextualized in the narrative of God's self-communication as a possibility of positively acknowledging the embodiment, the historicity, the sociality and the linguistic character of human reason.[53]

Such dissenting voices could not hide the fact that the concept of revelation and its theological foundations were pushed into the background by the main strands of the Enlightenment. Once revelation was shown to be consonant with reason and subject to the critical judgment of human reason, there seemed few good reasons to engage with revelation. It was precisely the self-critical examination of reason's own claims to absolute fundamentality that led to a revival of the concept of revelation in the works of the Idealist philosophers. The essence of the Spirit is in Hegel's philosophy the revelation of reality as such which discloses the process of nature as an on-going revelation insofar as the Spirit transcends itself into the other of itself only to return to itself in the structure of being-itself-for-itself. True religion is revealed religion, disclosing this movement of the Spirit, and the Spirit is disclosed in Christianity as revelatory religion, the religion in which the essence of religion is disclosed. Schelling's philosophy

53 Cf. Bayer, Oswald, *Contemporary in Dissent. Johann Georg Hamann as Radical Enlightener*, Grand Rapids, MI: Eerdmans, 2012.

reaches its climax in the *Philosophie der Offenbarung* (1854) in which the insight into the inability of philosophy as critical enterprise (negative philosophy) leads to a reassessment of the history of religions and the history of dogma without which philosophy, it is claimed, cannot grasp its own foundation and subject-matter, since it is only given in revelation (positive philosophy). The movement of negative philosophy to pursue the question of the foundations of reason must be retained and worked through again and again, in order to see positive philosophy not as a replacement of the project of negative philosophy, but as its continuation with different means and on different foundations. For Schelling, revelation is, not primarily the source of knowledge, but the object of philosophy because it is the way in which being itself is disclosed and demands a way of reflection in keeping with the way this object is disclosed. The rediscovery of the concept of revelation by the philosophers in the 19$^{th}$ century, and the sophisticated concepts of divine self-revelation which both Hegel and Schelling, each in their own way, developed, is the background for the role of revelation as the "key concept" of theology in the 20$^{th}$ century.[54]

## 3.5 Revelation as the Key Concept of 20$^{th}$ Century Christian Theology

### 3.5.1 The Debates on Revelation in Roman Catholic Theology

The clarification attempted in the 19$^{th}$ century in response to the criticism of the Enlightenment and its critical refutation in the philosophy of German idealism form the background of the debates on revelation in the 20$^{th}$ century. In Roman Catholic theology, Johann Adam Möhler (1794–1838) of the "Tübingen school" presented in his *Symbolik* (1832) a view of revelation as the dynamic self-manifestation of God in history culminating in the incarnation and continued in the Church as the "extension of the Incarnation". Similar emphases can be found in John Henry Newman (1801–1890), whose theology, which became very influential in 20$^{th}$ century Roman Catholic theology, emphasized the limits of human knowledge and the remaining mysteriousness of revelation where it is not illuminated by God himself. Möhler and Newman attempted each in his own way to overcome the influence of rationalist tendencies in Roman-Catholic theology, often called "semi-rationalism" and associated with Georg Hermes (1775–1831) and Anton Günther (1783), and of their fideist and tra-

54 Cf. Eicher, Peter, *Offenbarung. Prinzip neuzeitlicher Theologie*, Kösel: München, 1977.

ditionalist counter-parts, G.A. de Bonald and Félicité de Lammenais. In 1864 Pope Pius IX. proposed a *Syllabus of Errors*, excerpted from his earlier utterances (DH 2901–2980). This condemnation of what was seen as clear "errors" formed the background of the restatement of Roman-Catholic doctrine in the dogmatic constitution *Dei Filius* of the first Vatican Council, promulgated on the 24th of April 1870. The Council teaches with reference to Rom. 1:20 the doctrine of the Roman Catholic church that God "can be known with certitude by the natural light of human reason from created things". This is immediately supplemented, this time with reference to Heb. 1:1, with the statement that it has pleased God "to reveal Himself and the eternal decrees of His will in another supernatural way" (DH 3004). While the natural light allows in divine things, which are accessible to human reason, certain knowledge, supernatural revelation is nevertheless "absolutely necessary" because God "has ordained man for a supernatural end, to participation, namely, in the divine goods which altogether surpass the understanding of the human mind" (DH 3005). This argument, which is of course reminiscent of Thomas Aquinas, deems supernatural revelation to be necessary for the achievement of the supernatural destiny of human, i.e. their participation in "goods" which surpass the human mind. This supernatural revelation, the Council continues by citing the Council of Trent, is "contained in the written books and in unwritten traditions" (DH 3006). Scripture and tradition must be understood in the "true sense which Holy Mother Church held and holds, whose office it is to judge concerning the true understanding and interpretation of Scripture" (DH 3007).

The next section describes the nature of faith (DH 3008–3014). Revelation which is rooted in the being and will of God (DH 3001–3003) is oriented toward the constitution of faith. It is the way in which faith receives its object. The necessity of faith is grounded in the dependence of human creatures on God the creator. Therefore, human reason is "wholly subject to divine truth". For this humans are bound by faith "to give full obedience of intellect and will to God who reveals" (*Deo revelanti*). God in his revelation is therefore the real object of faith, and "full obedience" is demanded, because the truths of revelation should not be believed because they can be justified by natural reason, "but because of the authority of the God who reveals them, who can neither deceive nor be deceived" (DH 3008). God is the subject and object of revelation. Therefore, it seems at least a restrictive interpretation when *Dei Verbum* is seen as an example of propositional revelation. It is not the view of the Council that God does not reveal Godself, but only propositions about God. Rather God's self- revelation occurs in the form of propositions. The characterization of faith emphasizes, first of all, that it is "consonant with reason." For this reason, God has combined the internal aid of the Holy Spirit (illumination) with the evidence of "external proofs", i.e. the miracles reported in Scripture (DH 3009). In this sense, it is emphasized that faith is not a "blind movement of the intellect" but a "gift of God, and its act pertaining to salvation" (DH 3010). This balancing of external revelation and the internal aid of the Holy Spirit is then summarized in the formula:

> Further, by divine and Catholic faith, all those things must be believed (*credenda*) which are contained in the written word of God and in tradition, and those which are proposed by the Church, either in a solemn pronouncement or in her ordinary and universal teaching power, to be believed as divinely revealed (*tamquam divinitus revelata credenda*). (DH 3011)

This characterization of the object of faith gives a cumulative account of Scripture, tradition and the teaching office of the Church. The object of faith therefore includes everything that is proposed by the church in its teaching office, as the wording seems to suggest, on the same level as the written word of God and tradition. This is an enormous strengthening of the role of the Church and its teaching office in revelation. If this is applied to faith, constituted in this way, it is evident that faith, accepting faith in the act of obedience and of preserving it, is necessary for salvation. For this purpose the church has been instituted as "guardian and teacher of the revealed word" (DH 3012). Obedience to the church is in this way necessary for salvation.

The anti-Protestant emphasis of these statements is obvious. On the basis of this view of revelation, which has its origin and authority in God, is mediated in Scripture and tradition and promulgated by the church, it is not possible to claim that Scripture alone is the authority in all matters of doctrine or to insist that God himself in the internal testimony of the Spirit confirms the external word of Scripture, proclaimed in preaching as the truth of God's revelation in Christ. The so-called exclusive particles of "Scripture alone," "through Christ alone", "by grace alone" and "in faith alone" are effectively summarized by the new exclusive particle *sola ecclesia*, "in the church alone." The difference is not to be seen in the fact that the church has no place in accounts of revelation in Reformation theology. Rather, the difference can be located in the view that in Reformation theology the unity of revelation is seen in the threefold self-giving of the triune God who envelopes Scripture, tradition and the ministry of the church as the means of this divine self-giving (*tamquam per instrumenta, Augsburg Confession art. V)* in order to create faith. If, as in the definitions of the Council, revelation includes the teaching office of the church on the same level with Scripture and tradition, and as an element of the one process of God's self-revelation, there is the basis for the dogma of papal infallibility. The formal definition of the Council's declaration *Pastor Aeternus*, promulgated on 18th of July 1870, simply spells that out:

> And so We, adhering faithfully to the tradition received from the beginning of the Christian faith, to the glory of God, our Saviour, the elevation of the Catholic religion and the salvation of Christian peoples, with the approbation of the sacred Council, teach and explain that the dogma has been divinely revealed:
>
> that the Roman Pontiff, when he speaks ex cathedra, that is, when carrying out the duty of the pastor and teacher of all Christians by virtue of his supreme apostolic authority he defines a doctrine of faith or morals to be held by the universal Church, through the divine assistance promised him in blessed Peter, operates with that infallibility with which the divine Redeemer wished that His church be instructed in defining doctrine on faith and morals; and so such definitions of the Roman Pontiff from himself, but not from the consensus of the Church, are unalterable. (DH 3073/3074)

After the definition of the way in which faith is constituted by revelation, the first Vatican Council proposed a definition of the relationship between faith and reason. It states that there is a twofold order of knowledge, according to which natural reason and faith are both distinct in principle and in object. While there are certain things that can be known by natural reason, nevertheless, there is more, namely, "mysteries hidden in God are proposed to us for belief which had they not been divinely revealed, could not become known" (DH 3015). Natural reason can "with the help of God" attain some understanding of the mysteries of faith: from the analogy of the things it knows by means of natural reason; from the "connection of the mysteries among themselves", i. e. their systematic coherence; and even with regard to the ultimate destiny of humans, the supernatural end of natural human life. Nevertheless, natural reason can never attain knowledge of the divine mysteries in the same way and to the same extent in which it can attain knowledge of the natural world. Even where they are "handed down by revelation and accepted by faith, they nevertheless remain covered by the veil of faith itself" (DH 3016) until we attain the beatific vision.

This description of the relationship between faith and reason leads to a number of important conclusions. First of all, there can never be "true dissension" between faith and reason because they have their origin in the same God, and God can never contract himself (DH 3017). There may be apparent contradictions when the dogmas of faith are not interpreted "according to the mind of the church" or when reason deteriorates to mere opinion. Therefore, secondly, the church has "the right and duty of proscribing knowledge falsely so called" (3018). There is, thirdly, however, also a mutual constructive task, since right reasoning demonstrates (*demonstrat*) the foundation of faith and "illumined by its light perfects the knowledge of divine things"; conversely, faith "frees and protects reason from error" (DH 3019).

It is clear that the twofold order of knowledge does not posit two separate sources of knowledge. They both have their origin in the one God. However, it is also clear that the two orders exist within the one framework of revelation. Only because of that it can be claimed that the church has the function of being the guardian and protector of all true knowledge. This, however, leads to the question of whether it can be consistent when it is claimed that natural reason "proves" the foundation of faith. It would be more appropriate that it can only explicate the foundation of faith – and that is a task that is still demanding enough. Understanding revelation as the framework within which the Council differentiates between faith and reason, also implies that the doctrine of faith does not fall into the category where a natural progress of knowledge occurs as in the sciences. Rather, "it has been entrusted as a divine deposit to the Spouse of Christ, to be faithfully guarded and infallibly interpreted" (DH 3020). Therefore, if there is progress in knowledge and understanding "let it be solely in its own genus, namely, in the same dogma, with the same sense and the same understanding" (cited DH 3020).

Much of the discussion of Roman Catholic theology on revelation in the 20th century is concerned with finding the right interpretation for these statements and with developing a philosophical or theological theory that fits the boundaries defined by the Council. Following the Council, revelation was mostly understood as divine self-communication and its mode of communication as the personal self-presentation of God and not as an instruction with revealed true propositions. There remains, however, the question of how revelation, occurring in this mode, can bring forth the power to obey the revelation of God, the *obsequium rationale*, the rational submission to the truth revealed in Jesus Christ. Can the revelation in Jesus Christ be shown to be the condition of the possibility of the assent of faith? An answer to this question was made more difficult by a particular interpretation of the relationship of the natural and the supernatural that was established in the Thomistic school in early modern times. In his commentaries to the works of Thomas Aquinas, Cajetan introduced, what amounted to a new understanding of 'nature' as 'pure nature,' in order to emphasize the gratuity of grace. Does this include that one could speak of a natural end of humanity? If so, then grace and revelation can only be added to a nature that is complete in itself as a supernatural addition. All the major thinkers of the so-called Nouvelle théologie, exemplified in Henri de Lubac's *Surnaturel*, and the transcendental Thomists, as exemplified in Karl Rahner's philosophical theology, argued that since they are created in the image of God, human persons are from the beginning directed towards a supernatural end, and this orientation which implies that human nature always transcends itself towards grace, is fulfilled in Jesus Christ.[55] Looking back from the revelation in Jesus Christ, human persons can understand the relationship to revelation in creation, since the created destiny of human persons that is now fulfilled in Jesus Christ, in such a way that it makes the rational submission to Christ possible. Rahner famously claimed that all human persons are characterized by a "supernatural existential", a dimension of existence which enables existence to understand itself. This supernatural existential is fulfilled in Jesus Christ so that Christians can now understand the orientation of transcending their given nature towards receptiveness to the grace of God as something characterizing nature from the beginning which is now fulfilled in Jesus Christ. From this perspective, one can understand the background of Rahner's famous characterization of people of other faiths as "anonymous Christians".[56] Considerations such as these form the background for the model of construing the relationship of the Roman Catholic Church to other faiths in *Nostra Aetate* in a series of concentric circles.[57]

It should be noted in passing that with regard to the question about the relationship between the revelation of God in creation and the revelation of God in Christ we encounter a structural analogy to the view of Islam that accepting Islam is returning to the religion of Adam, the one religion of humankind.

### 3.5.2 The Discussions on Revelation in Protestant Theology

The complex history of the debates on revelation following the Enlightenment's criticism of revelation and the critique of the criticism of the Enlightenment in the philosophies of Romanticism and German Idealism which entails the re-appropriation of revelation as a philosophical category also forms the background of the debate within Protestant theology. With regard to the content and process of revelation the discussion focuses, like the debate in Roman Catholicism on the relationship between God's revelation in creation and God's revelation in Christ. The particular Protestant conceptuality on which this problem is considered is, following the Reformation, no longer the relationship between nature and grace, but the new paradigm of the relationship between law and Gospel.

55 Cf. Rahner, Karl, "Concerning the Relationship between Nature and Grace," in: id., *Theological Investigations*, vol. 1, Baltimore: Helicon, 1961, 297–317.
56 Cf. the exploration of this notion in: D'Costa, Gavin, "Karl Rahner's Anonymous Christian. A Reappraisal," *Modern Theology* 1 (1985), 131–148.
57 Cf. Schwöbel, Christoph, "The Same God? The Perspective of Faith, the Identity of God, Tolerance, and Dialogue," in: Miroslav Volf (ed.), *Do We Worship the Same God? Jews, Christians, and Muslims in Dialogue*, 1–17, Grand Rapids/Cambridge: Eerdmans, 2012.

The common starting-point for the discussion within Protestant theology is the experience of the First World War as a turning point in the sequence of historical time, a radical discontinuity which leads to the necessity of finding a new starting-point for living the Christian faith and elucidating the Christian Gospel. Whether in the theologies of the "theologians of crisis", or in "the other departure"[58] of the Luther-Renaissance, or in the theologies trying to retrieve the core of critical and Idealist philosophies under new circumstances (e.g. Neo-Kantianism, Neo-Hegelianism etc.), the awareness of the necessity of a new start is similar. The awareness of standing "between the times" is shared by almost everybody in German-speaking theology. Perhaps this is one of the reasons why the engagement with the concept of revelation, also expressing a new start, a discontinuity in the epistemic matrix of believers, is such a central concern for all theologians after the First World War.

#### 3.5.2.1 Karl Barth

For the theologians of crisis, most notably Karl Barth (1886–1968) the First World War signifies the breakdown of conventional academic theology in which he grew up. The self-criticism of natural reason that had already been developed in the response of Romanticism and Idealism to the Enlightenment has been radicalized. For Barth, this must not only include reason and "Wissenschaft", but also religion, as far as it is understood as the human capacity for relating to God. For theology, this confronts with the challenge of finding new foundations and of developing a theological method for which this self-criticism becomes foundational. The reorientation on the "strange new world of the Bible" and the dialectical method are for Barth the only viable response. In contrast to the view developed by Vatican I and then followed by many Roman Catholic theologians, the breakdown of natural reason and the failure of religion to relate to the reality of God is for Barth's theology constitutive. It is the "No!" over against which God speaks the "Yes" of the revelation in Christ. In his lecture of 1922 "Das Wort Gottes und die Aufgabe der Theologie" he phrases that in a stark dialectic: "As theologians we ought to speak of God. We are human, however, and so cannot speak of God. We ought therefore to recognize both our obligation and our inability and by that very recognition give God the glory. This our perplexity."[59]

---

58 Cf. Assel, Heinrich, *Der andere Aufbruch. Die Lutherrenaissance – Ursprünge, Aporien und Wege: Karl Holl, Emanuel Hirsch, Rudolf Hermann (1910–1935)*, Göttingen: V&R, 1994.

59 This is a corrected version of the English translation of Barth's lecture which translates of "ministers" where Barth speaks of "Theologen." There is no question that Barth saw the ministry as the paradigmatic form of theology. The challenge, however, goes further, because Barth

This perplexity can only be overcome, theology's task to speak of God can only be fulfilled, Barth intimates at the end of the lecture, where and when God himself speaks.[60] This stark dialectic indicates that Barth radicalizes the philosophical self-criticism of natural reason, which he had inherited, so that speaking of God becomes a human impossibility and a divine actuality. Barth's magnum opus, the *Church Dogmatics* can be understood as the attempt to point to the resolution of the dilemma by trying to repeat the way how God himself speaks and so overcomes the human impossibility of speaking of God. Therefore, the doctrine of the Trinity has a central place in the *Prolegomena* of Barth's *Church Dogmatics*. God's Word is here described as God himself in his revelation in the unity and distinction of Revealer, Revelation and Revealedness. God *is* his revelation and so also his knowability. This implies, of course, that natural theology becomes an impossibility. According to Barth "God is who He is in the act of His revelation",[61] and therefore the attempt to know God by means of natural reason is really the denial of God. The radical character of this can only be understood, if one understands Barth's theology as a consistent attempt to overturn the paradigm of modernity. He challenges two of the paradigmatic shifts that characterize the transition from pre-modern to modern thought. Barth does not accept that the primary question in philosophy or theology is an epistemological one: How can we know what something is? Barth rejects the modern dogma that before we can know what something is, we must establish how we can know about it. Furthermore, Barth also challenges the modern view that before we can think of the actuality of something we must consider the conditions of its possibility – the transcendental turn in Kantian and post-Kantian philosophy. Barth suggests here a twofold inversion of the modern paradigm with his proposal to look at being before knowing and to start with actuality and from this to construct the conditions of its possibility.[62] Applied to theology, this means that the being of God is the ground for knowing God. If "God is who He is in the act of His revelation", theology must start from the actuality of his revelation in Jesus Christ. If God's revelation in Christ acquires this exclusive position, God's reve-

---

attempts to formulate a dilemma that applies to the ministry, but also to academic theology, and indeed to every human attempt to speak of God. Cf. Barth, Karl, "The Word of God and the Task of the Ministry," in: id., *The Word of God and the Word of Man*, 183–217, London: Hodder and Stoughton, 1928, 186.

**60** Cf. *ibid.*, 214.

**61** Barth, Karl, *The Church Dogmatics* II/1, ed. by Geoffrey William Bromiley/Thomas Forsyth Torrance, Edinburgh: T&T Clark, 1957, 257.

**62** Cf. Schwöbel, Christoph, "Theology," in: John Webster (ed.), *The Cambridge Companion to Karl Barth*, Cambridge: Cambridge University Press, 2000, 17–36.

lation in creation becomes the preparation for God's self-revelation in human history in the incarnation. Barth's famous slogan that Creation is the external ground of the covenant and that the covenant is the internal ground for creation receives in this way an exclusively Christological interpretation.

From this perspective, one can understand Barth's vehement contradiction against the argument of his one-time ally Emil Brunner that revelation needs a "point of contact" in humanity, perhaps in what Brunner understood as the "formal" imago Dei.

Even more radical is Barth's rejection of all attempts to give priority to God's revelation in creation as the framework for locating and giving significance to God's revelation in Christ. For Barth, this amounts to a displacement of God in his revelation by the "orders of creation" or by the transformation of cultural life in modernity which brings forth the categories in which the Christ event is to be understood (Emanuel Hirsch). Such an attempt brings with it the risk to ascribe a revelatory quality to other entities, like the "Volk", race or even the "national revolution".

#### 3.5.2.2 Rudolf Bultmann

One could, of course, raise the question whether Barth's dogmatic account of the understanding of revelation remains too narrowly bound to what he rejects, the optimism of modernity to be able to define the true canons of knowledge in defining criteria for true knowledge. Would there be another way to understand revelation, not by contrasting it to other modes of knowledge which seem incompatible with Christian faith but by elucidating the account that the New Testament itself gives of revelation. Could it be that we find in the biblical sources themselves the right guidance for understanding revelation? This was the attempt of Rudolf Bultmann to show that the New Testament itself offers an understanding of revelation which can be described as the transition from an understanding of human existence which remains largely implicit to a self-understanding that is shaped by the truth of the *kerygma* of Christian proclamation.[63] The contemporary believer repeats in her own experience, in the transformation of her self-understanding when she is confronted with the proclamation of the Gospel, the process that has led to forming the Christian *kerygma* as it comes to expression in the New Testament. The task of "demythologization", which was at the heart of much controversy when Bultmann's reading of the New Testament was first

63 Cf. Bultmann, Rudolf, "The Concept of Revelation in the New Testament (1929)," id., *Existence and Faith*, 67–106, London: Collins Fontana, 1964.

proposed, is nothing but the way in which the mythological language of the New Testament is interpreted in an existential way, not as a description of mythical realities out there, but as a way of expressing in which way our self-understanding is held captive until it is liberated by the truth of Christian proclamation and comes to the certainty of faith. Bultmann's attempt was to develop the concept of revelation from the New Testament sources alone and to show that this is still a valid account of revelation for today.

#### 3.5.2.3 Wolfhart Pannenberg

The attempts at reconstructing the concept of revelation in the theologies of the Word of God, most notably Barth and Bultmann, were forcefully criticized by the programmatic collection of essays, published under the title *Revelation as History*.[64] The systematic contribution to the collection by Wolfhart Pannenberg expressed an alternative to the approach favored by Barth and Bultmann. Pannenberg agrees with Barth, Bultmann and the majority of theologians that revelation must consistently be interpreted as "self-revelation." Pannenberg attributes this understanding of revelation to Hegel who also first saw its implications. If there is only one God, there can be only one self-revelation in which God is both the author, the content and the medium of revelation. If there is only one self-revelation of God, the concept can only refer to the ultimate and final revelation at the end of history. From the perspective of this eschatological revelation, every event before it, indeed the whole of reality, receives its meaning. This eschatological perspective secures the universality of revelation. Therefore Pannenberg questions where God's self-revelation as it is witnessed in the biblical testimonies can be understood as God's direct self-disclosure, e.g. in God's Word. God, Pannenberg maintains, reveals himself *indirectly* in the events and processes of history. For Pannenberg, it is the decisive claim of Christian faith that God reveals himself fully in the resurrection of the crucified Jesus. However, against the background of understanding revelation as God's ultimate self-revelation at the end of history which Pannenberg attributes to Jewish apocalypticism, the resurrection of Jesus must be seen as the anticipation of the end of history. In Jesus' resurrection the end of history is proleptically present and this, Pannenberg argues, is the central claim of Christian faith. If God's self-revelation is truly universal, the proleptic event of the resurrection of Jesus must be accessible for anybody, it must be open for all who have eyes to see. Faith cannot be based on the address of the *kerygma*, it must be based on historical fact. These historical facts

---

64 Pannenberg, Wolfhart (ed.), *Revelation as History*, London: Sheed and Ward, 1969.

must be such that they vindicate the claims made for Jesus Christ as God's self-revelation. Therefore, historical facts as well as anthropological considerations can be adduced to support the claims made by Christian faith.

With Pannenberg's proposal we seem to be back to an earlier debate about the sufficiency of natural reason which is now understood as historical reason. Is this the way in which the assertions of Christian faith can satisfy the criteria knowledge, constitutive for the understanding of knowledge in modernity? In the course of developing his theological approach of revelation as history, Pannenberg has developed a number of further arguments to show that the claim that the end of history has proleptically occurred in Jesus' resurrection, can be supported by additional considerations. From anthropology he shows that humans are characterized by an openness to the world which, conceived radically, must be interpreted as their openness for God. In every act of human self-transcendence God is implicitly presupposed as the infinity of horizon in which all being finds its fulfilment. This thought is extended into a metaphysical principle: Everything is what it becomes in the end, and our knowing of reality is the anticipation of the completion of this process of becoming. In this way God's self-revelation becomes the key to a comprehensive understanding of reality.

#### 3.5.2.4 Eilert Herms

The most comprehensive reconstruction of the understanding of revelation in Protestant theology has been developed by Eilert Herms. Prepared by studies spanning over 30 years,[65] Herms has now presented the comprehensive account of his understanding of revelation in the first volume of his magisterial *Systematische Theologie.*[66] Herms views Christian faith as the *exemplar* of a religious form of life which is characterized by a comprehensive and action-directing certainty, rooted in revelation. "Revelation" here refers to the contingent event, which can be characterized as disclosure or discovery or as laying open something which had been hidden, in which something is given for our understanding and results in what he characterizes as a "situation of disclosure" (Erschlossenheitslage) that is determinative of our personal presence, for the whole of our orientation in the world, locating us as agents in a specific "now" and "here",

**65** Cf. Herms, Eilert, *Offenbarung und Glaube. Zur Bildung des christlichen Lebens*, Tübingen: Mohr Siebeck, 1992; id., *Phänomene des Glaubens. Beiträge zur Fundamentaltheologie*, Tübingen: Mohr Siebeck, 2006.

**66** Herms, Eilert, *Systematische Theologie. Das Wesen des Christentums: In Wahrheit und aus Gnade leben*, 3 vols, Tübingen: Mohr Siebeck, 2017, vol 1, part II: "Das christliche Leben. Sein Grundakt: Glaube. Dessen Grund und Gegenstand: Offenbarung," 75–556.

characterized by the enduring characteristics of our being in the world. Every actual disclosure experience refers back to the conditions of its possibility, comprising our relational being in four relations: the relation to ourselves, the relation to our environment, the relation to our world and the relation to the power of the origin which shapes the whole relational existence of every human person and of everything there is. The philosophical point of this phenomenological starting-point for the explication of revelation is that it allows Herms to circumvent the knotty problems of the so-called subject – object division that has exercised so much of modern philosophy and theology. Analyzing our being in the world in this way overlooks that we ourselves and our world are always in every possible situation already preveniently given to us, challenging us to understand this relation. In this way, Herms steers a course between the Scylla of understanding the world as a constructive achievement of subjectivity and the Charybdis of understanding the human person as a product of objective material processes. Both ways of dissolving the subject-object-tension imply a displacement of what religious discourse refers to as God from the outset. We are in a radically passive way involved in this fundamental relationship between ourselves and the world in every "situation of disclosure." This is the condition for all our active relating to anything that is comprehended in this fundamental relationship.

Every disclosure event, Herms asserts, consists of six components.[67] First of all, it has a particular *content* that provokes our understanding. Secondly it has an *author* which we might for lack of better characterization call an accident, chance, a contingent event or other persons when they tell us a secret. Every disclosure experience has, thirdly, a *recipient* who is challenged by what is disclosed. It occurs, fourthly, in a particular *situation.* Being bound to a particular situation implies – that is the fifth point – that a disclosure experience confronts the recipient in the totality of her *embodied existence.* The medium of revelation is therefore always bound up with experiencing and remembering key scenes of one's life. Sixthly, a disclosure experience locates the recipient in the situation it discloses, in the situation that is created by this disclosure. If one looks back one sees that the *situation of disclosure* is dynamic, more and more is disclosed to us, and so the process of disclosure is the story of the becoming of who we are as persons, the discontinuity of a new revelation discloses anew continuity when we understand our past differently in the light of the revelatory experience and have to adjust our expectations for the future.

67 Herms, *op. cit.*, 126–7.

How can religious revelation be understood in the framework of such a general theory of revelation? Herms maintains that religious revelations are not distinguished from other revelations by an extraordinary mode of occurrence. They fit the same pattern as all other revelations. The only difference is their content. This content always concerns our relationship to the power of the origin of all being. However, because the content of the relationship concerns the relationship to the power of the origin which is the foundation of all being and meaning, including the being and meaning of the recipient of revelation. The only effect which revelation in this sense demands is faith as the acknowledgement of the truth that has been disclosed. This is the basis for faith in the power of the origin, in God. According to this account, revelation is the foundation of all human rationality. All rational responsibility is rooted in disclosure situations. Rationality is therefore not to be understood as a specific faculty of human beings as rational animals, but comprises all conditions of the comprehensive-embodied self-understanding of humans.

This systematic account of revelation as the basis of all human knowing throws a new light on the history of interpreting revelation in the history of Western theology and philosophy.[68] For Herms, the terminological narrowing of the meaning of revelation when it becomes a technical term in Western theological and philosophical thought indicates a serious problem. In the theory of the two sources of knowledge "revelation" is reserved for supernatural knowledge of God's essence. The existence of God can be established by natural reason alone which reigns in the realm of worldly knowledge. Revelation has become irrelevant for our knowledge of the world. The implications of the narrowing of the meaning of "revelation" has further consequences for the way revelation is witnessed in the church. On the basis of this distinction, supernatural knowledge of God's essence is only revealed to a few, although it is for everybody of soteriological significance. If supernatural knowledge is only revealed to a few, it must be believed on the authority of the recipients of supernatural revelation. The question of the transmission of this supernatural knowledge assumes paramount significance. Authority in the church as the witness of salvific revelation shapes the nature of faith. It assumes the character of obedience to this divinely invested "apostolic" authority. Herms interprets the Reformation as a significant protest against this understanding of revelation. It is a criticism of the danger of the displacement of the authority of the revealing God by the authority of the church. According to the Reformers faith has salvific significance because it is rooted in the threefold self-giving of God. It has its foundation

**68** Cf. *op .cit.*, 239–47.

and its object in the self-communication of the "fatherly heart of God" in his incarnate Son which is made certain for believers by the Spirit of truth. By replacing the dichotomy of nature and grace with the dialectics of law and Gospel Reformation theology challenges the view that there can be truthful knowledge of the world independent and separate of God's revelation.

In Herms' interpretation the Enlightenment takes over the medieval distinction of natural reason and supernatural revelation, and radicalizes and generalizes it. Natural reason now becomes the measuring-rod for all claims to supernatural revelation, and it challenges the view that supernatural knowledge is necessary for the fulfilment of the human destiny. Consequently, reason and faith are interpreted as logically exclusive: reason is defined by the independence from faith; faith is defined as being located outside human rationality. For Herms the scholastic definition of supernatural revelation becomes the basis for the radical revolt against revelation in the name of reason which is now defined only in terms of human epistemic activity. Combined with the claim that reason is one, this view leads to the marginalization of all religious communities in a society whose rules and regulations are defined by reason alone, and religious beliefs, claiming to be based on revelation, are excluded from the public sphere of rational discourse.

There are for Herms no good reasons for accepting this view of revelation and reason and to try to accommodate the religious life to the canons of Enlightenment reason. Rather, the task consists in showing that this view rests on an abstract understanding of rationality, ignoring that all epistemic activity rests on the foundation of what is disclosed to human knowers and actors. It consists furthermore, in showing that the Enlightenment view is based on an equally abstract understanding of revelation, which restricts the understanding of revelation to the communication of supernatural truths. This denies the fundamental role of disclosure situation for the whole of human being in the world. In contrast, Herms tries to show that the logical consequence of a unified ethos of rationality in the wake of the Enlightenment becomes highly problematical in our pluralistic situation. We cannot overlook that in fact we are confronted with a variety of styles of rationality, be they religious or non-religious or even anti-religious, each rooted in particular ways in which the basic orientation of people is rooted in the disclosure experiences that occurred to them. Understanding the constitution of our certainties in disclosure experiences includes therefore the commandment to treat the certainties of others with respect, and to expect that such disclosure-based forms of rationality are nevertheless capable of developing mutual understanding, a culture of understanding that is different from the claims of one unified form of rationality and is open for the discovery of differences and commonalities.

If one applies the critical motto of the Enlightenment "sapere aude" ("dare to be wise") to the Enlightenment and its dogmatic view to the relationship of revelation and reason, one will see, Herms hopes, that both its view of rationality and of revelation cannot be confirmed in careful attention to the ways in which all our knowledge presupposes that we live in disclosure situation. This, in turn, challenges us to restrict the understanding of revelation not to the communication of supernatural truths but to see it as a condition given with every form of human being in the world.

One could raise the question whether this detailed reconstruction of the understanding of revelation is itself a general theory of revelation, designed as the philosophical framework for a Christian theological account of revelation. This objection does not do justice for the full account of revelation which Herms develops in his *Systematic Theology.* He claims that the account he offers is indeed based on the revelation of Christ and has its ultimate basis in the experience which is summarized in the Gospel of Luke in the sentence: "The Lord has risen indeed, and has appeared to Simon!" (Luke 24:34) If one takes the revelation in Christ seriously, then it opens up a view of the whole of creation as the self-disclosure of the God the creator. Therefore, Herms introduces his discussion of revelation with the thesis that Christian faith is the *exemplar*, the paradigmatic case of how faith has its foundation and object in disclosure situations.

# 4 Phenomena, Signs and Concepts: A Heuristic Model for Investigating the Structure of Revelation

The complex history of the discussion of revelation in Christianity offers ample illustrations of the systematic questions that have fueled the debates on revelation from the beginning in the early church. The answers given to the set of questions that we raised at the beginning of this chapter have been summarized by presenting them as different models of revelation, picking out the constitutive features of each account of revelation. Avery Dulles has analyzed the use of the concept of revelation in terms of five models, that arrange the answers given to the leading questions in patterns that serve as an interpretation of the wealth of accounts of revelation in the biblical writings and in the debates in the Christian communities.[69] In his reconstruction there are five models:

a) Revelation as doctrine, where revelation is found "in clear propositional statements attributed to God as authoritative teacher".[70] While certain strands in Protestantism would associate this view primarily with the *Bible* as the source of all knowledge of God and the world, in Roman Catholic theology it is primarily associated with the *magisterium*, the teaching office of the Church regarded as "God's infallible oracle."[71]
b) Revelation as history, according to which God's revelation occurs primarily in God's "mighty acts" which are the content and the ultimate sphere of justification for all statements about God, God's being and God's will.
c) Revelation as inner experience in which revelation is neither a set of propositions nor a series of events, but the interior transformation of humans when they are drawn into communion with God.
d) Revelation as "dialectical presence" is the name Dulles gives to the view of the "dialectical theologians" who emphasize both the sovereignty and gratuity of God's self-revelation and the impossibility of gaining knowledge of God by the independent capacities of human reason, so that revelation remains God's prerogative to such an extent that even in revelation there remains an element of concealment.
e) Revelation as inner awareness where revelation is understood as an expansion of consciousness or a shift of perspective due to which reality appears in a new light.

While the attempt at summarizing the distinctive features of theological theories of revelation is certainly useful, it also underlines that the features singled out as distinctive for the different models can be found in every experience of revelation. Revelation, even where it is not understood as the handing down of true propositions but as a personal encounter, must result in a disclosure of truth, opening up a new way in which we understand "what is the case". This seems to be already implied in the concept of revelation. Even where revelation is not understood as the communication of propositions, its result must be able to be expressed in propositions. Furthermore, even where the understanding of revelation is not restricted to God's acts in history, it is nevertheless clear that revelation is always embedded in the texture of contingent events in the

---

**69** Dulles, Avery S.J., *Models of Revelation*, New York: Doubleday & Company, 1983; Maryknoll, NY: Orbis, 17th imprint, 2011.
**70** Ibid., 27.
**71** Ibid.

spatio-temporal order of experience. Therefore, revelation is always located in a narrative: the narrative of the life of the recipient of revelation, the narrative of how the content of revelation rearranges the narrative structure of the life of believers and their communities, and the narrative of God's interaction and conversation with creation. At the same time, it is always clear that the impact of revelation always transcends the moment in which it occurs and illumines other aspects of the experience of reality, changing both the order of remembering and the expectation of the future. A similar observation can be made with regard to the model of revelation as an inner experience. It belongs to the very character of a revelation that it cannot merely remain in the external sphere of human experience, it must engage the interior dimension of human life. However, revelation also questions whether the distinction between the "inner" and the "outer" dimension of existence is a valid one. Revelation always includes that the "inner" structure of experience is confronted with encountering a reality that it did not constitute itself, and that what has been interiorized has the power of transforming all dimensions of human life from within. The model of "dialectical presence", in which Dulles summarizes the view of the "dialectical theologians" points to the critique that the understanding of revelation is implied with regard to any account of human reason or insight as actively constituted in human acts of knowing. This critical point, however, may not be overemphasized. Even if revelation is received in utter passivity, it nevertheless changes all the dimensions of active human action with the world and with God. Furthermore, while it is right to insist that God is and always remains "the Lord" in his revelation, that there does not occur a "change of subject" in revelation so that humans take over the communication of the content of revelation with God as the "object", it must nevertheless be emphasized that revelation changes the *relationship* between the author and the recipient of revelation. The emphasis on the sovereignty and hiddenness of God in his revelation may not call the effect of the revelation into question. Moreover, there is a theological tradition, of which Martin Luther is an important representative, that emphasizes that God conceals in order to reveal. The "naked majesty" of God remains inaccessible. However, when God reveals the "depths of his fatherly heart", he conceals it, often under the opposite, i. e. in the cross of Christ or in creaturely means of communication.[72] With regard to the model of "inner awareness" it seems similarly necessary to see this as an aspect of revelation, but to emphasize at the same time that revelation is never a simple "expansion" of consciousness but includes its transformation. In short, while the different models may be a helpful device

**72** Paulson, Stephen D., "Luther on the Hidden God," *Word and World* (1999), 363–371.

for distinguishing different theories of revelation, they are in danger of offering a restricted understanding of revelation, if the theoretical emphases are projected back onto the phenomena of revelation.

Is there another way of characterizing revelation that does do justice to its structure and allows for the variety of revelatory phenomena and experiences? Such a way would have to account for the structural features that underlie the history of debates on revelation. We can try to clarify the structure of revelation with the help of following formula for a disclosure event:

> The author (A) discloses in the situation (B) the content (C) for the recipient (D) with the effect (E).[73]

Revelation can only be described where a revelation has occurred. The formula is therefore a retrospective description of the disclosure experience and presupposes its effect. A stands for the author of revelation, B for the situation in which the revelation occurs. Speaking of a "medium" of revelation is an incomplete description. The situation in which the disclosure occurs includes the personal bodily involvement of the recipient of a revelation in the disclosure situation at a particular place and a particular point in time. This disclosure event occurs contingently at a particular point in the life of the recipient of revelation. It connects with the preceding history and shapes the following events in the life of the recipient. However, the author of the disclosure experiences must also be seen as involved in this situation. Disclosure experience involves a sense of the author becoming present in this situation, of relating in active communication with the recipient and using the circumstances and the capacities of the recipient for the disclosure. The content C that is disclosed in this situation can cover a variety of modes of communication and a variety of contents. Crucial is that it establishes a relationship between the author and the recipient of revelation that obligates the recipient. It is an address that demands a response. It is a directed form of communication that expresses the intention of the author of revelation and the way in which the disclosed content of revelation serves the realization of the intention of the author of revelation. Even where revelation is not

73 The formula was first introduced in my book *God. Action and Revelation*, Kampen: Kok Pharos: Kampen NL, 1992. One of the main inspirations was Eilert Herms' study "Offenbarung" (1985), now in: *Offenbarung und Glaube*, 168–220. For a further development cf. Schwöbel, Christoph. "Revelation," in: Hans Dieter Betz [et al.] (eds), *Religion. Past and Present*, vol. 11, 162–163; 169–170; 172–173, Leiden: Brill, 2011. Cf. Charry, Ellen T., "Revelation," in: Chad Meister/Paul Copan (eds), *The Routledge Companion to Philosophy of Religion*, 609–615, London: Routledge, $^{2}$2013.

explicitly characterized as self-revelation, it always contains these elements of a communicative encounter that creates communion. The content that is being disclosed therefore always includes the person and the life of the recipient in such a way that the life of the recipient is also disclosed through the content of revelation. The content is in this way self-involving for both the author and the recipient of revelation. This also applies to the recipient of the disclosure experience. The experience brings the recipient through the content into a communicative relationship with the author of revelation. The effects of the disclosure experience depend on the content of the disclosure experience. If it is a commission or a command, as in the case of Moses at the burning bush (Exod. 3), the intended effect is the willingness to obey the command. If it is a question, as in Paul's account of his encounter with Christ on the road to Damascus (Acts 22:6–12), an answer is required which may consist in a completely new direction of the life of the recipient. Again, it is important that the effect always implies a relationship to the author of revelation. It is never enough to simply to receive information. The power of the disclosure event is that it does indeed forge a relationship that now becomes determinative for the orientation of the recipient of revelation. This orientation now includes a relationship to the author of revelation. If, for instance, the effect of revelation is described as faith, this includes both the element of *trust in* and *believing that*. The recognition of the truth of what has been disclosed combines both elements, the truth of the message and the trustworthiness of the one who communicates it.

The formal structure that I have suggested offers many possibilities of inserting concrete content for the place-holders of the formula. As such it can be used to distinguish everyday disclosure experiences from religious disclosure experiences which concern the origin, meaning and destiny of human existence and of creation as a whole. It serves to illustrate that in all situations of life, our orientation in everyday matters and in matters of ultimate significance depends on disclosure experiences.

The formula provides a heuristic tool for describing experiences, for instance analyzing and interpreting the disclosure experiences that we encounter in the Bible. However, this should not disguise the fact that for most Christians, as well as for Jews and Muslims, such disclosure experiences occur through the mediation of the engagement with Scripture. It is in engaging with Scripture in the context of worship, study and meditation or in the context of proclamation, religious instruction or engagement with the Christian message that believers claim to receive orientation for their lives. Can these experiences of gaining insight and finding orientation for one's life also be described as disclosure experiences? Can the Scriptures that report disclosure experiences of the protagonists of the biblical narratives be the communicative context in which disclosure experiences occur today?

Our basic formula allows for extending the description of the situation of a disclosure experience in such a way that it refers to situations in which the witness of God's revelation in the witnesses of Scripture and in the proclamation of the Gospel, in catechetical instruction and pastoral care part of the disclosure situation. The encounter with the biblical traditions then becomes a way in which God communicates the truth of the revelation Christ to believers today. We already find disclosure experiences mediated in a context in which the knowledge of Scripture plays in many places in the New Testament and in the places in the Hebrew Bible where inter-textual references are explicitly or implicitly made. The central claim of Christ's resurrection is both presented as a tradition and as "in accordance with the scriptures" in Paul's use of an early in confessional formula in 1Cor. 15:3–5:

> For I delivered to you as of first importance what I also received, that Christ died for our sins in accordance with the scriptures, that he was buried, that he was raised on the third day in accordance with the scriptures, and that he appeared to Cephas, then to the twelve.

After the enumeration of more witnesses, Paul refers to his own disclosure experience: "Last of all, as to one untimely born, he appeared also to me." (1Cor. 15:8) The story of the disciples in Luke's gospel (Luke 24:13–35) who encounter a stranger on their way to Emmaus after Jesus' death and the unbelievable stories that he had risen illustrates in the description of a disclosure event the same interplay between the interpretation of Scripture, the celebration of a meal and opening of the eyes of the disciples which made them aware of the "burning of their hearts." This story probably also gives an account of how Luke thought Christian worship should be celebrated with the exposition of Scripture and a shared meal with thanksgiving.

It is the effect of disclosure experiences that these experiences, the circumstances in which they occurred, the effect which they occasioned and the insight which they open up become part of a living process of oral and then written tradition. In such a tradition the view of reality they disclose and the way of life they are handed on from generation to generation in a community in which these traditions become part of their life of worship, of their beliefs and ethical orientations and of their identity-definition. The fact that disclosure experiences are contingent events in space and time which cannot be repeated, implies that they have to be witnessed in order to become part of a tradition. The non-repeatability of the tradition-initiating disclosure experiences is an important element for their being preserved in written traditions. This process has quite a number of important presuppositions. On the one hand, disclosure experiences have to be understood as a process of sign-giving. They constitute a semiotic universe that becomes crucial for the way a community interprets its vision of life and view of reality, its view of God, of the human destiny and of the purpose of the world. On the other hand, the fact that these testimonies in their various literary forms are handed on from generation to generation implies that the truth of what they witness to has been vindicated from one generation to another. In this way they provide the semiotic material in which new experiences of their truth can be made. The distinction in Reformation theology between the external word of Scripture and Christian proclamation and the internal testimony illustrates the two requirements of a living religious tradition very well. What is needed is both the transmission of the world of signs in which experiences can be made and the motivation for doing so which can only come from the experience that the reality to which these texts witness has become true and certain for another generation.

There are many contexts in which the witness to revelation is communicated and cultivated. All the different dimensions of religion are suffused with the witness to revelation and so provide the context of new disclosure experiences. The point in the life of the church where these different dimensions come together is the act of worship. Gathered in the name of the triune God and sent into the world with the blessing of the triune God, the Christian community hears in worship the address in the name of God, the witness to God's revelation in the exposition of Scripture in Christian proclamation in the hope that God the Holy Spirit vindicates the witness to revelation by creating and confirming the certainty of faith – and responds by addressing God the Father in petition, lament and praise in the Spirit and through the Son. In this context the Eucharist is celebrated as the reconciliation of a community broken and distorted by sin and reconstituted by God's grace to be again brought on the way to the New Jerusalem, the perfected communion of God with his reconciled creation. It is in the context of worship that the witness of Scripture to God's revelation is proclaimed in the hope that God might use this witness to bring about new disclosure situations and so to create faith. The liturgical use of Scripture reveals more than any other its significance as the witness to God's revelation that is used in the hope that God might use it again as an occasion of revelation.

We can summarize the features of a disclosure experience analyzed in this way in the following way:

1. Revelation is a "success word" (Gilbert Ryle) and as such it points to the fact that we can only speak of revelation when a revelation has in fact occurred for the recipient. A revelation can only be identified and described retrospectively. It is a contingent event which does not necessarily follow from a set of conditions that can be antecedently known. Therefore, revelation is

often characterized as a miracle by its recipients. However, revelation always implies the challenge to understand its conditions by giving an account of the author, the content and the effect of revelation.

2. Revelation is polymorphic. It can occur in visions, auditions and in ways which engage the whole range of human experiences. No form of experience is to be privileged from the outset. The fact that all forms of experience can be engaged in revelation points to the fact that revelation is holistic and engages every dimension of human being and can occur in any aspect of the world.
3. Revelation is always relational. It establishes a relationship, occurs within a relationship or transforms a relationship in such a way that one cannot go back behind a revelation once it has occurred. Revelation begins and shapes a history.
4. Revelation is always asymmetrical. The relationality of revelation is such that its occurrence, form, content and effect is entirely dependent on the activity of the author of revelation. The recipient of revelation is passively involved in the event of revelation. This passivity involved in the asymmetry of revelation provokes and engages the activity of its recipients, even shaping their capacity for action in all spheres of action whether they are interpretative or symbolizing actions, organizational actions or physically effective actions.
5. Revelation always has a holistic impact, it engages all dimensions of human existence and their understanding.
6. Revelation must therefore be seen as constituting a new constellation for human life, it extends to all dimensions of human being as relational being. Therefore revelation can always be specified in its theological (What does it say about God?), anthropological (What does it say about human being?) and cosmological dimension (What does it say about the world?) and their constellation.
7. Revelation is always self-transcending with regard to its impact. The effect of revelation cannot be contained in one revelatory event, it spreads throughout our understanding of reality.
8. Revelation must be understood as an act of sign-giving, of providing new means of signification with regard to the reality it discloses. As such it modifies the way in which the recipients of revelation already understand their world. Examples can be found in the way in which the self-identification of God as "I will be who I will be" (Exod. 3:14) is explicitly related to the older understanding of God as the "God of your fathers" (3:15) or in which Jesus as the last word of God is related to the other occasions where God has spoken (cf. Heb. 1:1).

9. Revelation in history always calls for interpretation. Every disclosure experience provokes interpretation and at the same time restricts interpretation by imposing rules of adequacy on interpretation. Revelation gives us something to understand and this evokes the necessity of interpretation. The fact that disclosure experiences occur within the context of interpretations also means that they are subject to the critical power of tradition. This limits the risk of misconstruals.
10. Revelation has an ontological import. Revelation does not leave our understanding of reality unchanged, it transforms and modifies it in such a way that revelation cannot simply be understood in epistemological terms. Revelation does not only concern the question of how we can know what there is but also affects the question of what there is.
11. Revelation creates in its recipients certainty with regard to the author and content of revelation on the basis of the way in which revelation discloses to them the truth about their own lives. Certainty implies that the insight it grants has become for the recipients of revelation without alternative – until it is modified or corrected by another disclosure experience.
12. Revelation constitutes a community of witness and interpretation, of celebration and communal action. The specific character of this community as a community of faith consists in the fact that for each member of this community faith has the character of a personal certainty which defines the character of the community as one where personal particularity and social commonality are not to be seen as opposites.

When we now turn to the concept of revelation in Christian theology, it must be kept in mind that it summarizes the phenomena and the signs of revelation in order to elucidate their conceptual structure. The starting-point for such an elucidation can only be Christian faith as the effect of the self-communication of the triune God that gives believers insight into their true self-understanding and into the world of which they are a part. Christian faith experiences itself as a gift, as constituted by God. The certainty of faith is not achieved by means of human argument or any other epistemic effort but by the illuminating work of God. This illumination occurs where the Gospel of Christ, the witness to God's revelation in the life and death of Jesus of Nazareth, is experienced as the personal truth for the life of the believer. The truth of the Gospel makes believers' lives transparent for themselves. The truth of the Gospel has become the truth for their own lives.

This illumination, the enlightenment of the human person with the truth of the Gospel, has as its content the testimony of the Gospel as it is proclaimed and vindicated as a promise for believers today. It comprises the witness of Jesus' life in proclaiming the coming of the Kingdom of God in his person into which all are included who let themselves be drawn into community with Jesus. In the Easter experience Jesus' message of the coming of the Kingdom is disclosed as vindicated in his own person. God overcomes all resistance against his will of salvation for humankind by taking the effects of human contradiction against the will of God upon himself. The resurrection of the crucified Jesus is therefore experienced as the unconditional revelation of God's grace and truth, of grace creating justice where there was the injustice of the human revolt against God and of truth overcoming the self-deception of human self-love, possessive desire and pride, assuming the place of God. Living in the truth of this promise implies for Christian believers that they live in a continuous community with the risen Jesus as the living Lord, a community which is confirmed by the promise of the Gospel in proclamation and celebration of the Eucharist.

In the resurrection of the crucified Jesus, God the creator discloses his faithfulness to his will to bring his human creatures into communion with himself in the Kingdom of God. There is nothing that can stand in the way of the fulfilment of the promise implied in creation that the destiny of all creatures will be fulfilled in communion with God. Human creatures as the images of God will find the fulfilment of their destiny in cooperation with the will of God the creator and not in contradiction to it. For human creatures this means that they have to acknowledge their createdness by trusting in God's will. Faith as it is enabled by God the Spirit as trusting in the truth of the Gospel of Christ discloses in this way the right guidance for human creature. It discloses to them that they cannot find orientation by themselves, but are dependent on insight that is granted as a gift. In faith they gain insight that their own will is not capable of autonomous self-direction but must find its direction in the will of the creator. It is also made clear to them that the desires of the human heart must be set on God and his gifts and not on what humans can achieve by following their desires apart from being directed by the will of God. The disclosure experience of faith in this way includes a redirection of human knowledge through what is disclosed to them, the transformation of the human will from its radical self-directedness and the restructuring of human desires so that all desires find their place in the dynamics of the love of God.

In the language of systematic theology, the ground and content of the disclosure experience of faith are described as the self-disclosure or self-communication of God. This conceptuality emphasizes that God does not communicate information about God's being and will but that God communicates Godself in order to bring about the perfected communion with God's reconciled human creatures. The concept of God's self-disclosure or God's self-communication would, however, become abstract if it were to be interpreted in such a way that this self-communication somehow concerns God's "self" apart from the relationship to the believer so that the "self" of the believer could somehow be envisaged apart from God's self-communication. In a similar way faith would be misconstrued if it would be understood as the human capacity to relate to God apart from God's prevenient communication to the believer. God's self-communication always intends communion, its content is not God in Godself but God in relation to his creatures. Disclosure is aimed at a recipient of that disclosure; God's communication has an addressee. If revelation is analyzed as God's self-disclosure or self-communication this always presupposes, on the one hand, God's relationship to his human creatures and, on the other hand, the asymmetry of this relationship where God's self-disclosure for God's creatures is the condition for the possibility that they can become disclosed to themselves in relation to God.

We can at this point see why the Christian theological tradition past and present is so insistent on the relationship between the understanding of revelation and the doctrine of the Trinity.[74] This relationship is emphasized when the illumination of the believer by the Holy Spirit has as its content the Gospel of Christ which, in turn, is the disclosure of true God's true being and will. This emphasis safeguards the distinction between God as the author of the disclosure experience and the created means and instruments of this disclosure experience. Where the Spirit creates faith this is really God's work, even where God employs human witnesses to the truth of the Gospel. Therefore, faith as the unconditional trust in God is the only appropriate response to being illumined by God the Spirit. Where the human contradiction against God and against their own createdness is overcome in the cross and resurrection of Christ this is God's work in Christ alone. The creation as the creation of a history that leads to its consummation in the Kingdom of God is similarly the free will of God alone. When we try to express this in the order of being, revelation always has the order of the self-disclosure of God the Father, through the Son, in the Spirit. It follows the structure already expressed by Basil of Caesarea according to which in everything that God does the Father is the unoriginated cause, the Son the originating cause and the Spirit the perfecting cause.[75] If revelation in the divine economy is rooted in God's immanent triune being, this secures the freedom of God in rev-

74 Cf. Schwöbel, Christoph, "The One and the Three in Christian Worship and Doctrine: Engaging with the Question of Divine Unity in the Elaboration of Christian Doctrine," in: L. Mosher/D. Marshall (eds), *Monotheism and Its Complexities. Christian and Muslim Perspectives*, 63–91, Washington, DC: Georgetown University Press, 2018.

75 St. Basil the Great, *On the Holy Spirit*, transl. David Anderson, Crestwood, NY: St. Vladimirs Seminary Press, 1980, XV, 38.

elation. It makes the point that God is already relational before he relates to what is not God by creating a world in order to lead God's created image, God's human creatures into communion with their creator and by overcoming every obstacle on the way to this goal.

The question of the relationship between God's special revelation in Jesus Christ and God's general revelation in creation has been a consistent theme in the discussions of doctrinal history. On the basis of the sketch of a Christian Trinitarian understanding of revelation this relationship can be expressed in such a way that God's revelation in the incarnation of the Creator Logos discloses the whole of creation again as God's revelation. The revelation in Christ overcomes the contradiction of sin which had obscured creation as the revelation of the creator. In the Incarnate Word creation can again be understood as the address of the creator to his human creatures. This has a number of important implications for the understanding of creation. Everything that exists belongs to God's vocabulary; everything that is, has meaning; the *phainomena* of the created world are the *legomena* of God's creative speech act. Our understanding of the world is therefore not an attempt to detect the mechanical regularities of deaf and dumb forces interacting with one another. Rather, it becomes an exercise of reading in the book of creation, of listening to the polyphonic symphony in which the heavens and every creature praises God the creator.

# 5 Revelation in Denominational Diversity and Ecumenical Community

## 5.1 The Understanding of Revelation in the Eastern Orthodox Churches

The views on revelation in the different Christian denominations mirror the debates in the history of doctrine on revelation. They often appear as a synchronic picture of the diachronic narrative of the debates on revelation. In Eastern orthodoxy revelation is understood as a cumulative concept that combines the sacred scripture and tradition as they are integrated in the Holy Liturgy. Since the separation between the Eastern churches and the Western churches took place before the medieval debates on revelation and reason, their theology is less shaped by the debates on the relationship between natural reason and revelation than the debates in Western theology. One could perhaps say that for Eastern Orthodox theology questions of revelation are not so much a question for philosophical debates but for the liturgical life of the church and the spiritual life of the believer. It is in this context that the major debates presupposing a view on revelation occurred. In the middle of the heated debates on the veneration of icons at the seventh ecumenical council 787 CE it was maintained that Holy Scripture is the icon of Christ, thereby steering the debate away from the media of the experience and worship of God to the reality to which they point. Eastern Orthodox theology has maintained consistently that the essence of God cannot be known. The only access to knowledge of God is God's Trinitarian self-revelation in which God himself makes himself known in the *divine energeiai*. The debate between Barlaam of Calabria (ca. 1290–1348) and Gregory of Palamas (ca. 1296–1359) which concerned the question whether the monks on Mount Athos could during the prayer of the heart in a form of spiritual vision see the uncreated divine light that had illumined the burning bush and in which Jesus appeared in the transfiguration still shapes the understanding of revelation in large parts of Eastern Orthodoxy.[76] Barlaam, who had originally come to the East to defend the Eastern view that the Holy Spirit proceeds only from the Father and not from the Father and the Son (*filioque controversy*), had polemicized against the claims of the hesychast monks. In his defense of the spiritual practice of the monks in his work *The Triads*[77] Palamas attacked the philosophical method of Barlaam's criticism as presenting a negative theology based on a philosophical view of the human inability to know God's essence and defended the practice of "sacred quietude" (*hesychiasmós*). In his view the uncreated glory of God is communicated through God's Trinitarian self-revelation in the divine energies (*enérgeiai*) in such a way that it can be disclosed in spiritual practice, engaging the whole human person, and not just the intellect. In effect, this was a refutation of two sources of knowing, reason, and divine revelation and an argument for the unitary source of all knowing in God. The spiritual experience of God both in personal devotion as well as in the sacramental life of the Church shapes the process of the deification (*theosis*) of the human person towards its destiny of finding fulfilment in communion with God's trinitarian life. This view was gradually accepted in the Orthodox Church and found powerful advocates in 20$^{th}$ century Orthodox thinkers like Vladimir Lossky (1903–1958) in his classic *The Mystical Theology of the Eastern Church* (1957).[78] The question of revelation is here located not in a theory of knowledge but in the practice of spirituality, both in personal piety and in the life of the Church, which is regarded as

---

**76** Cf. Meyendorff, John, *St Gregory Palamas and Orthodox Spirituality*, New York: St Vladimir's Seminary Press, 1974.

**77** Cf. Palamas, Gregory, *The Triads*, ed. by John Meyendorff, Mahwah, NJ, 1983.

**78** Lossky, Vladimir, *The Mystical theology of the Eastern Church*, Cambridge: James Clarke 1991, esp. 217–235.

the source of all dogmatic theology. In many ways the Holy Liturgy is the catechism of the Eastern Orthodox Church regard to the understanding of revelation.

## 5.2 The Teaching of Revelation in the Roman Catholic Church

In the Catechism of the Roman Catholic Church (CCC) the exposition of the understanding of revelation is prefaced by an anthropological statement about the human desire to know God: "The desire for God is written in the human heart, because man is created by God and for God; and God never ceases to draw man to himself. Only in God will he find the truth and happiness he never stops searching for." (CCC 27) Therefore the teaching of Vatican I is affirmed: "Our holy mother, the Church, holds and teaches that God, the first principle and last end of all things, can be known with certainty from the created world by the natural light of human reason." (CCC 36, quoting Dei Verbum 2 [DH 3004]) The natural light of reason can come to knowledge of the existence of a personal God through his observation of the world and the reflection of the human person. (CCC 31–35) However, this is not sufficient to achieve personal communion with God: "But for man to be able to enter into real intimacy with him, God willed both to reveal himself to man, and to give him the grace of being able to welcome this revelation in faith." (CCC 35) Moreover, the knowledge of God granted by the natural light of reason is hampered "not only by the impact of the senses and the imagination, but also by disordered appetites which are the consequences of original sin." (CCC 37, quoting the encyclical *Humani Generis* by Pius XII., DH 3875) The consequence is clear: "This is why man stands in need of being enlightened by God's revelation" (CCC 38). Therefore, it is affirmed: "By natural reason man can know God with certainty, on the basis of his works. But there is another order of knowledge, which man cannot possibly arrive at by his own powers: the order of divine Revelation." (CCC 50) God reveals himself in the unity of his words and deeds in the stages of salvation history where he provides "constant evidence of Himself in created realities" (CCC 54), from creation, to Noah and Abraham, and from the formation of the people of Israel to Jesus Christ, the Incarnate Word, "the mediator and fullness of all revelation" (*Dei Verbum* 2). Therefore two statements must be made: "God has said everything in his word." And: "There will be no further revelation." (CCC Part I, III) Therefore the content of revelation must be handed on by the "the transmission of revelation" "in the apostolic preaching, continued in apostolic succession" (CCC 75/76). With regard to the "transmission of revelation" two qualifications are added: "This living transmission, accomplished in the Holy Spirit, is called Tradition" (CCC 78), because it is distinct from Scripture, though not unrelated to it. Furthermore tradition is asserted as a mode of the self-communication of the triune God: "The Father's self-communication made through his Word in the Holy Spirit, remains present and active in the Church" (CCC 79). In this sense it can be asserted that tradition and sacred scripture form a differentiated unity since they have the same origin in the self-communication of the triune God, but they are "two distinct modes of transmission": "Sacred Scripture is the speech of God as it is put down in writing under the breath of the Holy Spirit." However, the authority of Scripture functions always together with the tradition under the direction of the church: "... the Church, to whom the transmission and interpretation of Revelation is entrusted, 'does not derive her certainty about all revealed truths from the holy Scriptures alone. Both Scripture and Tradition must be accepted and honored with equal sentiments of devotion and reverence.'" (CCC 82, quoting *Dei Verbum* 9) Because the church is in this defined as part of the process of revelation, handing on what is completed in Christ, it can be asserted: "The Church's Magisterium exercises the authority it holds from Christ to the fullest extent when it defines dogmas, that is, when it proposes truths contained in divine Revelation or also when it proposes in a definitive way truths having a necessary connection with them." (CCC 88) However, the teaching of "truths contained in revelation" that is in this way proposed is still in need of being received in the appropriate way by all believers in the "sense of faith": "All the faithful share in understanding and handing on revealed truth. They have received the anointing of the Holy Spirit, who instructs them and guides them into all truth." (CCC 88)

Only after this mode of the transmission of revelation by the teaching office of the church is introduced, Scripture is discussed, with regard to its inspiration (CCC 105–1089), and with respect to the Holy Spirit as the "interpreter of Scripture" (CCC 109–119), which includes an affirmation of the fourfold sense of Scripture (cf. CCC 118). There is a clear sense of the priority of the apostolic tradition over Scripture: "It was by the apostolic Tradition that the Church discerned which writings are to be included in the list of the sacred books." (CCC 120) After the description of the place of Scripture in the life of the church, the Catechism turns to the constitution of faith by God's revelation as it is transmitted through the apostolic teaching, Scripture and the teaching office of the church. Faith is described in its most fundamental characteristic as obedience: "To obey ('from the Latin ob-audire, to hear or listen to') in faith is to submit freely to the word that has been heard, because its truth is guaranteed by God, who is Truth itself." (CCC 144) This does not prevent faith from being interpreted both as "a grace" and "as a human act" (CCC 153) which is required if faith is understood primarily as obedience. Nevertheless, it's emphasized that faith is certain:

"It is more certain than all human knowledge because it is founded on the very word of God who cannot lie." (CCC 157)

In a sense all beliefs of the Christian faith are in some way connected to revelation. Of particular significance for the understanding of revelation are, however, the affirmations of the Catechism to the teaching office of the Church. After stating that the bishops as the successors of the Apostles' have their primary calling in preaching the Gospel, the Catechism asserts: "In order to preserve the Church in the purity of the faith handed on by the apostles, Christ who is the Truth willed to confer on her a share in his own infallibility." (CCC 888) Infallibility, a characteristic of divine revelation is conferred to the Church because the Church has the central role in the transmission of tradition, which Christ instituted for the continuing communication of the revelation that is completed in Christ. The Catechism then repeats and affirms the statement of infallibility of the pope when teaching ex cathedra:

> The Roman Pontiff, head of the college of bishops, enjoys this infallibility in virtue of his office, when, as supreme pastor and teacher of all the faithful – who confirms his brethren in the faith he proclaims by a definitive act a doctrine pertaining to faith or morals.... the infallibility promised to the Church is also present in the body of bishops when, together with Peter's successor, they exercise the supreme Magisterium. (CCC 891 = *Lumen Gentium 25*)

This is then directly related back to God's revelation in Christ: "When the Church through its supreme Magisterium proposes a doctrine 'for belief as being divinely revealed' (*Dei Verbum* 10.2), and as the teaching of Christ, the definitions 'must be adhered to with the obedience of faith.' This infallibility extends as far as the deposit of divine Revelation itself." (CCC 891, *Lumen Gentium* 25.2) Here *Lumen Gentium*, the Dogmatic Constitution on the Church from Vatican II espouses and reaffirms the teaching of Vatican I.

## 5.3 Understandings of Revelation in the Protestant Churches

At the heart of the understanding of revelation in the churches of the Reformation and their modern off-springs is the emphasis on the distinction between divine work and human work and their proper distinction. Divine work and human work cannot be combined on the same level. God's work is always categorically distinct from all created agencies as the ground of their reality. The churches of the Reformation therefore criticized all instances where it seemed to be that the medieval Roman church had assumed divine authority. Since we are saved by Christ alone (*solus Christus*), the sufficiency of God's work in Christ forbids us to add any other agencies to the saving work of God in Christ. And because we are saved by God's grace alone the church cannot be understood as an institution which administers and distributes. God's grace can only be accepted in faith alone (*sola fide*). Faith is the comprehensive reorientation and reconstitution of the human capacity to act, the source from which all good acts flow. Because of that the claim that we are saved by faith *and* good works misunderstands faith and misconstrues their relationship. Therefore, the Reformers immediately attacked those practices and teachings where the church seemed to take the place of God as the sole authority for the truth of Christian teaching or as the sole source of grace and righteousness. This is why scripture becomes the sole authority for Christian faith and life (*sola scriptura*). However, this is not to be understood as the replacement of the pope in Rome with a paper pope. Rather, Scripture is the instrument by means of which God communicates himself, by proclaiming the truth of God's relationship to creation as the Gospel of Christ which is made certain by Godself in the Holy Spirit. The truth of Scripture has the character of a testimony to God in his revelation and it can only be made effective as God's revelation by God the Holy Spirit. If one sees the different exclusive particles summarized in the claim that God alone (*solus Deus*) creates, reconciles and perfects creation, revelation must be consistently understood as the self-presentation of the triune God, as God's threefold trinitarian self-giving which is the source of all truth, grace and being. The criticism is therefore nothing less than the charge of the displacement of God in the event and process of revelation. It is a charge of idolatry and false worship, epitomized by the claims made for the Pope in Rome.

The Confession of Augsburg of 1530, intended as an ecumenical confession, seeking approval not only among the princes and magistrates that had already joined the Reformation but also from those who refrained from doing so, begins with an article on the Trinity as the basis for every other aspect of Christian doctrine. The Council of Trent reaffirmed the divinely given teaching authority of the Church and the power of the Church to administer divine grace effectively. It had insisted on the veneration of the saints and had underlined the necessity of faith being supported by good works. Against this background, the so-called "scripture principle" became the focus of the debate. In this sense the Lutheran Book of Concord (1580) unequivocally states as its first sentence:

> We believe, teach, and confess that the only rule and guiding principle according to which all teachings and teachers are to be evaluated and judged are the prophetic and apostolic writings of the Old and New Testaments alone.[79]

---

**79** Book of Concord, 486.

This emphasis of Scripture as the primary authority in all matters of doctrine and life became the defining characteristic of the Protestant churches:

> Although the light of nature, and the works of creation and providence do so far manifest the goodness, wisdom, and power of God, as to leave men unexcusable; yet are they not sufficient to give that knowledge of God, and of His will, which is necessary unto salvation. Therefore it pleased the Lord, at sundry times, and in divers manners, to reveal Himself, and to declare His will unto His Church; and afterwards for the better preserving and propagating of the truth, and for the more sure establishment and comfort of the Church against the corruption of the flesh, and the malice of Satan and of the world, to commit the same wholly unto writing; which makes the Holy Scripture to be most necessary; those former ways of God's revealing His will unto His people being now ceased. (Westminster Confession 1643)

Against the criticism of the Reformation the Catholic Church consolidated itself as the Roman Catholic Church at the Council of Trent 1543. One way of interpreting the main points of divergence with regard to revelation is to trace them back to a difference in the understanding of the work and person of the Holy Spirit. For the medieval church, the Holy Spirit works through the offices and community of the Church. In the Western Church language of the person and operation of the Spirit came to be expressed in the terminology of grace. Therefore, it could seem that the work of the Holy Spirit is entirely bound to the church and its ministries. In the Reformation, the Spirit was not only seen as being immanent in the church (that was never denied, because God had remained faithful to the church even "under the papacy") but also as being transcendent to the Church, challenging the Church from outside its institutional structures. If that were not the case any Reformation would lose its theological, more precisely: its spiritual legitimacy. Therefore, the Holy Spirit is seen as perfecting the work of the triune God by granting insight into the truth of the Gospel of Christ as witnessed in Scripture as the truth of God's relationship to his creation, disclosing his being as love. This account is consistently developed where the Spirit of God is understood to be the source of all truth and the wellspring of all true insight and disclosure. In illuminating the believer with the truth of the Gospel God constitutes faith.

The understanding of the Spirit became in this way closely associated with the understanding of Scripture. The Spirit of God was seen as the "first author" of Scripture in inspiring the biblical authors and as its "ultimate interpreter" in creating certainty in the believer with regard to the truth of the Gospel. The external word of Scripture, the biblical text, understood in its literal sense, and the internal testimony of the Holy Spirit belong together because they have the same author. This understanding of the Spirit that gave spiritual authority to the liberation from what Martin Luther called in 1520 the "Babylonian captivity of the Church" explains the pluralism in the social organization of the Reformation Churches. If the Spirit is seen as working immanently in the Church through the consecration of those who hold an office in the church, and if this spiritual authority is seen as concentrated in the successor of Peter and in the Church of Rome, the Church will have a monocentric form of organization. Where this is denied and the Spirit is believed to work in many places, calling many persons into the ministry, the church will be organized in a polycentric fashion. Church order and oversight will take the form of a relational communion of churches. This is the feature which the Reformation churches share with the churches of Eastern Orthodoxy. This is not merely a sociological difference because it presupposes different views of revelation.

The understanding of the Spirit and its relationship to Holy Scripture, the relationship between the external and the internal word became the main factor in the many divisions of the Protestant churches. While the magisterial Reformation already had to deal with enthusiastic groups of radical Reformers, sometimes claiming spiritual authority over and above the authority of Scripture, the question of the external and the internal word became a main issue in the 17$^{th}$ century. While spiritualist movements relied on the primary authority of the internal testimony of the Spirit, the "inner light", other groups understood the Spirit to be contained entirely in the external word of Scripture so that Scripture became the inspired authority. The "verbal inspiration" of the Bible became, in many different variations, a feature of the Lutheran Reformed Orthodoxy in the 17$^{th}$ century. Among evangelicals in the United States it became the focus of a continuing debate about biblical inerrancy in the 19$^{th}$ century. Should the Bible be regarded as "absolutely" or "fully" inerrant, or as inerrant in a limited way? Is it an inerrancy of purpose rather than of content and form? Which Bible is inerrant, the "original" text in Hebrew and Greek or does inerrancy also extend to translations?[80] Looked at from an outsider's perspective, these debates within Protestantism are remarkably similar to the debates on papal infallibility in Roman Catholicism. Does it go too far to detect in these debates the danger of "displaced foundation" where faith in the triune God is replaced by faith in one of the media and instruments of his revelation? It would be difficult not to answer this question in the affirmative, if one looks at the "five fundamentals" which are the origin of the name of "fundamentalism" where the first article of faith is no longer faith in the triune God but in the inerrancy of the Bible, followed by believing the virgin

---

**80** A thoughtful discussion of these different view can by found in Erickson, Millard J., *Christian Theology*, Grand Rapids: Baker Academic, $^{3}$2013, 188–229.

birth of Christ.[81] If that is the case, then the only antidote to a fundamentalism that is in danger of committing the heresy of displaced foundation could only consist in a theological reflection on the understanding of the revelation. Do the biblical testimonies themselves offer a justification for a theory of the inerrancy of the Bible?

If one sees traditions which have a tendency of identifying revelation with the external word as one pole in the polarity between external and internal means of communication, the movements which stress the internal, subjective pole of the internal word form the other pole. We find this element of the emphasis of the subjective element in revelation in a large variety of Protestant churches. They all stress the primacy of Scripture as the authority of Christian doctrine, and see this view as rooted in revelation. The emphasis on the primacy of Scripture can have a variety of forms, ranging from stressing the reliability of God's communication in the witnesses of the Bible to acceptance of the principle of inerrancy. In the churches and religious movements which have their origin in the 18th century, we find an emphasis on the inner experience of transformation often called "evangelical conversion". In Methodism which started as a reform movement within the Church of England the prototype of this experience is the "Aldersgate experience" of John Wesley (1703–1791). While attending a meeting of the Moravian brethren on the 24th of May 1738, he found "his heart strangely warmed" by the assurance of God's grace in Christ. This was the impulse for a new evangelistic initiative which soon became a mass movement. While Methodism was first of a movement of evangelism and sanctification in the Church of England, it became a church in North America. Revelation is seen here as resulting in a transformation of the affections of the heart which leads to a new lifestyle of inward and outward holiness. The process of sanctification, often understood in sanative terms, could even include "entire sanctification" already in this life, before the Eschaton. The question which was raised by this movement and other movements in the various revivals of the 18th and 19th century is again the contribution of the human person to the transformation of the inner and outward life. Debates between Calvinist Wesleyans, emphasizing the significance of the doctrine of predestination and therefore the exclusive efficacy of God's action in salvation, and Arminian Wesleyans who, finding their orientation in the teachings of Jacobus Arminius (1560–1609), emphasize in contrast the contribution of the human will, characterize the internal conversation in the Methodist

**81** For a discussion of fundamentalism as a phenomenon of "displaced foundations" cf. Schwöbel, Christoph, *Gott im Gespräch. Theologische Studien zur Gegenwartsdeutung*, Tübingen: Mohr Siebeck, 2011, 39–68.

churches until today. It is this question which has been the impulse for many holiness movements and churches in all continents.

Pietism in continental Europe had a very similar emphasis on the personal conversion experience and must be seen as one of the factors that influenced the rise of Methodism. Originally a movement of the renewal of piety within the Lutheran churches, its influence has spread far beyond its original setting in central Europe, often existing as meetings within institutional churches. If one tries to see Pietism in the context of the understanding of revelation, it is the emphasis on the personal appropriation of revelation in personal conversion experiences that seems most characteristic.

The major new movement in the 20$^{th}$ century that is relevant in this overview is the rise of Pentecostalism, beginning with the Azuza Street Revival in Los Angeles in 1906. Pentecostalism is characterized by the claim that the gifts of the Spirit that were alive in early Christianity have not ceased, but continue to be poured out today. The Pentecostal Movement has gained tremendous momentum throughout the 20$^{th}$ century and continues to grow rapidly especially in the global South. Its spread in Latin and South America has been one of the most influential factors of social change. The main emphasis is on the holistic character of the gifts of the Holy Spirit which include faith healing and speaking in tongues, which follow the baptism in the Holy Spirit. Pentecostal churches have proved to be able to transcend boundaries of race, culture, class and education very successfully, and adapt to the conditions of the global South in a situation where the majority of Christians now live in the Southern hemisphere. This raises the question whether the traditional forms of theological thinking developed to a large extent in the academic contexts of the Northern hemisphere can be helpful in offering the resources for Christians in the global South to reflect theologically on their experiences and to employ theological reflection as a tool for shaping their life.

Important elements of Pentecostalism have been taken up in the Charismatic Movement which has found a place within other Protestant churches since around 1960 and has also become a movement within the Roman Catholic church since the late 1960s. In contrast to views of revelation according to which revelation constitutes a deposit of faith which is then handed on through the generations by the traditions of the church, revelation in Pentecostalism and in the Charismatic Movement is a present reality, often interpreted as the "first fruits of the Spirit" (cf. Romans 8: 22), an anticipation of the future Kingdom. Revelation is seen as coming from the future to affect reality with the gifts of the Spirit, which are all anticipatory signs of the future consummation of everything. Compared to the technical debates on the concept of revelation since the High Middle Ages, we have here the return of phenomena associated with revelation in the early church. The presence of these phenomena in the Pentecostal churches and in the Charismatic Movement challenges the traditional conceptualizations of revelation.

The 20th century is the century of Christian ecumenism. The success of the ecumenical movement has demonstrated that the beliefs of Christians, often thought to be only divisive and leading to strategies of exclusion have led to new forms of community, understanding and common action across the boundaries of cultures, political forms of organization, socio-economic contexts. Compared to political or economic endeavors to forge connections between different communities across the divide of cultures, ecumenism has had a resounding success. At the beginning of the 21st century much of the original enthusiasm and energy of the ecumenical movement seems to be less vibrant and lively. At least part of this is due to the fact that the ecumenical movement has to re-imagine and reorganize itself in view of the rapid changes in worldwide Christianity.

If one considers the dynamics of these developments in the context of reflection on the concept of revelation, it seems less promising to apply the sophisticated conceptual tools from the history of reflection on revelation to the rich and varied world of the Christian churches and movements in the first quarter of the 21st century. The task seems to consist rather in rebuilding the conceptuality of revelation on the basis of the experience of the various Christian denominations and Christian movements worldwide. In all of them the appeal to revelation is a pervasive feature. The task of theology consists in such a situation in the attempt of working through the processes of the formation of central Christian concepts again. With regard to revelation this means to reconstruct on the basis of the phenomena, the world of signs which forms the basis for the theological concepts. For Christianity there seems to be only one starting point for this: the celebration of Christian worship in which Scripture is used in various ways that shape the patterns of worship. Especially the growth of the Pentecostal churches are a reminder that Christian faith is not only a reflective faith, developing theologies, but also ethical faith, shaping the ethos of Christian communities. It is also a faith that has its life in worship, and it is here that reflection of revelation has to begin again and again. Do the ways in which we relate to God in worship mirror the ways in which God has related to us, do they conform to the mode and content of God's self-communication?

Does this mean that in view of these challenges the complex histories of the development of theories of revelation can be set aside? The opposite seems to be the case. In the globalized situation in which the world religions exist today, we all become heirs of one another's histories and that includes the history of dogma. The question for the future will be to what extent the problems, complexities and attempted clarifications of the past can serve as resources for understanding the present challenges and for attempting to shape the future. It may be that in such a situation the primary forms of doing theology as we find them in patristic times, scriptural exegesis, the explication of liturgies and the formulation of catechisms, acquire new significance.

# 6 Divine Self-Communication in Interreligious Conversations: Perspectives for the 21st Century

At the beginning of the 21st century we live in a situation of religious and ideological pluralism, globally, locally and in the fusion zone of the global and the local which socialists describe as the "glocal", pointing to the simultaneous dynamics of universalizing and particularizing tendencies. For the world religions this means that they live in situations of close encounter in almost every context, mirroring the situation of religiously pluralist situations of encounter and conflict in which Judaism, Christianity and Islam have coexisted for most of their histories. The apparently mono-cultural situations, which often were the result of the formation of national states in modernity, seem to have been an episode in the history of the interaction of Judaism, Christianity and Islam. In the situation of pluralism there exists a dialogical imperative.[82] Most of our situations are characterized by the absence of a common ground of values and norms that we could take for granted. In such a situation we have to negotiate common aims that encapsulate the common good for societies characterized by difference, by differences which matter since they concern the fundamental orientations of individual persons and of communities in pluralist societies. Believers of different religious traditions may have very different justifications for achieving these common aims. The deeper these justifications are rooted in the respective faith traditions, the stronger is their obligatory power to persuade members of faith traditions to achieve these common goals. In a pluralist society we need agreement about common aims, but agreement about the justifications of trying to achieve these goods is not needed. Can we achieve these common aims within a framework of common rules which regulate our interactions with one another in justice and peace? Again, the reasons for agreeing to such rules and for abiding by them may be quite different, but the respect for the rules should be a shared concern.

**82** Cf. on the following issues Schwöbel, *Gott im Gespräch.*

Does the appeal to revelation help in a situation characterized by the dialogical imperative? Is it conducive for the dialogical exchange that is focused on common aims and is directed at finding means of cooperation to achieve them? Or does it impede a constructive exchange? It is the insight into the constitution of their own basic orientations, their action-directing certainties which oblige religious believers to respect and tolerate the basic convictions of others. When we believe that our fundamental insights are rooted in revelation we are aware that they are constituted *for us* and not *by us* by a process of reflection and argument. And we believe that this form of constitution of faith applies to every human person. This insight should help us to accept that the basic orientations of others have been constituted in a similar way. The accounts of revelation in Judaism, Christianity and Islam all imply that we are not ourselves the authors of our true insights *and* that this applies to all human creatures, not just to the members of our own faith community. The particular revelation which Christians experience as the constitution of certainty with regard to the truth of the Gospel in Jesus Christ opens up the insight that this mode of gaining true insight through the disclosure of truth by God is universally true for every human creature. As human creatures we cannot actively disclose ultimate truth concerning the origin and meaning of human life to ourselves. Where we encounter the conviction that orientation has been granted to our fellow humans of another faith, we can tolerate and respect them and their beliefs, because we know that our beliefs which we believe to be true have come about in the same way. Tolerance between religions is always tolerance on the basis of faith, rooted in one's own faith and in recognition of the faith of the other. Understanding human beings as creatures who are destined to live not by their own lights, but by the light that has been granted and so live by the light of their revelation is the basis for mutual respect and toleration. Abraham Heschel has famously remarked that interfaith dialogue presupposes faith. This implies that interfaith dialogue presupposes revelation that has created faith. We engage in interfaith dialogue on the basis of what is disclosed to us, on the basis of how God discloses his will and being and so discloses us to ourselves as we are in relation to God. If interfaith dialogue presupposes faith, then it should be possible to apply our formula for God's self-disclosure – A discloses in the situation B C to D with the effect E – also to interreligious conversation.

A. What can we say about the author of revelation? Jews, Christians and Muslims believe in one God who is the ground and *telos* of all being, meaning and perfection. If God is omnipresent and omnipotent we cannot deny the presence of God in the religion of the other. Christians cannot profess in the Creed: "We believe in one God, the Father Almighty, maker of heaven and earth, of all things, seen and unseen" and then deny the presence of God in the religions of the others and the believers of other faiths. Believing in God the Creator implies that the other faiths are not enemy territory, but belong to the one creation of God, they are not an accident in the history of salvation but their existence is enveloped in God's promise for creation. Christians believe that this God is the author of revelation. If, however, the creator is also the author of revelation, whatever God reveals to us also in some way includes all his other creatures. There will not be a particular revelation that contradicts God being the creator, reconciler and perfecter of everything there is. Rather, revelation belongs to the way in which God achieves the divine purpose for the whole of creation. Relating to the religion of others with the expectation to find the presence of God in them, is a necessary implication when we believe that the author of the revelation that constitutes our faith is the omnipresent and omnipotent creator.

B. What can we say about the situation of revelation? Jews, Christians and Muslims believe that God reveals his identity and will by communicating with the creatures he created in the context of the created world. In Christian faith it is emphasized that creation occurred through the divine Word who was made flesh in Jesus. This implies that human creatures are created for communication with God and with one another. Humans are dependent, conversational, rational creatures. As creatures they are dependent on the communication with the creator for finding orientation in the world, they have their being as language creatures who find the meaning of their existence in conversation with God and with one another. Therefore their rationality is in a very basic sense always dialogical, never reduced to solitary self-reflection. Furthermore, Jews, Christians and Muslims believe that the world is a created order which has meaning, because the creator spoke it into being and uses it now as a means of addressing his creatures. For Christians the belief that the creative Word became a human being has a special poignancy here. It implies that every human being not only presents us with an image of God but also with an image of God's communication to us. No human face is devoid of this divine address. The situation in which God addresses us in revelation is therefore always one in which God already communicates in other persons and in every creature. Every "special" revelation discloses God's "general" revelation, the God who is always already there in the situation of disclosure.

C. How can we characterize the content of revelation? Jews, Christians and Muslims believe that God communicates his will in order to guide human creatures on the right path, in conformity with God's purposes. For Christians the content of God's revelation is God's being as love which commits Christians to love God in such a way that this love of God includes love of neighbor even love of the enemy. The primary question for interreligious conversations is not whether what God reveals through the Hebrew Scripture and in the Qur'ān is the same as in the Christian revelation. Interreligious dialogue is not about the lowest common denominator between the revelations for Jews, Christians and Muslims. Rather, the question is: If that is the revelation which is contained in Christian faith how does it commit a Christian to relate to Jews, Muslims and, indeed, to all people? What does the unconditional character of God's love mean for the love of Christians to their neighbors, be they Jews, Christians or Muslims? How does the content of revelation change our outlook on the people around us? How can our love for our neighbor reflect in a creaturely form the way God loves God's human creatures? That is one of the questions which the revelation of God's love raises for us.

D. Do the reflections about the recipient of revelation have any significance for interreligious dialogue? The most important insight that the understanding of revelation has to contribute to interreligious dialogue is that in revelation, the disclosure experience constitutes the recipient of revelation, transforms their view of life, of God, of themselves and of their world. Revelation always occasions a radical change, a change which discloses also that the recipient of revelation has been on the wrong way, was caught up in misleading orientations and is now directed on the right path. Where a disclosure experience occurs it invariably provokes repentance, liberation from self-deception and reorientation. On the other hand, disclosure experiences imply, because of their radical asymmetry, that God who is the author of revelation and who discloses his relationship to the recipient of revelation, always remains beyond human control. Recipients of revelation can never possess what is revealed to them. Disclosure situations are therefore always situations of radical dispossession. Because God is the author and content of revelation, its ground and object, human recipients of revelation can never avail themselves of revelation so that it could be at their disposal. This exactly is the nature of the certainty which revelation creates, it is without alternative, not malleable to the shaping of human insights, because it is a contingent gift. Humans can therefore never assume the authority of God as the ground and object of revelation. Paradoxically, the certainty that is created in disclosure situations only comes with the corollary of epistemic modesty, never being in possession of what is in this way revealed.

E. When we look at the effect of a disclosure situation, the effect which from a Christian perspective must be characterized as faith, as unconditional trust in God, this brings to interfaith dialogue precisely the condition which makes it a dialogue between believers. It is important to recognize that faith as the effect of a disclosure experience has always a critical thrust. Having faith in God implies never being able to turn God into an instrument for the achievement of our own purposes, or into an argument supporting our own views. Faith – and that would be something Jews, Christians and Muslims can readily agree on – means letting God be God. In this sense, the significance of the concept of revelation for interfaith conversations is already affirmed when we say with Abraham Heschel: "The first and most important prerequisite of interfaith is faith."[83] If faith is constituted in revelation and if revelation means being addressed by God and being called to respond in all the relationships that make up our lives, then our conversations with one another belong inextricably to our response to God.

## Bibliography


Anselm of Canterbury, *The Major Works. Including Monologion, Proslogion, and 'Why God Became Man.'* Oxford: Oxford University Press, 1998.

Assel, Heinrich, *Der andere Aufbruch. Die Lutherrenaissance – Ursprünge, Aporien und Wege: Karl Holl, Emanuel Hirsch, Rudolf Hermann (1910–1935)*, Göttingen: V&R, 1994.

Audi, Robert, *Epistemology. A Contemporary Introduction to the Theory of Knowledge*, London: Routledge, 2003.

Avis, Paul (ed.), *Divine Revelation*, London: Darton, Longman & Todd, 1997.

Barth, Karl, "The Word of God and the Task of the Ministry," in: id., *The Word of God and the Word of Man*, 183–217, London: Hodder and Stoughton, 1928.

Barth, Karl, *The Church Dogmatics* II/1, Geoffrey William Bromiley/Thomas Forsyth Torrance (eds), Edinburgh: T&T Clark, 1957.

St. Basil the Great, *On the Holy Spirit*, transl. David Anderson, Crestwood, NY: St. Vladimirs Seminary Press, 1980.

Bauckham, Richard, "Jesus the Revelation of God," in: Paul Avis (ed.), *Divine Revelation*, 174–200, London: Darton, Longman & Todd, 1997.

Bayer, Oswald, *Contemporary in Dissent. Johann Georg Hamann as Radical Enlightener*, Grand Rapids, MI: Eerdmans, 2012.

Bergmann, Sigurd, *Creation Set Free. The Spirit as Liberator of Nature*, Grand Rapids MI: Eerdmans, 2005.

Brunner, Emil, *Offenbarung und Vernunft.* Zürich: Theologischer Verlag Zürich, 1941; 2nd edition Zürich: Zwingli Verlag, 1961; reprint Wuppertal: TVG Brockhaus, 2007.

Bultmann, Rudolf, "The Concept of Revelation in the New Testament (1929)," id., *Existence and Faith*, 67–106, London: Collins Fontana, 1964.

Calvin, John, *Institutes of the Christian Religion*, trans. Henry Beveridge, Grand Rapids, MI: Eerdmans, 1989; reprinted 1995.

Chadwick, Henry (ed.), *Lessing's Theological Writings*, Stanford: Stanford University Press, 1957.

Charry, Ellen T., "Revelation," in: Chad Meister/Paul Copan (eds), *The Routledge Companion to Philosophy of Religion*, 609–615, London: Routledge, 22013.


83 Heschel, Abraham Joshua, "No Religion is an Island," in: Harold Kasimov/Byron L. Sherwin (eds), *Abraham Joshua Heschel and Interreligous Dialogue*, 3–22, Maryknoll, NY: Orbis, 1991.

Dalferth, Ingolf U., "Die Mitte ist außen. Anmerkungen zum Wirklichkeitsbezug evangelischer Schriftauslegung," in: Christoph Landmesser/Hans-Joachim Eckstein/Hermann Lichtenberger (eds), *Jesus Christus als die Mitte der Schrift. Studien zur Hermeneutik des Evangeliums*, 173–198, Berlin/New York: De Gruyter, 1997.

Dalferth, Ingolf U., "Understanding Revelation," in: Ingolf U. Dalferth/Michael Ch. Rodgers (eds), *Revelation. Clarment Studies in Philosophy of Religion Conference 2012*, 1–25, Tübingen: Mohr Siebeck, 2014.

Dalferth, Ingolf U., "Creative Grace. The Spiritual Revolution of the Reformation," *Neue Zeitschrift für Systematische Theologie* 59 (2017), 548–71.

D'Costa, Gavin, "Karl Rahner's Anonymous Christian. A Reappraisal," *Modern Theology* 1 (1985), 131–148.

Dulles, Avery S.J., *Models of Revelation*, New York: Doubleday & Company, 1983; Maryknoll, NY: Orbis, 17$^{th}$ imprint 2011.

Dunn, James D.G., "Biblical Concepts of Revelation," in: Paul Avis (ed.), *Divine Revelation*, 1–22, London: Darton, Longman & Todd, 1997.

Edwards, Mark, *Catholicity and Heresy in the Early Church*, Farnham, Surrey: Ashgate, 2009.

Eicher, Peter, *Offenbarung. Prinzip neuzeitlicher Theologie*, Kösel: München, 1977.

Erickson, Millard J., *Christian Theology*, Grand Rapids: Baker Academic, $^{3}$2013.

Farrow, Douglas, "St. Ireanaeus of Lyons. The Church and the World," *Pro Ecclesia* 4,3 (1995), 333–55.

Freemantle, Ann, *The Age of Belief. The Medieval Philosophers*, selected with introduction and interpretive commentary, Boston: Houghton and Mifflin, 1955.

Al-Ghazālī, *The Incoherence of the Philosophers*, a parallel English-Arabic text trans., introduced and annotated by Michael E. Marmura, Provo UT: Brigham Young University Press, 1997/2000.

Gay, Peter (ed.), *Deism. An Anthology*, Princeton, NJ [et al.]: van Nostrand, 1968.

Gunton, Colin E., *A Brief Theology of Revelation. The 1993 Warfield Lectures*, Edinburgh: T&T Clark, 1995.

Hadot, Pierre, *Philosophy as a Way of Life. Spiritual Exercises from Socrates to Foucault*, Oxford: Wiley-Blackwell, 1995.

Hadot, Pierre, *What is Ancient Philosophy?* Cambridge, MA: Harvard University Press, 2004.

Halevi, Yehuda, *The Kuzari*, with an introduction by Henry Slonimsky, New York: Schocken Books, 1966.

Hall, Stuart G., *Doctrine and Practice in the Early Church*, London: SPCK, $^{2}$2005.

Harmless, William S.J., "Mystic as Cartographer," in: id., *Mystics*, 79–105, Oxford/New York: Oxford University Press, 2007.

Helm, Paul, *The Divine Revelation. The Basic Issues*, London: Marshall Morgan & Scott, 1982.

Herms, Eilert, *Offenbarung und Glaube. Zur Bildung des christlichen Lebens*, Tübingen: Mohr, 1992.

Herms, Eilert, "Offenbarung V. Theologiegeschichte und Dogmatik," in: Gerhard Müller (ed.), *Theologische Realenzyklopädie*, vol. XXV, 146–210, Berlin/New York, De Gruyter, 1995.

Herms, Eilert, *Phänomene des Glaubens. Beiträge zur Fundamentaltheologie*, Tübingen: Mohr Siebeck, 2006.

Herms, Eilert, *Systematische Theologie. Das Wesen des Christentums: In Wahrheit und aus Gnade leben*, 3 vols, Tübingen: Mohr Siebeck, 2017.

Heschel, Abraham Joshua, "No Religion is an Island," in: Harold Kasimov/Byron L. Sherwin (eds), *Abraham Joshua Heschel and Interreligous Dialogue*, 146–210, Maryknoll, NY: Orbis, 1991.

Jenson, Robert W., "Once More on the *Logos asarkos* (2011)," in: Robert W. Jenson, *Theology as Revisionary Metaphysics. Essays on God and Creation*, ed. by Stephen John Wright, Eugene, OR: Cascade Books, 2014.

Kolb, Robert/Wengert, Timothy J., (eds), *The Book of Concord. The Confessions of the Evangelical Lutheran Church*, trans. Charles Arand [et al.], Minneapolis: Fortress Press, 2000.

Locke, John, *An Essay Concerning Human Understanding*, New York: Dover Publications, 1947.

Lossky, Vladimir, *The Mystical Theology of the Eastern Church*, Cambridge: James Clarke 1991.

Lutz-Bachmann, Matthias/Fidora, Alexander (eds), *Juden, Christen und Muslime. Religionsdialoge im Mittelalter*, Darmstadt: Wissenschaftliche Buchgesellschaft, 2004.

Maimonides, Moses, *The Guide of the Perplexed*, trans. with an introduction and notes by Shlomo Pines. With an introductory essay by Leo Strauss, 2 vols., Chicago/London: University of Chicago Press, 1963.

Marenbom, John, *The Philosophy of Peter Abaelard*, Cambridge: Cambridge University Press, 1997.

Marty, Martin E./Appleby, R. Scott, *The Fundamentalism Project*, 5 vols., Chicago: University of Chicago Press, 1991–1995.

Meyendorff, John, *St Gregory Palamas and Orthodox Spirituality*, New York: St Vladimir's Seminary Press, 1974.

Möhler, Johann Adam, *Symbolik, oder Darstellung der dogmatischen Gegensätze der Katholiken und der Protestanten nach ihren öffentlichen Bekenntnisschriften*, Frankfurt a. M.: Minverva, $^{6}$1895.

Nielsen, Jan T., *Adam and Christ in the Theology of Irenaeus of Lyons. An Examination of the Function of the Adam-Christ Typology in the Adversus Haereses of Irenaeus, against the Background of the Gnosticism of His Time*, Assen: von Gorkum, 1968.

Origen, *On First Principles*, ed. by John Behr, Oxford Early Christian Texts, Oxford: Oxford University Press, 2017.

Pannenberg, Wolfhart (ed.), *Revelation as History*, London: Sheed and Ward, 1969.

Pannenerg, Wolfhart, *Systematic Theology*, vol. 1, trans. Geoffrey W. Bromiley, Grand Rapids MI: Eerdmans, 1991.

Palamas, Gregory, *The Triads*, ed. by John Meyendorff, Mahwah, NJ, 1983.

Paulson, Stephen D., "Luther on the Hidden God," *Word and World* (1999), 363–371.

Preuß, Horst Dietrich, "Offenbarung II. Altes Testament," in: Gerhard Müller (ed.), *Theologische Realenzyklopädie*, vol. XXV, 117–128, Berlin/New York, 1995.

Rahner, Karl, *Theological Investigations*, vol. 1, Baltimore: Helicon, 1961.

Runia, David T., *Philo in Early Christian Literature*, Assen: van Gorcum, 1993.

Schffczyk, Leo/Waldenfels, Hans, *Offenbarung. Von der Reformation bis zur Gegenwart*, in: Helmut Hoping/Gerhard Kardinal Müller (eds), *Handbuch der Dogmengeschichte*, vol. 1, facicle 1b:, Freiburg: Herder, 2014.

Schwöbel, Christoph, *God. Action and Revelation*, Kampen: Kok Pharos, 1992.

Schwöbel, Christoph, "Theology," in: John Webster (ed.), *The Cambridge Companion to Karl Barth*, Cambridge: Cambridge University Press, 2000.

Schwöbel, Christoph, "God as Conversation. Reflections on a Theological Ontology of Communicative Relations," in: Jacques Haers (ed.), *Theology of Conversation. Towards a Relational Theology*, BEThL 172, 43–67, Leuven [et al.]: Peeters Publishers, 2003.

Schwöbel, Christoph, "Offenbarung, Glaube und Gewissheit in der reformatorischen Theologie," in: Eilert Herms/Lubomir Žak (eds), *Grund und Gegenstand des Glaubens nach römisch-katholischer und evangelisch-lutherischer Lehre*, 119–55, Tübingen: Mohr Siebeck, 2008.

Schwöbel, Christoph, *Gott im Gespräch. Theologische Studien zur Gegenwartsdeutung*, Tübingen: Mohr Siebeck, 2011

Schwöbel, Christoph, "Revelation," in: Hans Dieter Betz [et al.] (eds), *Religion. Past and Present*, vol. 11, 162–163; 169–170; 172–173, Leiden: Brill, 2011.

Schwöbel, Christoph, "The Same God? The Perspective of Faith, the Identity of God, Tolerance, and Dialogue," in: Miroslav Volf (ed.), *Do We Worship the Same God? Jews, Christians, and Muslims in Dialogue*, 1–17, Grand Rapids/Cambridge: Eerdmans, 2012.

Schwöbel, Christoph, "Martin Luther and the Trinity," in: *Oxford Research Encyclopedia on Martin Luther*, Oxford, 2017, http://religion.oxfordre.com (last accessed Nov 4, 2019).

Schwöbel, Christoph, "Justice and Freedom. The Continuing Promise of the Reformation," *Neue Zeitschrift für Systematische Theologie* 59 (2017), 595–614.

Schwöbel, Christoph, "The One and the Three in Christian Worship and Doctrine: Engaging with the Question of Divine Unity in the Elaboration of Christian Doctrine," in: L. Mosher/D. Marshall (eds), *Monotheism and Its Complexities. Christian and Muslim Perspectives*, 63–91, Washington, DC: Georgetown University Press, 2018.

Schwöbel, Christoph, "'We Are All God's Vocabulary.' The Idea of Creation as a Speech-Act of the Trinitarian God and Its Significance for the Dialogue Between Theology and Sciences," in: Andrew B. Torrance/Thomas H. McCall (eds), *Knowing Creation. Perspectives from Theology, Philosophy, and Science*, vol. 1, 47–68, Grand Rapids, MI: Zondervan, 2018.

Seybold, Michael, *Offenbarung. Von der Schrift bis zum Ausgang der Scholastik*, in: Helmut Hoping/Gerhard Kardinal Müller (eds), *Handbuch der Dogmengeschichte*, vol. 1, facicle 1a, Freiburg: Herder 2014.

Smart, Ninian, *Dimensions of the Sacred. An Anatomy of the World's Beliefs*, Berkeley/Los Angeles: University of California Press, 1999.

St. Thomas Aquinas, *Summa Theologica* (vol. 1), trans. the Fathers of the English Dominican Province, Westminster, Maryland: Christian Classics, 1981.

Trigg, Joseph Wilson, *Origen*, New York: Routledge, 1998.

Van Ess, Josef, *The Flowering of Islamic Theology*, Cambridge, MA: Harvard University Press, 2006.

Williams, Rowan, *Arius. Heresy and Tradition*, revised edition, London: SCM Press, 2009.

## Suggestions for Further Reading

Abraham, William J., *Crossing the Threshold of Divine Revelation*, Grand Rapids, MI/ Cambridge, UK: Eerdmans, 2006.

Dalferth, Ingolf U./Rodgers, Michael Ch. (eds), *Revelation. Claremont Studies in Philosophy of Religion*, Tübingen: Mohr Siebeck, 2014.

Dulles, Avery, *Models of Revelation*, Maryknoll: Orbis, 1883, [7]2001.
Gunton, Colin, *A Brief Theology of Revelation. The 1993 Warfield Lectures*, London: T&T Clark, 1995.
Helm, Paul, *Divine Revelation. The Basic Issues*, Vancouver: Regent College Publishing, 2004.
Herms, Eilert, *Offenbarung und Glaube. Zur Bildung des christlichen* Lebens, Tübingen: Mohr Siebeck, 1992.
Herms, Eilert, *Systematische Theologie. Das Wesen des Christentums: In Wahrheit und aus Gnade leben*, vol. 1, Tübingen: Mohr Siebeck 2017, 3–550.
Jenson, Peter, *The Revelation of God*, Downers Grove, IL: IVP Academic, 2002.
Levering, Matthew, *Engaging the Doctrine of Revelation. The Mediation of the Gospel through Church and Scripture*, Grand Rapids, MI: Baker Academic, 2014.
Schwöbel, Christoph, *God. Action and Revelation*, Kampen: Kok Pharos, 1992.
Wenz, Gunter, *Offenbarung. Problemhorizonte moderner evangelischer Theologie*, Göttingen: Vandenhoeck & Ruprecht, 2005.

Asma Afsaruddin

# The Concept of Revelation in Islam

Revelation is an extremely important concept within Islam. Within the Abrahamic religious tradition, the truth of Islam is perhaps uniquely anchored in a scripture directly revealed from God, as Muslims believe, preserved in its original Arabic language for subsequent generations of believers. In the Islamic context, revelation is a multidimensional and multivalent concept that binds humans to their Creator.

In this chapter, I will discuss ten primary aspects of revelation that are particularly significant in the Islamic context but also in a dialogic context involving the other two Abrahamic religions – Christianity and Judaism. These aspects are drawn from the Qurʾān and elaborated upon by referring to the rich Qurʾān commentary literature (*tafsīr*) and other extra-Qurʾānic discussions of revelation when relevant. The ten aspects are: a. revelation as communication between God and humans – language and divine truth; b. revelation as invitation to – and not imposition of –faith; c. revelation as oral and written text and the merits of its recitation; d. revelation as beautiful and inimitable text: the doctrine of *iʿjāz al- Qurʾān*; e. revelation as primordial text; f. revelation as manifestation of divine mercy and justice; g. revelation as a message of hope and guidance to humanity; h. revelation as reminder; i. revelation as mediation of the tension between inclusivism and exclusivism; and finally, j. revelation as affirmation of monotheism as common ground between Muslims, Christians, and Jews.

These aspects are now discussed in detail below.

## 1 Revelation as Communication between God and Humans – Language and Divine Truth

The Arabic word for the phenomenon of revelation is *waḥy* and is, strictly speaking, applied to the Qurʾān alone. *Waḥy* more broadly means to send a message, often secretly, by means of a gesture, through written transmission, or by inspiration. In the Qurʾān, the term *waḥy* and its derivatives occur seventy-eight times. Except for five instances, all of these occurrences pertain to God as the one who sends down revelation.

The Qurʾānic revelation consists of words received directly from God and is set apart from the whimsical statements of human beings. Three verses (Qurʾān 53:3–5) make this very clear. They state:

https://doi.org/10.1515/9783110476057-004

He [sc. the Prophet Muḥammad] does not speak out of his own desire
It [sc. the Qur'ān] is nothing but revelation (*in huwa illā waḥyun yūḥyā*)
Which one endowed with strength taught him

Similarly, in Qur'ān 69:38–48, God speaks:

So I do call to witness what you see, and what you see not. That is indeed the word of an honored messenger (sc. Muḥammad), it is not the word of a poet; Little it is that you believe!

The cluster of verses in Qur'ān 26:192–196 also asserts the divine provenance of Islam's central scripture and the role of the angel Gabriel, who is not otherwise explicitly named, in the transmission of revelation, here referred to as *tanzīl:*

Indeed, it is a transmission (*tanzīl*) from the Lord of the Worlds
Which the trustworthy spirit has brought down
Upon your heart so that you may be one of the warners
In plain Arabic speech
And indeed it is in the scriptures of those who have preceded

The well-known twelfth/sixth century theologian Abū 'l-Muʿīn an-Nasafī (d. 1114/508) describes the nature of the Qur'ānic revelation in the following manner:

The Qur'ān is God's speaking, which is one of His attributes. Now God in all of His attributes is One, and with all His attributes is eternal and not contingent, (so His speaking is) without letters and without sounds, not broken up into syllables or paragraphs. It is not He nor is it other than He. He caused Gabriel to hear it as sound and letters, for He created sound and letters and caused him to hear it by that sound and those letters. Gabriel, upon whom be peace, memorized it, stored it (in his mind) and then transmitted to the Prophet, upon whom be God's blessing and peace, by bringing down a revelation and a message, which is not the same as bringing down a corporeal object and a form. He recited it to the Prophet, upon whom be God's blessing and peace, the Prophet memorized it, storing it up (in his mind), and then recited it to his Companions, who memorized it and recited to the Followers.[1]

The Qur'ān as direct divine revelation to humanity is furthermore protected from alteration and falsification. The Qur'ān thus describes itself as "an unassailable scripture" and that "Falsehood cannot come at it from before or behind, [for it is] a revelation (*tanzīl*) from the Wise, the Praiseworthy" (Qur'ān 41:42). God Himself

1 An-Nasafī, "Sea of Discourse," cited in: F. E. Peters, *A Reader on Classical Islam*, Princeton: Princeton University Press, 1994, 173.

guarantees the Qur'ān's incorruptibility: "We have, without doubt, sent down the Message; and We will certainly guard it (from corruption)" (Qur'ān 15:09).

The celebrated exegete Muḥammad b. Jarir aṭ-Ṭabarī (d. 923/310) comments that according to Qur'ān 54:3–5, God first imparted the Qur'ānic revelation to the angel Gabriel, described as "one endowed with strength," who then communicated it to the Prophet.[2] In Qur'ān 26:193, he notes that Gabriel, according to a consensus of early exegetes, is identified as "the trustworthy spirit" who transmits the words of God to the Prophet.[3]

Another well-known commentator Fakhr ad-Dīn ar-Rāzī (d. 1210/606) comments that Qur'ān 54:3 provides a clear rebuttal to those who accused the Prophet of being a mere soothsayer or a poet; that is to say, someone who merely strings words together for magical effect.[4] Ar-Rāzī pays particular attention to the term *waḥy* and explains the term as follows:

> It is both a noun whose meaning is "the Book" and a verbal noun (gerund) which connotes "transmission" (*al-irsāl*) and "inspiration" (*al-ilhām*), as well as writing (*al-kitāba*), speech (*al-kalām*); allusion (*al-ishāra*); and instruction (*al-ifhām*), all of which constitute references to the Qur'ān.[5]

Ar-Rāzī also pays special attention to the term *tanzīl* occurring in Qur'ān 26:192. It means, he says, "that which is sent down" (*al-munazzal*) indicating the transmission of God's words to the Prophet via Gabriel referred to as the "trustworthy spirit." He further comments that the divine assertion "Indeed it is a revelation from the Lord of the Worlds" points to the eloquent and inimitable nature of the Qur'ānic revelation, as well as to the fact that accounts of bygone generations of people are transmitted directly to Muḥammad by God and not via human learning and transmission.[6]

To explain the distinction between *waḥy* and *tanzīl*, it is worth quoting from a well-known modern scholar of Islam, Mahmoud Ayoub on the specific significations of these two terms. Ayoub states,

> *waḥy* is a general expression denoting in this context urgent divine communication to prophets, messengers, and other righteous persons, such as the prophet Zachariah and his son John the Baptist, Jesus and his mother Mary, and the mother of Moses. *Tanzīl*, in

2 Aṭ-Ṭabarī, Muḥammad b. Jarīr, *Tafsīr aṭ-Ṭabarī*, Beirut: Dār al-Kutub al-ʿilmiyya, 1997, 11:504–505.

3 Aṭ-Ṭabarī, *Tafsīr*, 9:477. Gabriel is similarly described in Qur'ān 81:20.

4 Ar-Rāzī, Fakhr ad-Dīn, *At-Tafsīr al-kabīr*, Beirut: Dār iḥyā' at-turāth al-ʿarabī, 1999, 10:235.

5 Ibid., 10: 235–237.

6 Ibid., 8:530.

> contrast, is God's sending down revelation over a specified period of time, as was the case with Moses, who received the Torah over a forty-day period on Mt. Sinai, or Muḥammad who received the Qur'ān through the angel Gabriel over a period of more than two decades. It must be observed that the revelation of the Qur'ān combines both *waḥy* – direct communication by Gabriel on God's behalf – and *tanzīl* – Gabriel coming down to him from God with revelations.[7]

More briefly, *waḥy* may therefore be understood as the actual phenomenon of divine communication and *tanzīl* as the content of that communication that is revealed over a period of time.

In a critical verse, the Qur'ān explains the various ways in which God chooses to communicate with humankind. The verse (42:51) states:

> It is not vouchsafed to any mortal that God should speak to him except by revelation, or from behind a veil, or through a messenger sent and authorized by Him to make known His will. Exalted is He, and Wise.

In his exegesis of this verse, aṭ-Ṭabarī comments that God does not speak to mortals except through revelation as he sees fit, or through inspiration (*ilhām*). If he should speak to a human being from behind a veil, it means the recipient can hear him but not see him, as was the case with Moses. Or he may send one of his emissaries, that is to say, one of his angels like Gabriel or others, in order to reveal his commandments and other aspects of his revelation.[8]

It is noteworthy that aṭ-Ṭabarī mentions the word "inspiration" (*ilhām*) in connection with revelation because in the Qur'ānic context there seems to be considerable overlap between the two concepts, especially when *waḥy* and its derivatives are applied to non-humans. Thus the Qur'ān says, "Then He completed and finished their creation (as) seven heavens, and He inspired (*awḥā*) in each heaven its affair" (41:12). This may be regarded as a reference to the natural laws which govern the orbits of the planets and the rotation of the earth, and so forth.

Similarly God "inspires" animals and imprints upon them their essential nature and instincts. Thus Qur'ān (16:68 – 69) relates, "And your Lord inspired the bee, saying, take as habitations mountains, and in the tree and in what (mankind) builds, then, eat of all fruits, and follow the ways of your Lord." This signifies the natural animal instinct that every creature is endowed with; bees, for example, instinctively build their hives and search for nectar from flowers.

---

7 See his "History of the Qur'an and the Qur'an in History," *The Muslim World* (2014), 430.
8 Aṭ-Ṭabarī, *Tafsīr*, 11:162.

God also inspires the angels to carry out His commands. The Qur'ān (8:12) says, "(Remember) When your Lord inspired (*idh yuḥy*) the angels, 'I am with you, so keep firm those who have believed.'"

*Waḥy* is furthermore used more in the sense of inspiration than revelation in the case of some human recipients who are not prophets, such as Moses' mother. Thus the Qur'ān (28:7) says, "And we inspired (*wa-āwḥaynā*) the mother of Moses, 'Suckle him! But when you fear for him, then cast him into the river and fear not, nor grieve.'" Here God inspires the mother of Moses to undertake a certain course of action with out actual words spoken to her through the medium of an emissary as would have been the case with a revelation to a prophet.

In one case, it is a human being – albeit a prophet – who inspires his people to engage in praise of God. Qur'ān 19:11 refers to Zechariah who after having been forbidden from speaking for three days, "emerged before his people and inspired/signaled to them (*awḥā ilayhim*) to glorify God morning and night." But since Zechariah was a prophet, ultimately we may understand his inspiring act to go back to God himself.

Depending on the agent, the term *waḥy* and its derivatives need not always have a positive connotation. The word is also used in connection with devils or malicious creatures who "inspire (*la-yuḥūna*) their cohort [among humans] to dispute with you" (Qur'ān 6:121). And again, "And thus We have appointed for every prophet an enemy – evil humans and jinns, who suggest (*yuḥy*) to one another alluring words of deception ..." (Qur'ān 6:112).

The Arabic verb *alhama* which is the usual word that means "to inspire" is used only once in the Qur'ān (91:8) to refer to God who fashions the human soul and inspires it with discernment of good and evil. *Alhama* here would then be connected with the notion of *fiṭra* or the human inborn disposition, about which more will be said later.[9]

---

9 Outside of the Qur'ān there is a general distinction maintained between *waḥy* as divine revelation vouchsafed only to select prophets and *ilhām* or inspiration that may also be of divine provenance but is provided to select righteous people for private guidance. Such righteous people may include ordinary piety-minded folk and pious scholars, as well as righteous rulers and other caretakers with more mundane responsibilities.

## 2 Revelation as Invitation to – and Not Imposition of – Faith

According to the Qur'ān, there is only one infraction that God will not forgive in the hereafter: the sin of associationism or polytheism (*shirk*) (Qur'ān 4:48; 5:72). Monotheism is repeatedly affirmed through revelation and its salvific efficacy is underscored in a number of passages in the Qur'ān. Nowhere is this articulated more starkly and powerfully than in the fifth verse of the first or opening chapter (*al-Fātiḥa*) of the Qur'ān. This verse states: "It is [only] You we worship; it is [only] You we ask for help." The original Arabic emphatic particle (*iyyāka*) in this verse clearly affirms that no contender to the one and only God may be imagined, who alone is adored by the believer and beseeched for help.

The well-known exegete Muḥammad b. Jarīr aṭ-Ṭabarī quotes the famous Companion ʿAbdallāh b. ʿAbbās who glossed "It is [only] You we worship" to mean "It is only You Whom we declare to be one and to hold in awe and in Whom we place our hope – O our Lord, there is none other than you!"[10] As for the next part of the verse which states "It is [only] You we ask for help," aṭ-Ṭabarī expansively expounds on its meaning thus:

> It is You, O our Lord, Whom we beseech for help in our adoration of only You and our obedience of You in all our matters – there is absolutely none beside You – in contrast to those who do not believe in You and who ask the idols that they worship instead of You for help in their affairs. We however ask You for help in all our matters sincerely dedicating our worship to You.[11]

The Qur'ān insists that God's unicity is absolute. The 112th chapter of the Qur'ān – called the Chapter on Sincerity (*al-Ikhlāṣ*) and on the Unicity of God (*at-Tawḥīd*), among other names – declares this unambiguously and fittingly reflects the first chapter's emphasis on God's singularity. This chapter also contains a distillation of the essential message of the Qur'ān, predicated as it is on the invitation to humans to glorify and supplicate the One God alone. Chapter 112 is therefore declared by the Prophet Muḥammad to be equivalent to a third of the Qur'ān, whose frequent recitation confers untold merit on the believer.[12]

One of the occasions of revelation provided by aṭ-Ṭabarī for Qur'ān 112 is as follows. According to the Companion Ubayy b. Kaʿb, the Arab polytheists asked

---

**10** Aṭ-Ṭabarī, *Tafsīr*, 1:99.

**11** Ibid.

**12** Al-Bukhārī, *Ṣaḥīḥ*, Qāsim ash-Shammāʿī ar-Rifāʿī (ed.), Beirut: Dār al-qalam n.d., "Kitāb at-Tawḥīd," 8:778.

the Prophet if he could "provide for us the genealogy of your Lord." In response, the chapter was revealed. Variant versions attributed to Qatāda b. Diʿāma (d. 736/117) and Saʿīd b. Jubayr (d. 714/95), among others, state that it was a group of Medinan Jews who asked the Prophet a similar question and further demanded to know that since God had created Creation who had created God? Aṭ-Ṭabarī comments that in this context, *Sūrat al-Ikhlāṣ* may be understood to constitute a categorical response to such queries about God's pedigree, his attributes, and his existence. It instructed the Prophet to respond as follows: "He is the one God (Allāh) who is the object of worship of all things; absolutely no one else is worthy of worship but Him."[13]

The Arabic statement *Allāh aḥad* ("God is one") in Qur'ān 112:1 is a stark affirmation of God's oneness. The well-known late twelfth/sixth century exegete ar-Rāzī comments that the name *Allāh* as used here may be understood to signify the totality of positive divine attributes (such as possessing all knowledge and power) while *aḥad* connotes the totality of negative divine attributes (for example, being without corporeal form and substance). The phrase *Allāh aḥad* therefore conveys a full theological understanding of God. As ar-Rāzī puts it, "The entire Qur'ān is an oyster, and the pearl is His statement 'Say, He, God is One.'"[14]

God's singularity and sole sovereignty is furthermore established in the Qur'ānic revelation because he alone is proclaimed to be the Creator of all things and he alone is in charge of everything (Qur'ān 6:102). He never sleeps or tires and, while transcendant, can be found everywhere; "the East and the West belong to God; wherever you turn, there is His Face," declares the Qur'ān (2:115). His glorious throne encompasses all of creation and no one may serve as an intercessor except by his leave, as stated in Qur'ān 2:255. This verse has justly become famous for invoking the ineffable majesty of the Divine Being in incomparably beautiful Arabic. Known in the commentary literature as "the Verse of the Throne" (*āyat al-kursī*), it is recited by Muslims on many occasions in reverential awe of the Almighty and as talismanic protection against the adversities that assail humans in this world. A *ḥadīth* refers to the Verse of the Throne as the "Mistress of the Verses of the Qur'ān." The well-known mystical theologian al-Ghazālī (1058–1111/450–505) in his commentary titled *Jawāhir al-Qur'ān* explains why this verse has achieved such an elevated status. "The Verse of the Throne," he says, is so called because it

13 Aṭ-Ṭabarī, *Tafsīr*, 12:740–741.

14 Seyyed Hossein Nasr et al. (eds), *The Study Qur'an. A New Translation and Commentary*, New York: HarperOne, 2015, 1578–79.

> "is concerned with the divine essence, attributes and works only; it contains nothing other than these..." Now when you reflect on all these meanings [contained in the Verse of the Throne] and then recite all other verses of the Qur'an, you will not find all these meanings – divine unity, sanctification, and explanation of high attributes – gathered together in a single one of them.[15]

Scriptural emphasis on the soteriological efficacy of monotheism historically became reflected in the principle of *irjā'* which evolved in roughly the eighth/second century of the Common Era in the Muslim world. The root of the Arabic term *irjā'* connotes both "hope" and "deferment." Because of a number of doctrinal schisms that developed in the early period, some Muslim theologians wisely came to see immense virtue in postponing or deferring to God any definitive judgment on the correctness of a particular dogma that was not explicitly referred to in the Qur'ān or *ḥadīth*. This principle was specifically formulated in contradistinction to the notion of *takfīr* ("accusation of unbelief"), resorted to by the seventh/first century schismatic group, the Khawārij. The Khawārij had mutinied against ʿAlī b. Abī Ṭālib, the fourth caliph, when the latter agreed to human arbitration to resolve the dispute between him and Muʿāwiya, the governor of Syria, over the issue of leadership of the community. The Khawārij (lit. "the seceders") claimed that arbitration was the prerogative of God alone and human arbitration was unwarranted in this case. They considered those Muslims (the overwhelming majority) who disagreed with them to have lapsed from the faith and thus to be fought against until they capitulated (a chilling harbinger of today's minoritarian extremist views).[16]

In contrast to the fissiparous doctrine of *takfīr*, the principle of *irjā'* stated that any Muslim who proclaimed his or her belief in the one God and the prophetic mission of Muḥammad (that is, affirmed the basic creedal statement of Islam) remained a Muslim, regardless of the commission of even gravely sinful actions, thereby holding out the hope and promise of moral rehabilitation in this world and of forgiveness in the next. A sinning Muslim was liable for punishment for criminal wrong-doing but could not be labeled an unbeliever by his co-religionists. Those who subscribed to such views were known as the Murji'a.[17]

---

15 Al-Ghazālī, *The Jewels of the Qur'an. Al-Ghazali's Theory*, trans. Muhammad Abu al-Quasem, Kuala Lumpur: University of Malaya Press, 1977, 75–77.

16 For a still useful broad overview of this group, see Salem, Elie Adib, *Political Theory and Institutions of the Khawārij*, Baltimore, MD: Johns Hopkins Univ. Press, 1956.

17 For a useful overview of these broad historical trends, see Watt, W. Montgomery, *Islamic Political Thought*, Edinburgh: Edinburgh University Press, 1968, 54–63.

These views became influential and came to undergird the majoritarian Sunni accommodationist world-view.

How should Muslims react when others spurn the Qur'ān's call to monotheism? A cluster of verses (Qur'ān 6:106–108) establishes a protocol of conduct in these circumstances. Qur'ān 6:106 clearly instructs Muslims to "Follow what has been revealed to you from your Lord, there is no God but Him," and to "Turn away from those who join other gods with Him." The following verse (Qur'ān 6:107) counsels the Prophet that it is not part of his worldly mission to turn people towards monotheism; his is one of preaching the divine message that he was entrusted with that others can embrace or reject, for "We have not made you their guardian, nor are you their keeper." The last verse in this cluster (Qur'ān 6:108) furthermore categorically proclaims a directive for interfaith conduct and a mandate for civility in the midst of religious difference that is of particular significance. It states, "Do not revile those [idols] they call upon beside God in case they revile God out of hostility." The verse therefore stresses that it is not for human beings to pronounce on the rectitude of religious doctrines since that leads to dissension and strife in this world. The Prophet Muḥammad himself is clearly warned that it is not among his duties to chastise people for their beliefs contrary to Islam, including idolatry, which represents the polar opposite of the fundamental Islamic tenets of monotheism and iconoclasm.[18]

A sampling of exegeses of this verse establishes that this fundamental message of non-compulsion in religion was emphasized by the large majority of Qur'ān commentators. The early exegete Muqātil b. Sulaymān (d. 767/150) in his brief exegesis of Qur'ān 6:107 states that if God had so willed, he would have prevented the Meccans from being polytheists. But he did not appoint the Prophet their guardian nor is he their guardian if they refuse to believe in the one God. As for Qur'ān 6:108, it informs us that the early Muslims used to curse the idols of the Meccans and God forbade them from doing so lest they curse God in their ignorance.[19]

Aṭ-Ṭabarī similarly comments that Qur'ān 6:107 affirms that if God had willed, the people of Mecca would have not have disbelieved in God and his messenger, but the Prophet Muḥammad was sent only as an emissary and summoner to people and not as an overseer of their actions or as one who is responsible for their maintenance and welfare. The next verse forbids Muslims from reviling the idols of the polytheists for that would cause them to revile God in their igno-

---

**18** See my further discussion of these verses in Afsaruddin, Asma, *Contemporary Issues in Islam*, Edinburgh: Edinburgh University Press, 2015, 199–200.

**19** Muqātil b. Sulaymān, "Tafsīr Muqātil b. Sulaymān", ʿAbd Allāh Maḥmūd Shiḥāta (ed.), Beirut: Muʾassasat at-Taʾrīkh al-ʿArabī, 2002, 1:573.

rance.[20] Similar commentaries are given by az-Zamakhsharī (1075–1144/467–538),[21] ar-Rāzī,[22] and Ibn Kathīr (d. 1373/774).[23]

The modern exegete Muḥammad ʿAbduh (1849–1905) reproduces many of the essential points made by his pre-modern predecessors in connection with these two verses. But he goes further than his predecessors in asserting that Qurʾān 6:107 makes clear that God, despite being the Guardian and Overseer of humanity, does not force humans to believe in and obey Him. If he were to do so, humans would no longer be humans but become a different specie; that is to say, humans by virtue of their humanness have freedom of choice in religious matters.[24] The implication is that those who heed both reason and revelation are bound to embrace monotheism of their own free and rational volition.

The Qurʾān's invitation to faith and affirmation of the human right to choose to believe – or not – is categorically expressed in verse 56 of the second chapter, which has justly become famous in the contemporary period. This verse states, "There is no compulsion in religion." In practically any discussion of toleration in an Islamic context today, this verse will be foregrounded by many Muslims. Its obvious and unambiguous meaning is that no one may be coerced into adopting a religion against his or her will. A quick survey of some exegetical views is revealing however of a range of views on this critical verse. Aṭ-Ṭabarī in the late ninth/third century documents a spectrum of views concerning the meaning of this verse. According to one of the earliest strands of exegeses, this verse was understood to be revealed in regard to the situation of some of the early Medinan Muslims, known as the Anṣār or the Helpers, who were previously raising their children to be either Jews or Christians. When the preaching of Islam began, they wanted to forcibly convert their children to Islam. The verse was consequently revealed to specifically prohibit them from doing that and to foreground instead free volition in the selection and practice of a religion. This was the commentary offered by early Companions like Ibn Abbās, Saʿīd b. Jubayr, and others.[25]

According to the late first/seventh century exegete Mujāhid b. Jabr (b. 642/21), as cited by aṭ-Ṭabarī, the verse was revealed in reference to another group of Medinan Muslims who had grown up among the Banū Qurayza, a Jewish

---

**20** Aṭ-Ṭabarī, *Tafsīr*, 5:304–5.
**21** Az-Zamakhsharī, *Kashshāf*, 2:385.
**22** Ar-Rāzī, *Tafsīr*, 5:108–111.
**23** Ismāʿīl b. ʿUmar Ibn Kathīr, *Tafsīr al-qurʾān al-ʿazīm*, Beirut: Dār al-Jīl, 1990, 2:156.
**24** Riḍā, Rashīd, *Tafsīr al-qurʾān al-ḥakīm*, Beirut: Dār al-Kutub al-ʿilmiyya, 1999, 7:548–49.
**25** Aṭ-Ṭabarī, *Tafsīr*, 3:15–16.

tribe, and who now wished to forcibly convert its members to Islam.[26] The verse was revealed to forbid them from doing so. Both "causes of revelation" (*asbāb an-nuzūl*) clearly establish that Qur'ān 2:256 prohibits the forcible conversion of non-Muslims to Islam and allows them instead to continue in their religious practices.

However, aṭ-Ṭabarī also documents that by the time we get to the second generation of Muslims, other less tolerant views had begun to surface. He quotes the Successor (from the second generation of Muslims after the Companions) Ibn Zayd (d. 798/182) who had asserted that the commandment "There is no compulsion in religion" had been abrogated. Although Ibn Zayd is not explicitly quoted as saying it, the implication is that the verse had been abrogated by the verses that give the command to fight the pagan Arabs. Earlier, another Successor Qatāda b. Diʿāma had maintained that Qur'ān 2:256 applied primarily to the People of the Book (Jews and Christians) who, upon payment of the *jizya* or poll-tax to the Muslim authorities, could continue to practice their religion but it did not apply to the Arab polytheists. For them their only option was to accept Islam or face the sword. Similar views were expressed by the Successor aḍ-Ḍaḥḥāk b. Muzāḥim (d. 723/105).[27]

Aṭ-Ṭabarī's own preferred interpretation in the late ninth/third century is that Qur'ān 2:256 is not to be regarded as abrogated because it applies only to Jews, Christians, and Zoroastrians; Arab idolaters however were obligated to embrace Islam or be fought against.[28] Aṭ-Ṭabarī also underscores that the Arabic word used for "religion" in the verse is *ad-dīn*, the definite article *al-* signifies that it is a reference to Islam alone.[29] Aṭ-Ṭabarī's commentary became quite influential after him and in many ways became the predominant view at least among certain exegetes and jurists.

Historically speaking, it is not hard to understand why this perspective gained ground in influential, official circles. Qur'ān 2:256 in Arabic states, "*La ikrāha fī d-dīn.*" In its very simplicity and transparency, the verse clearly and unequivocally mandates that all humans have freedom of religion and that no one may be compelled to either accept or reject religion – any religion – since Islam is not specifically indicated, despite aṭ-Ṭabarī s attempt to derive this meaning from the verse. So transparent in fact was its mandate that some scholars, by no means all, felt compelled already by the second century of Islam to declare this verse to be abrogated, as we saw, so as to legitimate a more triumphalist

**26** Ibid., 3:16–17.
**27** Ibid., 3:17–18.
**28** Ibid., 3:18.
**29** Ibid., 3:19.

world-view that asserted the superiority of Islam over all other religions, often for political reasons. Aṭ-Ṭabarī, it should be noted, was very close to the Abbasid ruling elite of his time; for the purposes of empire-building, it was useful to promote Islam as a conquest-based world religion which perspective then could be deployed, at least in certain contexts, as a mandate for expanding the imperial realms.

Such scholars have been challenged by others, both in the pre-modern and modern periods, who categorically stated that this verse remained normative for all times and its basic injunction of non-compulsion in religion could never be violated. Criticism of some of the classical exegeses of Qurʾān 2:256 and of the principle of *naskh* in general, has, not surprisingly, been the sharpest in the modern period when freedom of conscience has become a moral desideratum.[30] *Naskh*, it should be noted, refers to the principle of abrogation, which, according to many pre-modern exegetes, allows for certain earlier verses to be superseded or nullified by later verses.

Another verse which clearly conduces to tolerance is Qurʾān 5:48 which states,

> For every one of you We have appointed a law and way of life. And if God had so willed, He could surely have made you all one single community, but (He willed it otherwise) in order to test you by means of what He has given you. So hasten to do good works!

Turning to aṭ-Ṭabarī once again, he fully recognizes that every religious community or nation (*qawm*) has its own religious law or tradition (*shirʿa*) and way of doing things (*minhaj*). He quotes Qatāda b. Diʿāma who had stated that religion is one but religious laws or traditions (*sunan*) are many. Thus the Torah has its own religious law (*sharīʿa*), as does the Gospel and the Qurʾān, which prescribes and proscribes various things so that God may know those who obey Him from those who do not. However, the religion that was proclaimed by numerous prophets through time is one and it is the only one acceptable to God: that is to say, the religion that is founded on monotheism and sincere belief in God.[31]

Contraposed to this inclusivist view of religious traditions is that of others who averred that the verse actually referred only to those who embraced Islam as having a religious law and tradition. Among these exegetes was Mujāhid b. Jabr who maintained that only the Qurʾān, and no other scripture, had such a religious law and way. Once again, we see exclusivist views beginning to arise already in the second century of Islam which directly contradicted the prima

---

**30** See my discussion of these issues in Afsaruddin, *Contemporary Issues*, 124–128.
**31** Aṭ-Ṭabarī, *Tafsīr*, 4:610.

facie meaning of Qur'ānic verses, such as 5:48. Revelation became the site for such contestations that had considerable implications for self- and communal identity.

# 3 Revelation as Oral and Written Text and the Merits of Its Recitation

In later theological texts, the Qur'ān is specifically referred to as *al-waḥy al-matlū* ("the recited revelation") while the *ḥadīth* (sayings of the Prophet Muḥammad) is referred to as *al-waḥy ghayr al-matlū* ("the unrecited revelation"). This distinction between the Qur'ān and *ḥadīth* on the basis of whether it is recited or not underscores the liturgical role of the Qur'ān in Muslim worship. The name 'Qur'ān' after all refers to a text that is both recited and read – and points to both its oral and written modalities. William Graham, among others, has rightly emphasized the Qur'ān's role as an oral text in Muslim religious life and the primacy of its orality over its written form in Islam's early centuries.[32]

The Qur'ān's role as a liturgical text explains, at least partially, why chronology was not a factor in the final redaction of the sacred text after the Prophet's death in 11/632. Compared to both the Hebrew and the Christian Bible, the entire Qur'ān is meant to be recited. Muslim worshippers recite selections from the Qur'ān in their daily obligatory prayers, during special occasions marking the passages of life – birth, marriage, death, etc. – and during other mundane, quotidian events. The Qur'ān after all served as both an oral and written texts from its very beginning. Traditional sources inform us that while the Prophet orally communicated the revelations received by him, his Companions committed them to writing. Even after the codification of the sacred text, its oral dimension remained (and remains) an integral part of the Qur'ānic revelation.

A possible tension may be discerned in early Islamic literature that refers to the oral and written dimensions of the Qur'ānic revelation and how the faithful accommodated themselves to these dual dimensions. This tension sometimes comes through in the literary genre known as the *faḍā'il al-Qur'ān* which discusses the merits or excellences of the Qur'ān. One may read into many of the

32 Graham, William A., *Beyond the Written Word. Oral Aspects of Scripture in the History of Religion*, Cambridge, Eng.: Cambridge University Press, 1993, 88–92; Graham, William A., "The Qur'an as Spoken Word: An Islamic Contribution to the Understanding of Scripture," in: Richard Martin (ed.), *Approaches to Islam in Religious Studies*, 23–40, Tucson: University of Arizona Press, 1985.

reports contained in the *faḍā'il al-Qur'ān* works the insecurities generated in a society that is rapidly making the transition from a society based on oral transmission to that based on written transmission. Starting with Nabia Abbott, modern scholars have marshalled impressive arguments and a considerable body of evidence to indicate that this transition occurred much earlier than has been commonly assumed and that written documents were prevalent as early as the late first/seventh and early eigth/second centuries. Such a transition brought about an attendant transfer of religious authority and social power from the traditional piety-minded elite to an emerging professional class of religious scholars, whose expertise was defined in large measure by mastery of the written text. Abbott has pointed to this historical tension between oral and written transmission in Islam's first century which found moral overtones. She states that those groups who represented "pious scholarship" and, therefore, were "orthodox," were the ones who "struggled to hold onto the idea of the absolute primacy of oral transmission." [33] This attitude is believed to have stemmed primarily from 'Umar's edict against the writing down of *ḥadīth* as reported by some sources.[34]

The early resistance to dealing with the Qur'ān as primarily a written text is encoded in a number of *faḍā'il al-Qur'ān* works. One report nicely encapsulates the apprehension generated by the ascendancy of the *muṣḥaf* (the written Qur'ān copy) over oral transmission. The account states that when 'Ikrima b. Abī Jahl (d. 723–24/105) heard that the *muṣḥaf* had become widespread, he swooned and, apparently, on coming to, lamented, "It is the speech of my Lord (*kalām rabbī*); it is the speech of my Lord!" The emphasis on speech (*kalām*) draws attention to what Brinkley Messick has termed "a culturally specific logocentrism" in Islam. This logocentrism privileged the spoken word for "while recitation was thought to maintain a reliable constancy of meaning, the secondary medium of writing was seen as harboring a prospect of misinterpretation."[35] Such a recitational logocentrism would be severely challenged by the rise to prominence of a class of professional scholars and scribes by the ninth/third century whose discursive medium became the written word.

The trend towards a preference for written transmission of sacred revelation finds reflection in a statement by the thirteenth/seventh century Shāfi'ī jurist scholar Yaḥyā b. Sharaf ad-Dīn an-Nawawī (1233–1277/631–676) who exhorts

---

33 Abbott, Nabia, *Studies in Arabic Literary Papyri. Historical Texts*, Chicago: University of Chicago Press, 1957, 1:131; 2:24.

34 Al-Khaṭīb al-Baghdādī, *Taqyīd al-'ilm*, Yūsuf al-'Ishsh (ed.), Beirut: Dār iḥyā' as-sunna an-nabawiyya, 1974, 2:19; 49–53.

35 Messick, Brinkley, *The Calligraphic State. Textual Domination and History in a Muslim Society*, Berkeley: University of California Press, 1993, 25.

the believer to recite from the *muṣḥaf* rather than from memory (*ʿalā ẓahri ʾl-qalb*) since "looking at the written text is a desirable [act of] worship," and, he continues, "it has been reported by many that the righteous forebears (*as-salaf*) would recite from the *muṣḥaf*."[36] This may in fact reflect historical truth. From another perspective, these reports clearly make a religious virtue out of the bookish erudition of the *ʿulamāʾ*, a trait that is grafted retroactively onto the moral exemplars of the early centuries of Islam to create a pious precedent.

The rich *faḍāʾil al-Qurʾān* literature is therefore a repository of some of these critical debates within the Muslim community and preserves for us the tension between the oral and written aspects of revelation and its consequences for the formation of individual and communal piety. This literature also attests to the growth of praise traditions specifically concerning the Qur'ān that exaggerated the recompense (*thawāb*) earned by the believer in reciting certain chapters from the holy book, such as *al-Fātiḥa* (chapter 1) and *at-Tawḥīd* (chapter 112), or specific verses, such as Qurʾān 2:255, which, as we previously noted, became known as the Verse of the Throne (*āyat al-kursī*).

The controversial nature of this issue is reflected in the following accounts recorded about the 112th chapter known as sura *at-Tawḥīd* or *al-Ikhlāṣ*. The unusual merit ascribed to this *sūra* is best exemplified in the prophetic report commonly related in regard to it, "Say, he is God the One," equals a third of the Quʾrān. The Andalusian scholar Ibn ʿAbd al-Barr (978–1070/368–463) reports that when the famous jurist Aḥmad b. Ḥanbal (780–855/164–241) was asked regarding the probative value of this report, he did not signify his approval of it. He also references Isḥāq b. Rāḥawayh (d. 853/238) who had explained this report in the following way: he said that when God made His speech more excellent than the rest of speech, He assigned greater recompense to the recitation of part of it [sc. His speech] in order that people would be induced to teach it. Ibn Rāḥawayh further dismisses the understanding of this tradition to imply that reciting it thrice earns for the reciter the reward of having recited the entire Qurʾān; "this would not be possible even if one were to recite it two hundred times." Ibn ʿAbd al-Barr himself counseled that "Silence on this matter is better than speech regarding it and more sound."[37] Clearly, there was a reluctance on the part of early scholars to consider parts of the Qurʾān to be more excellent than others. After all, was not all of God's speech equally excellent and beautiful?

36 Fakhr ad-Dīn al-Baʿalbakkī, *Mukhtaṣar Tibyān*, Ms. Leiden University Library, OR 1525, fol. 42b. For further discussion, see Afsaruddin, Asma, "The Excellences of the Qurʾān: Textual Sacrality and the Organization of Early Islamic Society," *Journal of the American Oriental Society* 122:1 (2002), 1–24.

37 As-Suyūṭī, *al-Itqān fī ʿulūm al-qurʾān*, Beirut: Dār ibn Kathīr, 1993, 2: 1140–41.

Jalāl ad-Dīn as-Suyūṭī (1445–1505/849–911) in his *al-Itqān fī ʿulūm al-qurʾān* poses the question that has troubled scholars in general: is there anything in the Qurʾān [to be considered] more excellent than something else [in the Qurʾān]? He notes that prominent scholars like Abū ʾl-Ḥasan al-Ashʿarī (ca. 873–ca. 935/260–324), Abū Bakr al-Bāqillānī (d. 1013/403), and Ibn Ḥibbān (d. 965/354) forbade such comparisons for "all [of it] is the word of God; otherwise, the preferred [portion] presumes the deficiency of the less preferred [portion]." It was said that the jurist Mālik b. Anas (d. 796/179) also disliked that any *sūra* be repeated more than others. On the other hand, certain scholars like the afore-mentioned Isḥāq b. Rāḥawayh, Abū Bakr b. al-ʿArabī (1076–1148/468–543), and al-Ghazālī, considered "preference" (*at-tafḍīl*) permissible on account of prophetic *ḥadīth*s to this effect. In fact, as as-Suyūṭī points out, al-Ghazālī in his *Jawāhir al-Qurʾān* comes out very strongly in favor of the permissibility of showing preference for some chapters over others and asserts the existence of prophetic precedence for it. He says,

> Follow the one who, peace and blessings be upon him, was entrusted with the message (*ar-risāla*), for he was the one to whom the Qurʾān was revealed, and the prophetic reports indicate the exalted status of certain verses and the doubling of reward in the case of certain revealed chapters. And he, peace and blessings be upon him, said further, "the Opening Chapter of the Book is the most excellent chapter of the Qurʾān; the Verse of the Throne is the mistress of the verses of the Qurʾān; Yā Sīn is the heart of the Qurʾān; and 'Say, He is God, the One' equals a third of the Qurʾān."

Despite the fact that a number of prominent scholars resorted to such exaggerated praise for certain sections of the Qurʾān, certain, and perhaps more punctilious, *ḥadīth* scholars from the later period took exception to this development. Ibn al-Jawzī (1126–1200/510–597), az-Zarkashī, and as-Suyūṭī, for example, expressed their dismay over the proliferation of *faḍāʾil* reports which assigned greater merit to certain portions of the Qurʾān over others and their recording by respectable scholars. They have questioned the motives of those who circulated these exaggerated accounts, mainly because critical scrutiny of the *isnād*s (chains of transmission) of such accounts have revealed the presence of transmitters with less than sterling reputations.

For example, Ibn al-Jawzī takes exception to the following *ḥadīth* attributed to the Companion Ubayy b. Kaʿb, related below at some length since it is frequently cited in this kind of literature:

> The Messenger of God, peace and blessings be upon him, displayed the Qurʾān to me twice in the year in which he died and said, "Gabriel, peace be on him, has commanded me to recite to you the Qurʾān and he recites greetings to you." ... When the Messenger of God,

> peace and blessings be upon him, recited to me, I asked him if I had a special [role to play]; "if so, impart to me specially the merit of the Qur'ān according to what God has taught you and informed you about." He replied, "Yes, Ubayy. Every time a Muslim recites the opening chapter of the Book, he is given as recompense the equivalent of having recited a third of the Qur'ān and of having given alms to every believing man and woman. Whoever recites al-ʿImrān is given safe passage on the bridge of Jahannam for every verse in it; whoever recites Sūrat an-Nisā' is given as recompense the equivalent of offering alms to each person who inherits from him; whoever reads al-Mā'ida is given ten rewards and ten demerits are wiped out ..." And he mentioned the rewards that accompanied each *sūra* until the end of the Qur'ān.[38]

Az-Zarkashī states that the above *ḥadīth* attributed to Ubayy b. Kaʿb regarding the merits of each *sūra* is a fabricated one. He further reports that Nūḥ b. Abī Maryam was once asked how he had come to relate a tradition from ʿIkrima reporting from Ibn ʿAbbās regarding the merits of the Qur'ān chapter by chapter (*fī faḍā'il al-Qur'ān sūratan sūratan*). He replied, "I saw people turning away from the Qur'ān and concerning themselves with the *fiqh* [jurisprudence] of Abū Ḥanīfa and the Maghāzī of Muḥammad b. Isḥāq and thus I fabricated these *ḥadīths* in their entirety."[39]

Az-Zarkashī goes on to criticize the Qur'ān exegetes, al-Wāḥidī (d. 1076/468) and ath-Thaʿlabī (d. 1035/427), who consequently came to list such praise accounts at the beginning of each *sūra* in their commentaries, with the exception of az-Zamakhsharī who appended these accounts to each chapter at the end. Ibn al-Jawzī passes a similar negative judgement on al-Wāḥidī and ath-Thaʿlabī for such a practice and says that this is not surprising on their part since they were not one of the *ahl al-ḥadīth* (a reference to hadith scholars; implying that they had less scruples about reporting unreliable traditions). Ibn al-Jawzī further rebukes Ibn Abī Dā'ūd as-Sijistānī (844–929/230–316) for having included this report in a work that he composed on the *faḍā'il al-Qur'ān* in spite of being aware of the spurious nature of the *ḥadīth*. Ibn al-Jawzī then goes on to impugn the reliability of some of the narrators who related this tradition; for example, Mukhallad b. ʿAbd al-Wāḥid who was described by Ibn Ḥibbān as "repudiated (*munkar*) of *ḥadīth*."[40] ʿAbd Allāh b. al-Mubārak (d. 797/181) was of the opinion

---

**38** Ibn al-Jawzī, *Kitāb al-mawḍūʿāt*, ʿAbd ar-Raḥmān Muḥammad ʿUthmān (ed.), Medina, 1966–68, 1:239; As-Suyūṭī, *al-La'ālī 'l-maṣnūʿa fī l-aḥādīth al-mawḍūʿa*, Beirut, n.d., 1:226 ff.

**39** Az-Zarkashi, *al-Burhān fī ʿulūm al-Qur'ān*, M. A. F. Ibrahim (ed.), Dar Ihya al-Kutub al-ʿArabiyya, 1957–9, 1:432.

**40** Ibn al-Jawzī, *Mawḍūʿāt*, 1:240.

that the *zanādiqa*[41] had fabricated the tradition attributed to Ubayy b. Kaʿb. Another report states that a certain *shaykh* related the above tradition from Ubayy to Mu'ammal b. Ismāʿīl (d. c. 821/206), a Baṣran scholar. The *shaykh*'s transmitters were traced back to the source who was discovered to be another *shaykh* living in ʿAbbādān who was one of the Ṣūfīs (*qawm min al-mutaṣawwifa*). When this *shaykh* was queried regarding his original transmitter, he replied, "No one related it to me. But when we saw that the people had turned away from the Qur'ān, we fabricated this tradition for them so as to turn their faces towards the Qur'ān."[42]

These reports may thus be seen as having been generated against the backdrop of a "battle of piety" waged by various interest groups as they jostled for prominence in a society that was still in flux, in which prominence was defined in terms of greater moral excellence (*faḍl/faḍīla*).[43] Moral excellence itself would come to be largely predicated on the possession of knowledge; how this knowledge should be defined provided the point of departure for laying claims to this kind of excellence. The *ahl al-Qur'ān* (Qur'ān scholars) insisted on the primacy and self-sufficiency of knowledge derived from close study of the Qur'ān itself and had little use for the organized, hierarchical system of knowledge developed by the professional scholars. Ultimately, the *ahl al-ḥadīth* and the *ahl al-fiqh* (jurists) would win the day; their elaborate taxonomy of the *ḥadīth* literature that could generate certain knowledge and thus help elucidate the revealed law made irrelevant, even seditious (hence the label *az-zanādiqa* as deployed by Ibn al-Mubārak) the less rigorous and relatively unschooled piety of other groups, such as the *ahl al-taṣawwuf* (the Sufis or mystics).

## 4 Revelation as Beautiful and Inimitable Text: the Doctrine of *Iʿjāz al-Qur'ān*

Because of its divine provenance, the Qur'ān also stresses that its language is in clear and eloquent Arabic that defies human emulation. Divine revelation

41 This was a term used "loosely for "heretic, renegade, unbeliever" and more specifically for a Manichaean; see the article "zindiḳ," *Encyclopaedia of Islam*, second edition, Peri Bearman et al. (ed.), online version.

42 Ibn al-Jawzī, *Mawḍūʿāt*, 1:240 – 241.

43 See my discussion of the importance of this concept in conjunction with *sābiqa* (precedence) in Afsaruddin, Asma, *Excellence and Precedence. Islamic Discourse on Legitimate Leadership*, Leiden: E. J. Brill, 2002.

must be both accessible to the human mind and clothed in elegant language. Qur'ān 55:1–2 states, "(God) Most Gracious! It is He who has taught the Qur'ān;" furthermore, "We know indeed that they say: 'It is a man that teaches him.' The tongue of him they wickedly point to is notably foreign, while this is Arabic, pure and clear" (Qur'ān 16: 103). Two more verses link the Arabic language with communication of wisdom and comprehensibility. Qur'ān 12:2 says, "We have sent it down as an Arabic Qur'ān, in order that you may learn wisdom;" and "A revelation from (God), Most Gracious, Most Merciful. A Book, whereof the verses are explained in detail, a Qur'ān in Arabic, for people who understand" (Qur'ān 41:2–3).

God's words are inevitably beautiful since he himself is beautiful; the faithful who fulfill the commands contained in revelation partake in this beauty. Several verses in the Qur'ān repeat the phrase "those who do what is beautiful" for referring to those who carry out good deeds and conduct themselves with honor and dignity in daily life: "The mercy of God is near to those who do what is beautiful (*al-muḥsinīn*)" (7:56). The Qur'ān also exhorts: "Do what is beautiful. God loves those who do what is beautiful" (*wa-aḥsinū; inna 'llāha yuḥibbu 'l-muḥsinīn*; 2:195).

The perfection of God's word in the Qur'ān may therefore be understood to be a reflection of divine beauty and uniqueness – just as God is without peer so are his pronouncements communicated to human beings. The inimitability of the Qur'ān (*iʿjāz al-Qur'ān*) consequently became a matter of dogma underscoring the peerless language of the sacred text reflecting its divine authorship. Although the Qur'ān testifies to the presence of miracles or signs given to various prophets, such as Moses and Jesus, it denies that the Prophet Muḥammad performed any miracles except for the transmission of the Qur'ān (29:50). When Muḥammad was accused by his enemies of having forged the revelations received by him, the Qur'ān came to his defense and challenged mere mortals to produce chapters similar in eloquence and wisdom to its own.

> This Qur'ān is not such as can be produced by other than God; on the contrary it is a confirmation (of revelations) that went before it, and a fuller explanation of the Book – wherein there is no doubt – from the Lord of the Worlds. Or do they say, "He forged it?" Say: "Bring them a chapter like unto it, and call (to your aid) anyone you can, besides God, if indeed you speak the truth!" (Qur'ān 10:37–38)

As Mohammed Arkoun remarks, "Revelation in the Qur'ān is at first a result of linguistic evidence: the syntactic, semantic, semiotic structure of the Qur'ānic discourse imposes a space of communication totally articulated to impose a notion and a content of Revelation."[44] The eloquent and mellifluous Arabic of scripture points to its divine author and establishes the centrality of language in communication between the divine and human realms.

In his exegesis of Qur'ān 10:37, aṭ-Ṭabarī underscores the significance of this internal linguistic evidence for the Qur'ān's divine provenance. He states that by the revelation of this verse, "the Exalted says that no one but God could have created this Qur'ān for no created being has such ability." The Qur'ān was revealed to "Muḥammad, His servant, so as to give the lie to those polytheists who remarked that 'this is [mere] poetry and divination.'"[45] The Qur'ān is furthermore a confirmation of scriptures revealed to previous prophets, including the Torah and the Gospels, and provides further amplification of the duties imposed upon humans.[46]

Az-Zamakhsharī in his exegesis of Qur'ān 10:37 similarly comments that the Qur'ān is a confirmation and elucidation of previous revelations by "the Lord of the worlds" (*rabb al-ʿālamīn*). The next verse (Qur'ān 10:38) challenges those who accused the Prophet of fabricating the revelations and prompts Muḥammad to address his detractors thus: "Since you are my peer in Arabic and eloquence, then produce a chapter like [a Qur'ānic chapter] that would equal its eloquence (*al-balāgha*) and its beauty of composition (*ḥusn an-naẓm*).[47] Az-Zamakhsharī concludes from this verse that no one but God could have produced such chapters of unparalleled beauty and eloquence. Those who disbelieved in their divine provenance were simply doing so out of rebellion and obstinacy (*tamarrudan wa ʿinādan*) and by blindly following in the footsteps of their forebears (*taqlīdan lil-abāʾ*).[48]

Ar-Rāzī in the early twelfth/sixth century is more forceful in asserting the miraculous nature of the Qur'ān's composition, particularly in light of the fact that Muḥammad was unlettered (*ummī*) and therefore incapable of producing such a text on his own. He compares Qur'ān 10:37 to Qur'ān 2:23, which similarly challenges the unbelievers to produce a chapter comparable to a Qur'ānic chapter. Ar-Rāzī comments that Qur'ān 2:23 invites the reader to ponder how a man like Muḥammad who had not studied with anyone nor read any books could have acquired the ability and the necessary knowledge to produce a text like the Qur'ānic text. In the face of such inability, the result must be a miracle (*ḥay-*

44 Havemann, Axel/Johansen, Baber (eds), *Gegenwart als Geschichte. Islamwissenschaftliche Studien*, Leiden: Brill, 1988, 67.
45 Aṭ-Ṭabarī, *Tafsīr*, 6:561.
46 Ibid.
47 Az-Zamakhsharī, *Kashshāf*, 3:137.
48 Ibid., 3:137–38.

*thu ẓahara al-ʿajz, ẓahara al-muʿjiz*). The verse suggests not so much that the *sūra* itself is a miracle but rather that the emanation of the Qurʾānic revelation from a man like Muḥammad who was unlettered and unschooled is to be regarded as a miraculous event. However, ar-Rāzī understands Qurʾān 10:37 to be asserting that Qurʾānic chapters in themselves are to be considered a miracle because human beings, however learned and well-trained and reflective, would be utterly incapable of reproducing God's compositional virtuosity.[49]

Ar-Rāzī's more detailed delineation of the concept of the inimitability of the Qurʾān indicates to us that by the twelfth/sixth century this concept had become doctrinally entrenched and widespread. This is corroborated by the fact that already by the tenth/fourth century, a new literary genre focused on the concept of the *iʿjaz al-Qurʾān* makes its appearance and becomes a fairly prolific one thereafter. The Muʿtazilī scholar an-Naẓẓām (ca. 845/230) was one of the first to deal with this topic and to pave the way for more treatises to be written on this topic. In the following century ar-Rummānī (909–994/296–384) composed his *an-Nukat fī iʿjāz al-qurʾān* and al-Khaṭṭābī (b. 931/319) wrote the *Bayān iʿjāz al-qurʾān*. A number of motivating factors may be identified for the emergence of this genre starting in the ninth/third century: 1) as a response to the general Muʿtazilī denial of miracles, a position that was shared by the philosophers; 2) as a challenge to the claim of those later termed Sufis to be able to perform miracles (*karamāt*), and 3) as a reaction to the rise of the Shuʿūbiyya movement spearheaded by non-Arabs, particularly Persians, who asserted their cultural superiority over the Arabs. Against these groups, mainstream Sunnī Arab scholars were compelled to articulate a clearer conception of the Qurʾān as Muḥammad's miracle which was different from the extraordinary feats that some Sufi luminaries claimed to have performed. Thus al-Bāqillānī wrote his *al-Farq bayna al-muʿjizāt wa-ʾl-karamāt* intended to elucidate the differences between these two categories of supernatural acts while others undertook the task of extolling the superiority of the Arabic language over other languages. The brilliant litterateur al-Jāḥiẓ (d. 869/255), although only half-Arab, took up cudgels against the Shuʿūbiyya in an effort to prove this point. Arabic of course was the language of the Qurʾān and therefore defense of the Arabic language led further to an espousal of the unparalleled aesthetic nature of the Qurʾānic text.[50]

There is another development starting in the aftermath of the ʿAbbasid revolution in the middle of the eighth/second century that is of particular interest to

---

**49** Ar-Rāzī, *Tafsīr*, 6:254.

**50** For this discussion, see Vasalou, Sophia, "The Miraculous Eloquence of the Qur'an: General Trajectories and Individual Approaches," *Journal of Qurʾanic Studies* 4 (2002), 23–53.

us since it concerns inter-faith relations. During this period we see the rise of apologetic and polemical writings against Islam on the part of Christian authors, like the Jacobite Ḥabīb b. Khidma Abū Ra'iṭa (d. ca. 851/236), who were alarmed by the prospect of increasing Christian conversions to Islam in the more inclusive society established by the ʿAbbasids.[51] This in turn instigated the writing of polemical treatises by Muslim authors against Christianity, such as the one by the Zaydī imām al-Qāsim b. Ibrāhīm (d. 860/246) and the afore-mentioned al-Jāḥiẓ, both of whom wrote works titled *ar-Radd ʿala an-naṣāra* in the ninth/third century. Needless to say, Christian apologetics focused on the miracles performed by Christ which were regarded as proving the truth of Christianity as opposed to Islam which lacked such authenticating miracles.[52] It is therefore possible to understand a greater Muslim preoccupation with the notion of the inimitability of the Qur'ān as at least a partial response to Christian apologetics in this period.

In the early period, there were two schools of thought regarding the constitution of the *iʿjāz al-Qur'ān*, based on whether their proponents were of the opinion that its inimitability was located within the sacred text itself or subscribed to the view that it emanated from a quality or factor extraneous to it. The well-known scholar of Qur'ānic sciences az-Zarkashī describes these two positions in his *al-Burhān fī ʿulūm al-Qur'ān*. Those who argued for an external impetus tended to be from the Muʿtazila; notably among them was an-Naẓẓām who stated that *iʿjāz* primarily referred to God preventing human beings from acquiring the ability to imitate the Qur'ān (*ṣarf*).[53] The theory of *ṣarfa* coincided to some extent with the Muʿtazilī belief in the created Qur'ān since that would preclude the possibility of continuous divine intervention in the worldly realm.[54]

A greater majority of scholars however drew upon internal textual evidence for establishing the inimitable nature of the Qur'ān, focusing primarily on stylistics and linguistic eloquence. One of the best-known exponents of this school of thought is the afore-mentioned al-Bāqillānī whose *Iʿjāz al-Qur'ān* provides a detailed analysis of this concept and has rightly become famous in literary and Qur'ānic studies. For al-Bāqillānī, the miraculous eloquence of the Qur'ān rests on the stylistic composition of the sacred text (*naẓm al-Qur'ān*) whose excellence does not derive from the usual rhetorical figures associated with *balāgha* (eloquence), such as metaphor, simile, hyperbole, conciseness, and others. Rather,

---

51 Griffith, Sidney, "Habib b. Khidma Abu Ra'itah, a Christian *mutakallim* of the First Abbasid Century," *Oriens Christianus* 64 (1980), 161–201.

52 Watt, Montgomery W., *Formative Period of Islamic Thought*, Edinburgh: Edinburgh University Press, 1973, 179.

53 Az-Zarkashi, *Burhān*, 2:90 ff.

54 Vasalou, "Miraculous Eloquence," 30.

the Qur'ān's inimitable nature is grounded in the fact that its compositional eloquence defies all existing literary forms. In other words, the Qur'ān's literary excellence is *sui generis* and is therefore proof of its miraculous inimitability which in turn points to its divine provenance.[55]

Another well-known work on *iʿjāz al-Qur'ān* is by ʿAbd al-Qāhir al-Jurjānī (d. 1081/474 or 1078/471), whose *Dalā'il iʿjāz al-Qur'ān* has become a classic in the field. Like al-Bāqillānī before him, al-Jurjānī also understands the Qur'ān's inimitability to inhere in its linguistic excellence, the evidence for which can be derived from the text itself. He particularly focuses on the syntactic features of the Qur'ānic text which confer upon it its unique stylistic form (*naẓm*) that cannot be replicated by any human being. This fundamental point is expressed by al-Jurjānī in the following way:

> What is this imposing excellence, this dazzling superiority and wondrous construction that occurred for the first time in the Qur'ān, such that it rendered all creatures, without exception, powerless, overcoming the powers and capabilities of the eloquent and articulate ones and binding notion and thought until the orators like braying he-camels went silent and the utterance of the speakers ceased to be, and until no tongue stirred and no clear speech manifested itself and no power helped and no flint yielded a spark for any of them and the point of no sword penetrated, and until it made the valley overflow upon them with inability and seized from them the outlets of speech forever.[56]

Al-Jurjānī's *Dalā'il* has been praised as a mature literary work that expounds a sophisticated theory of language and meaning in the context of elaborating the doctrine of the inimitability of the Qur'ān. It is also clear from this work that by this period a language-based discussion of the *Iʿjāz al-Qur'ān* could not be divorced from the larger theological issues of the time.[57]

Since the eleventh/fifth century, the inimitability of the Qur'ān – both in terms of its extraordinary content and literary excellence – has become an accepted doctrinal tenet for all Muslims and uniquely defines the Muslim's believer's relation to revelation. The prominent modern Egyptian Muslim scholar and reformer, Muḥammad Abduh (d. 1905), unambiguously articulates the importance of this doctrine in the following manner:

> The matchlessness of the Qur'ān is an actuality beyond the powers of humanity. Its eloquence remained unparalleled. We say deliberately "the powers of humanity." For the

55 Al-Bāqillānī, *Iʿjāz al-Qur'ān*, I.D. A. Haydar (ed.), Beirut, n.d., passim., Vasalou, "Miraculous Eloquence," 33–39.

56 Al-Jurjānī, *Dalā'il al-Qur'ān*, 9, trans. Margaret Larkin, "The Inimitability of the Qur'an. Two Perspectives," *Religion and Literature* 20/1 (1988), 31.

57 Larkin, "Inimitability of the Qur'an," 38 ff.

> Qur'ān came to an Arabic-speaking prophet. Writing was well-known among the Arabs everywhere at that time, to a degree of excellence already described, and in the context of intense hostility already noted. Yet for all that the Arabs quite failed to produce from their whole mental effort anything to oppose to it. It is then irrational to think that some Persian, or Indian or Greek, could have commanded such Arabic skill to achieve what had defeated the Arabs themselves. The powers of the Arabs quite failed them, despite their having comparable origins and education to Muḥammad, and many of them special advantages of science and study. All of this is proof positive that the words of the Qur'ān are in no way the sort of thing to originate from man. No! it was a unique Divine gift to him on whose lips it came. And so its statements about their inability to equal it and its readiness to meet head on all that their skill could contrive are plain proofs of its assurance as to its identity. The speaker is undoubtedly the Lord, who knows the unseen and the visible, and no man preaching and counselling in the ordinary way. This is the conclusion of all the evidences now accumulated, of contents quite impossible to merely human intelligence to sustain for so long. And thus, the great wonder of the Qur'ān is proved.[58]

For ʿAbduh, as for other theologians, the *iʿjāz al-Qurʾān* is an article of faith that underscored more than the aesthetic uniqueness of the sacred text in terms of its style and content – it was a formal and necessary acknowledgement of its miraculous provenance. For believers, revelation is, above all, a unique divine gift to humankind anchored in God's limitless solicitude for His creation.

## 5 The Qur'ān as Primordial Revelation

The Qur'ān's unassailability as scripture is connected with the concept of "the Preserved Tablet" (*al-lawḥ al-maḥfūẓ*) mentioned in the Qur'ān itself: "This is indeed a Glorious Qur'ān (inscribed) in the Preserved Tablet (*al-lawḥ al-maḥfūẓ*) (Qur'ān 85:21–22; cf. 56:77–78). The Qur'ān describes *al-lawḥ al-maḥfūẓ* as having everything – small and big – recorded in it (54:53). The Preserved Tablet is described elsewhere in the Qur'ān as *umm al-kitāb* ("the source of scriptural revelation"; cf. Qur'ān 13:39). According to aṭ-Ṭabarī, early exegetes like Mujāhid b. Jabr understood these terms to be identical.[59] Divine revelation is based on this celestial archetype, on account of which it is "protected from alteration and falsification," says aṭ-Ṭabarī.[60]

In extra-Qur'ānic literature, the process of revelation is often described as having taken place in three stages. Some scholars mention that in the first

**58** ʿAbduh, Muḥammad, *The Theology of Unity*, trans. Ishaq Musaʾad and Kenneth Cragg, London: George Allen and Unwin Ltd., 1966, 121.

**59** Aṭ-Ṭabarī, *Tafsīr*, 12:531.

**60** Ibid.

stage, the Qur'ān, the word of God, was written on the Preserved Tablet in the celestial realm. In the second stage God revealed the entire Qur'ān from the Preserved Tablet to the lower heavens, in a place called "The House of Majesty" (*Bayt al-ʿizza*). This revelation occurred in Ramadan, on the Night of Decree or Power (*laylat al-qadr*), as referenced in Qur'ān 2:185 which states, "The month of Ramadan is the month in which the Qur'ān was revealed;" and "We have sent it (the Qur'ān) down, on a Blessed Night" (Qur'ān 44:3). The Qur'ān later specifies this Blessed Night as "the Night of Decree/Power" (97:1).

The third stage represents the final stage of revelation when Gabriel brought those portions of the Qur'ān which God commanded him to bring to the Prophet Muḥammad. This gradual revelation occurred over a period of twenty-three years.[61] Primarily oral in nature during the lifetime of the Prophet, the revelation was also written down on pieces of bark or parchment, and other writing materials at hand, as the traditional sources inform us. The final codification of the Qur'ān would occur during the time of the third Rightly-Guided caliph, ʿUthmān b. ʿAffān (d. 655/35).[62]

A particular verse – Qur'ān 25:32 – is often invoked in the literature to explain why the Qur'ān was revealed piecemeal over a period of time to the Prophet Muḥammad rather than as a complete text all at once. This verse states, "And those who disbelieve say, 'Why was the Qurʿan not revealed to him all at once?' It is that way so that We may strengthen thereby your heart. And We have recited it in a measured way."

In his brief commentary on Qur'ān 25:32, aṭ-Ṭabarī records the views of a number of exegetes who affirm that this verse establishes the gradual, progressive nature of the Qur'ānic revelation in the course of over twenty years, so that it could be responsive to specific questions asked by people over time. The word *tartīl* ("gradual revelation") is understood to imply both gradualness and precision in reading/recitation. According to other authorities, among them ʿAbd ar-Raḥmān b. Zayd,[63] *tartīl* is glossed as "elucidation and explanation or commentary" (*at-tabyīn wa 't-tafsīr*). This view stresses the simultaneity of exegesis inherent in the act of recitation or reading itself and the importance of measured and

61 As-Suyūṭī, *Itqān*, 1:129 – 134.

62 Al-Aʿẓamī, Muḥammad Muṣṭafā, *The History of the Qur'anic Text. From Revelation to Compilation*, London: UK Islamic Academy, 2003.

63 This is the Successor ʿAbd ar-Raḥmān Ibn Zayd b. Aslam al-ʿAdawī al-Madanī, son of the well-known Companion Zayd b. Aslam, from whom the former transmitted *ḥadīth*s. Ibn Zayd was known to have composed a Qur'ān commentary, which was used by aṭ-Ṭabarī, as well as a work titled *Kitāb an-nāsikh wa-'l-mansūkh*; cf. Sezgin, Fuat, *Geschichte des Arabischen Schrifttums*, Leiden: E.J. Brill, 1967, 1:38.

deliberate reflection on the word of God, establishing a protocol for engaging Scripture.[64]

Az-Zamakhshari comments that in contrast to the three previous scriptures (the Torah, the Psalms and the Gospel, according to Muslim tradition) which came down all at once, the Qur'ān was revealed piecemeal over a period of time. He says that either the Quraysh or the Jews of Medina may have uttered this statement. Az-Zamakhsharī further remarks that it would have made no difference to the Qur'ān's inimitable nature or its cogency as a divine proof-text whether it came down all at once or *seriatim*. It was preferable however for the Qur'ān to come down gradually, he says, because it allowed the Prophet to memorize it more easily, particularly since, unlike the previous messengers, he could neither read nor write. Like aṭ-Ṭabarī, az-Zamakhsharī also emphasizes that the piecemeal revelation of the Qur'ānic verses allowed the Qur'ān to be responsive to specific historical circumstances and to the concerns of the believers, and also allowed for the possibility of the phenomenon of abrogation.[65]

Ar-Rāzī similarly gives several reasons for the gradual revelation of the Qur'ān, one of which is that since Muḥammad could not read nor write, this manner of oral revelation was conducive to memorization and allowed for accurate preservation of the words by the Prophet. This is in contrast to the written Torah which could be transmitted all at once and which the literate Moses could read. Another reason is that if the Qur'ān had been revealed all at once, says ar-Rāzī, then the entire divine law would have been imposed immediately on humans, which would have represented an unusual hardship for them.[66]

As-Suyūṭī similarly states that the phrase "We may strengthen thereby your heart" (*li-nuthabbita bihi fu'ādaka*) was understood by some scholars as referring to facilitating memorization on the part of the Prophet who was unlettered and who would therefore be able to commit to memory the revelation only if it descended *seriatim*. According to other scholars, the Qur'ānic text did not come down all at once because some verses were abrogated while others functioned as abrogating ones.[67]

It is worthy of note that in their understanding of this verse, our classical exegetes and scholars read not only particularity and singularity into the mode of the revelation of the Qur'ān – its piecemeal nature and rootedness in specific historical circumstances – but also affirmation of the finality of the Qur'ānic message and its comprehensiveness at the same time. Ar-Rāzī in particular em-

**64** Aṭ-Ṭabarī, *Tafsīr*, 9:387.
**65** Az-Zamakhsharī, *Kashshāf*, 4:347–48.
**66** Ar-Rāzī, *Tafsīr*, 8:457.
**67** As-Suyūṭī, *Itqān*, 1:134.

phasizes that revelation does not represent an imposition on human beings; so that the manner of the Qurʾānic revelation *ad seriatim* became an expression of divine solicitude for the well-being of human beings that took into consideration the frailty of human intelligence. As such, as God facilitates human receptivity towards revelation and fosters understanding of its content, the achievement of which represents the highest purpose of humankind. This may be understood then as a testament to the universality of the Qurʾānic message because it conforms to the human ability to understand and implement it everywhere and at any time.

## 6 Revelation as a Manifestation of God's Mercy and Justice

The revelation of the Qurʾān to the Prophet Muḥammad continues the process of God's self-disclosure to humanity through His revealed scriptures before the advent of the Qurʾān, as stated in Qurʾān 26:196. A cluster of Qurʾānic verses (4:163 – 65) names the various prophets who were vouchsafed divine revelation prior to Muḥammad:

> We have sent you revelation as we sent it to Noah and the messengers after him: We sent revelation to Abraham and Ismail, Isaac, Jacob and the tribes, to Jesus, Job, Jonah, Aaron, and Solomon, and to David We gave the Psalms. Of some messengers We have already told you the story; of others We have not – and to Moses God spoke directly. Messengers who gave good tidings as well as warnings, that humankind, after (the coming) of the messengers should have no proof against God; for God is Exalted in Power and Wise.

God's communication with humankind through direct revelation to His prophets through time is therefore an act of mercy which provides continual guidance to erring humans by bringing good tidings (*bushrā*) and warnings (*indhār*). It is furthermore a manifestation of his justice towards humanity, who can be held accountable for their deeds in the hereafter precisely because God has revealed his will and his design for creation through his selected emissaries.

In his exegesis of Qurʾān 4:163 – 65, ar-Rāzī stresses this aspect of divine justice and human accountability to God. He comments that in the absence of messengers sent by God, humans would have an excuse to abandon worship of God and obedience to him. He refers to the arguments of the Muʿtazila who had argued on the basis of such verses that God does not act capriciously[68] and that he does not burden human beings beyond what they can bear.[69]

God is indeed described as just in the Qur'ān (4:40), which is one of his ninety-nine "beautiful names" or epithets. The Qur'ān also states that God has prescribed mercy upon himself (Qur'ān 6:12; 54). Other essential attributes of God – his omniscience, his omnipotence; his generosity, etc. – are divulged in the Qur'ān. It is therefore through revelation that humans become aware of the Divine Being's attributes and which allows them to establish a knowing and loving relationship with him. The two most common names of God – *ar-Raḥmān* and *ar-Raḥīm* – emphasizing his mercy are mentioned in the Qur'ān 57 and 114 times respectively. The frequency of occurrence of these names in revelation conveys to the believer that God's mercy is limitless and envelops all those who sincerely attempt to do good but who inevitably fall short as fallible humans. "O my servants who have transgressed against their souls! Do not despair of the mercy of God: for God forgives all sins: for He is most forgiving and most Merciful," assures the Qur'ān (39:53).

As the bearer of God's message rooted in mercy and justice, Muḥammad himself is also described "as a mercy to all people" (*raḥmatan li-'l-ʿālamīn*) in Qur'ān 21:107. Aṭ-Ṭabarī in his commentary on Qur'ān 21:107 takes this description to be self-explanatory and does not comment on it further.[70] But aṭ-Ṭabarī indicates that the exegetes differed among themselves regarding the meaning of *li-'l-ʿālamīn* (in our translation "to all people") and therefore regarding the universality of the Qur'ānic revelation. Some of the exegetes had apparently questioned whether Muḥammad had been sent to both the believers and the unbelievers while others, like Ibn ʿAbbas, asserted that indeed it was so. ʿAbd ar-Rahmān b. Zayd however had maintained that *al-ʿālamūn* referred only to "those who believed in him [sc. the Prophet] and deemed his message true." Aṭ-Ṭabarī regards Ibn ʿAbbas' exegesis as more plausible and comments that the Prophet Muḥammad was a mercy to both the believers and the unbelievers. In the first instance, the believers were guided to faith and righteous action through the Prophet while in the second, the unbelievers, through his presence among them, were given a reprieve from the divine punishment that had befallen

**68** There is an implicit criticism here of some among the Ash'arites who maintained that God can behave as He wishes.

**69** Ibid., 4:268. Similar reasons are given by Az-Zamakhsharī, *Al-Kashshāf an Ḥaqā'iq ghawāmid at-tanzīl wa 'uyūn al-aqāwīl fī wujūh at-ta'wīl*, ʿĀdil Aḥmad ʿAbd al-Mawjūd and ʿAlī Muḥammad Muʿawwad (eds), Riyadh: Maktabat al-ʿUbaykān, 1998, 2:180.

**70** Aṭ-Ṭabarī, *Tafsīr*, 9:100.

other nations before them.[71] In Ibn ʿAbbās' and Ibn Zayd's differing interpretations as recorded by aṭ-Ṭabarī, we see particularity vying with universality in defining the scope and effect of the prophetic mission of Muḥammad and the scope of the revelation vouchsafed to him. While Ibn Zayd would restrict accessibility to the divine message conveyed by Muḥammad to the salvific community of Muslims alone, Ibn ʿAbbās' interpretation universalizes access to the same message, whose language and content cut across self-consciously erected confessional boundaries and speak, as we might put it today, to a globalizing world.

Az-Zamakhsharī takes it to be self-evident that Muḥammad was sent as a mercy to all people, Muslim and non-Muslim, good and bad. In his brief commentary on Qurʾān 21:107, az-Zamakhsharī maintains that the Prophet came equally to those who followed him willingly and thereby achieved happiness and to those who opposed him and refused to follow him, thereby ruining themselves in the process. In other words, everyone potentially had equal access to Muḥammad or, conversely, the Prophet made himself available to all. The people around him derived benefit – or not – from his presence and his message, according to their individual choices and actions. To better illustrate what he means, az-Zamakhsharī uses the example of a gushing spring which God has caused to spring forth and which is accessible to all. Some people use the water from this spring to irrigate their lands and water their livestock and thus prosper. Others fail to use the spring to water their lands and face financial loss. Despite these different consequences, says az-Zamakhsharī , the spring *qua* spring represents a blessing from God and a mercy to both groups of people. Idle people (*al-kaslān*), he says, are a trial to themselves since they willfully deprive themselves of a beneficial thing. Muḥammad is a source of mercy even to the morally reprobate (*al-fujjār)*, he stresses, because their punishment is averted by his presence in their midst and he grants them protection from being destroyed.[72]

Ar-Rāzī comments extensively on how and why the Prophet Muḥammad constituted, as he phrases it, "a mercy in religion and in the world". In brief, ar-Rāzī comments that at the time of his prophetic mission, the people in general lived in ignorance and error, and even the People of the Book were in despair and divided among themselves. Muḥammad summoned the people to the truth, showed them the path of salvation, and promulgated laws which clearly distinguished between what is licit and illicit. Although prior nations were destroyed for refusing to obey their prophets, ar-Rāzī references another verse, Qurʾān 8:33, which

**71** Ibid., 9:101.
**72** Az-Zamakhsharī, *Kashshāf*, 4:170.

states, "God would not punish them while you [i.e. the Prophet] are among them." Like his predecessors, ar-Rāzī therefore stresses that the Prophet's presence among the unbelievers had warded off divine retribution against them. Like aṭ-Ṭabarī, ar-Rāzī disagrees with Ibn Zayd that the Prophet was sent as a mercy only to the believers and affirms instead that his mercy extended to all. He cites a *ḥadīth* related by Abū Hurayra in which he [sc. Abū Hurayra] implores Muḥammad to inveigh against the polytheists, but the Prophet replies, "Indeed I was sent as a [source of] mercy and not as [a source of] affliction."[73]

In the discussion of all three exegetes above, mercy and compassion render Muḥammad's mission and legacy eminently pleasing and accessible to all and endows the revelation given to him with an enduring universality. God's imposition of mercy upon Himself and upon His Apostle is clearly articulated in the Qur'ānic revelation and invites humanity to find hope in this aspect of divine self-disclosure.

## 7 Revelation as a Message of Hope and Guidance to All Humanity

Revelation is described several times in the Qur'ān as a message (*risāla*) or messages (*risālāt)* from the universal God to all humanity conveyed by his various prophets through time. Although this message is fundamentally the same, it is also particularized by time and place. In Qur'ān 7:79, the prophet Ṣāliḥ affirms to his erring community "O my people, I have indeed conveyed to you the message of my Lord and offered you advice but you do not like advisors." Similarly, Noah tells his people, "I convey to you the messages of my Lord and advise you; and I know from God what you do not know (Qur'ān 7:62).

The Prophet Muḥammad is exhorted by the Qur'ān (72:23–24) to say to his community: "Indeed, there will never protect me from God anyone [if I should disobey], nor will I find in other than Him a refuge. I have for you but only messages from God, and His messages" (*risālāt*). The transmission of these messages is the primary aspect of Muḥammad's role as prophet, as it was of the prophets who preceded him, a role which the Qur'ān praises and affirms. "God praises those who convey the messages of God and fear Him and do not fear anyone but God. And sufficient is God as a reckoner" (Qur'ān 33:39).

In the context of this understanding of revelation as a message from God that is conveyed in verbal form to its recipient, the Qur'ān further refers to itself

73 Ar-Rāzī, *Tafsīr*, 8:193.

as "weighty speech" (73:5) and as "the word of God" (*kalām allāh*, Qur'ān 2:75; 9:6; 48:15), in addition to *tanzīl*, as mentioned earlier. The Qur'ān also refers to itself in several places as scripture or book – *kitāb* – which parallels previous revelations given to various apostles through time. Revelations given to Abraham and Moses are described as being preserved in scrolls (*ṣuḥuf*; cf. Qur'ān 87:19; 53:36–37). In all these revelations there is guidance for humanity, which the Qur'ān in turn confirms. Qur'ān 5:46 says:

> We caused Jesus, son of Mary, to follow in their footsteps, confirming what was before him, and We bestowed on him the Gospel in which there is guidance and light, confirming that which was before it in the Torah – a guidance and a reminder to those who are careful.

The Qur'ān in fact instructs the Prophet Muḥammad to declare to his listeners that Muslims must believe in the prior revelations vouchsafed to God's messengers who are equally righteous and blameless. The equality of God's messengers is a recurrent theme in the Qur'ān and in the Islamic tradition, even though a number of medieval Muslim theologians went on to articulate a doctrine of supersessionism vis-á-vis the Jewish and Christian scriptures, in explicit defiance of verses such as Qur'ān 3:84:

> Say: We believe in God and what is revealed to us and what was revealed to Abraham and Ishmael and Isaac and Jacob and the tribes, and what was entrusted to Moses and Jesus and the prophets from their Lord. We make no distinction between any of them, and to Him we have surrendered.

The Qur'ān further asserts that all the prophets submitted to a similar covenant with God and they proclaim the same essential message. The sectarian divisiveness among humans is a result of their faulty understanding over time of the divine eternal message that was faithfully conveyed by all of God's apostles. Thus Qur'ān 33:7–8 states:

> And when We exacted a covenant from the Prophets, and from you (O Muḥammad) and from Noah and Abraham and Moses and Jesus, son of Mary – We took from them a solemn covenant; that He may ask the loyal of their loyalty. And He has prepared a painful doom for the unfaithful.

And again, Qur'ān 42:13 states,

> He has ordained for you that religion which He commended to Noah, and that which We inspire in you (referring to Muḥammad), and that which We commended to Abraham and Moses and Jesus, saying, "Establish the religion and do not be divided in it."

The prophets are therefore innocent of the theological wrangling that ensued among their followers and the Qur'ān affirms that there is no fundamental disjunction between the Judeo-Christian revelation and the Islamic one.

In formal doctrinal explanations, the different aspects of the Qur'ān as heavenly revelation and its liturgical role in communal and individual worship are emphasized. As the popular treatise on Islamic dogma titled *al-Fiqh al-Akbar* attributed to Abū Ḥanīfa (d. 767/150) states, "The Qur'ān is the word of God Almighty (*kalām allāh taʿālā*), transcribed in written copies (*maṣāḥif*), preserved in hearts, recited on tongues, and revealed to the Prophet, peace and blessings be upon him."[74]

Revelation as God's speech and message is not however meant to be passively received by humans but rather to be engaged with spiritually and intellectually. The Qur'ān repeatedly calls on its hearers to use their reason in understanding its revelations. It challenges them to ponder it seriously and reflect on its internal consistency and the truth that it contains. "For had it come from any other source than God, they would have found in it much discrepancy" (Qur'ān 4:82). Moreover, "This is the book in which there is no doubt, [a source of] guidance to the God-fearing" (Qur'ān 2:2). Since the primary function of the Qur'ān is to guide humankind to God and the Good, its message must be understood, contemplated upon, and implemented in one's life.

To provide guidance for humanity, the Qur'ān contains detailed moral and legal precepts that demarcate what is permissible and what is impermissible for the faithful. It communicates its teachings through parables, similes and metaphors, and admonitions. It recounts stories of bygone nations and their prophets and the examples one may learn from their history. The Qur'ān announces divine promises to the righteous of the bliss of Paradise, and threats to the wrong-doers of punishment in hell. The Qur'ān furthermore establishes for the believing community specific religious obligations (*farā'iḍ*) which include prayer, almsgiving, fasting during the month of Ramaḍān, undertaking the pilgrimage (*ḥajj*) to the Kaʿba in Mecca if one is financially and physically capable, and in general striving in the path of God (*al-jihād fī sabīl allāh*) to better oneself and the society around them.

One of the persistent messages contained within the Qur'ān is that good must eventually triumph over evil. Revelation serves the purpose of reiterating this message to humanity through time and thus keep hope alive in the final vindication of truth and goodness, especially in times of despair. The Qur'ān there-

---

74 Abū Ḥanīfa, *al-Fiqh al-Akbar*, 4; available online at: www.mailofislam.com/uploads/Al-Fiqh_Al-Akbar.pdf (last accessed Nov 4, 2019).

fore frequently refers to earlier prophets and their role in the construction of this salvational history centered on hope. As the well-known modern scholar of Islam Fazlur Rahman ably phrased it.

> It is because of this basic line of thought concerning the final victory of good over evil that the Qur'ān refers constantly to the vindication of Noah, who was saved from the flood; of Abraham, who was saved from fire; of Moses, who was saved from Pharaoh and his hordes; and of Jesus, who was saved from execution at the hands of the Jews (hence the rejection by the Qur'ān of the crucifixion story). Muḥammad must equally be vindicated; he will not only be saved but his Message will be victorious. Hence he must proclaim the Message loudly and without reservations – even though he is by temperament a reserved and withdrawn person and the Message is revolutionary: "Proclaim loudly what you are commanded and become indifferent to [the machinations of] those who assign partner to God" (15:94).[75]

The message vouchsafed through revelation must above all be made known and heard and acted upon by humanity. Despite the perilous circumstances in which believers are called upon to receive the divine message and implement it in their lives, the Qur'ān assures them that success (*al-falāḥ*) and deliverance (*an-najāḥ*) awaits them, if not in this world, then certainly in the hereafter.

## 8 Revelation as Reminder: *Fiṭra* and Intrinsic Human Dignity

In chapter 41, the 42nd verse refers to the Qur'ānic revelation as a "reminder" (*dhikr/dhikra/tadhkira*), which is another important aspect of the God-human relationship. This reminder is sent by God as a sign of his inexhaustible mercy for erring humanity, who are urged to mend their ways and restore their relationship with the Almighty so as to be guided on the straight path. "And is it not enough for them that We have sent down to you the Book Which is rehearsed to them? Verily, in it is mercy and a reminder to those who believe" (Qur'ān 29:51).

And again, "And indeed, it is a reminder (*tadhkira*) for the righteous." (Qur'ān 69:48); "Then do you wonder that there has come to you a reminder (*dhikr*) from your Lord through a man from among you, that he may warn you and that you may fear God so you might receive mercy?" (Qur'ān 7:63). In his commentary on Qur'ān 69:48, aṭ-Ṭabarī says that "a reminder" is a reference to the Qur'ān which provides counsel and admonition for the righteous, who

---

75 Rahman, Fazlur, *Major Themes of the Qur'an*, Minneapolis: Biblioteca Islamica, 1989, 87.

avert God's punishment by carrying out his commands and refrain from disobeying Him.[76]

Revelation as a "reminder" may be fruitfully connected with the concept of *fiṭra* – which may be defined as a natural predisposition inspired in all human beings by God (as referenced above) that serves as an instinctive moral compass. This inborn nature predisposes humans towards belief in the one God and allows them to discern between good and evil. Qur'ān 30:30 states, "Observe religion in sincerity (*ḥanīfan*) which is the nature created by God upon which He created humankind (*faṭara an-nās*). There is no changing the creation of God. That is the right religion (*dīn*) but most people know not."

On account of this primordial disposition, humans are born with the need and desire to worship the one God. However, humans are often forgetful and as they advance through life, lose touch with their *fitra* and adopt blameworthy ways. Out of solicitude for humankind, God sends His prophets with revelation to remind human beings of their essential disposition and to exhort them to revert to their true nature. The Qur'ān stresses that the prophets and divine revelation only remind; humans have a choice in complying with this reminder: "Surely, this is a reminder (*tadhkira*); so whoever wills, let him make his way to his Lord." (Qur'ān 76:29). Failure to heed God's reminder however results in oppressing oneself for one cannot fully realize one's true potential as a human being. "Who is more of an oppressor [to one's self] than the one who is reminded by the verses of his Lord but turns away from them and forgets what his hands have sent on?" (Qur'ān 18:57)

Ar-Rāzī in his commentary on Qur'ān 76:29 says that Chapter 76 – with all that it contains of ordered symmetrical language and exquisite locutions, of exhortations and admonitions – serves as a reminder for those who reflect and provides insight to those who are perspicacious. So whoever wishes benefit for his soul in this world and in the hereafter will wend his way towards God, which means that he will seek to draw closer to Him.[77]

The universal significance of the Qur'ānic revelation finds quintessential expression in Qur'ān 38:87; in this verse the Qur'ān is described as "only a warning or reminder (*dhikr*) for all creation." In his very brief commentary on this verse, aṭ-Ṭabarī remarks that the Prophet was asked to assert before the Meccan polytheists that the Qur'ān was a reminder from God and that "all creation" referred

**76** Aṭ-Ṭabarī, *Tafsīr*, 12:224.
**77** Ar-Rāzī, *Tafsīr*, 10:761.

to humans and the jinn, who by virtue of their faith could save themselves from perdition.[78]

In his even briefer commentary, az-Zamakhsharī simply says that the verse refers to the Qur'ān as a reminder from God.[79]

Ar-Rāzī understands *dhikr* in relation to the Qur'ān as that which prompts "every sound mind and upright disposition" to attest to the truth and majesty of the divine law (*ash-sharīʿa*) and avoid what is false and corrupt.[80] This verse has a variant in Qur'ān 6:90 where the Qur'ān is described as "a reminder to all creation", which ar-Rāzī understands to be an affirmation that Muḥammad was "sent to all the people of the world," and not to any specific group of people to the exception of another.[81]

Ultimately, the Qur'ān explains, our fundamental humanness fashioned by a common Creator is what endows us with intrinsic dignity and makes us the equal of one another. This is unambiguously proclaimed in Qur'ān: "We have honored (all) the children of Adam with innate dignity (*karāma*); and provided them with transportation on both land and sea; and given them sustenance from the good and pure things in life; and favored them far above most of those We have created."

This distinctive Islamic concept of human dignity is furthermore illustrated in Qur'ān 32:9 which states: "[God] fashioned [the human being] in due proportion, and breathed into him something of His spirit (*wa nafakha fīhī min rūḥih*). Then He endowed you with [the faculties of] hearing and sight and feeling [and understanding]: but little thanks do you give!"

From this Qur'ānic perspective, living in this world with dignity for all – regardless of whether they are Muslim or non-Muslim, male or female, adult or child, rich or poor – should be a fundamental objective of the rightly-ordered society. Every human being has exactly the same intrinsic worth since each carries the divine breath within them. Revelation is a reminder of this fundamental truth and prods the human conscience into acknowledging and implementing the rights that accrue to every individual as a consequence of this divinely-mandated equality.

**78** Aṭ-Ṭabarī, *Tafsīr*, 10:608.

**79** Az-Zamakhsharī, *Kashshāf*, 5:285.

**80** Ar-Rāzī, *Tafsīr*, 9:416–17.

**81** Ibid., 5:58.

# 9 Revelation as Mediation of the Tension between Inclusivism and Exclusivism

The Qur'ān (3:84) directs Muslims to say:

> We have believed in God and in what was revealed to us and what was revealed to Abraham, Ishmael, Isaac, Jacob, and the Descendants, and in what was given to Moses and Jesus and to the prophets from their Lord. We make no distinction between any of them, and we are Muslims [submitting] to Him.

This verse appears to stand in tension with the very next verse which declares, "And whoever desires a religion other than Islam – never will it be accepted from him, and he, in the Hereafter, will be among the losers."

The well-known scholar of Islam Abdulaziz Sachedina addresses this tension by pointing to the contested interpretation of "islam" in Qur'ān 3:85 focused on the following question – does it refer to specifically the historical religion associated with the Prophet Muḥammad or does it refer in general to the "submission/surrender" of all believers to the one God, which is the word's basic meaning? Sachedina subscribes to the latter interpretation, which, he points out, accords better with how the Qur'ān itself deploys this term in a number of places. [82]

In corroboration of this inclusivist position, one may look at Qur'ān 3:67 which states,

> Abraham was neither a Jew nor a Christian, but he was one inclining toward truth, a Muslim [a person who submits to God]. He was not one of the polytheists." Another verse, Qur'ān 2:133 underscores the broader, generic meaning of *islam:* "When death approached Jacob, he said to his sons, 'Who will (you) worship after I am gone?' They answered, 'We will worship your God, the God of our forefathers, Abraham, Ishmael, Isaac, the One God. We will surrender ourselves unto Him (*muslimūn*).'

These and other similar verses clearly establish that *islām*/*muslim* is used in the Qur'ān frequently in the broadest sense of righteous believers who have surrendered to God, which impacts our understanding of Qur'ān 3:85. Most exegetes in the pre-modern period however understood this verse to have abrogated or superseded other verses that speak highly of righteous Jews and Christians and which extend to them the same salvific promise extended to Muslims (cf.

---

**82** Sachedina, Abdulaziz, *The Islamic Roots of Democratic Pluralism*, Oxford: Oxford University Press, 2001, 39, 44, and passim.

Qur'ān 2:62; 5:69). Abrogation (*naskh*) in fact became the preferred hermeneutical tool of exclusivist exegetes who wished to restrict salvation to Muslims alone and read such views back into scripture. The rich exegetical literature on the Qur'ān (*tafsīr*) sometimes indicates to us that inclusivist views vied with more exclusivist ones in Islam's formative period as Muslims struggled to articulate a communal identity in the multi-religious environment that they found themselves in. The process of identity formation that consequently ensued can be recuperated to some extent by undertaking a diachronic survey of the exegeses of two key Qur'ānic verses that describe a righteous faction among the People of the Book in highly positive terms.

The first of these verses is Qur'ān 5:66 which states:

> If they [sc. The People of the Book] had upheld the Torah and the Gospel and what was sent down to them from their Lord, they would have been given abundance from above and from below. Some of them constitute a balanced community (*umma muqtaṣida*), but many of them are prone to wrong-doing.

The literal meaning of the Qur'ānic term *umma muqtaṣida* used to describe a righteous contingent from among the People of the Book is "a balanced" or "moderate community/nation." In his commentary on this term, the eighth century exegete Muqātil b. Sulaymān (d. 767/150) says it refers to "a group (*'asaba*) of believers from among the people of the Torah and the Gospel who are just (*'adila*) in their speech." Among this group of Jews were 'Abd Allāh b. Salām (d. ca. 663/43) and his companions while the Christians "who had adhered to the religion of Jesus, the son of Mary (peace and blessings be upon him)" were comprised of thirty two men. Muqātil thus clearly understands *umma muqtaṣida* to refer to specific Jews and Christians who responded positively to the mission of the Prophet Muḥammad and embraced Islam.[83]

In the Qur'ān commentary attributed to Ibn 'Abbās known as the *Tanwīr al-miqbās*, *umma muqtaṣida* is glossed as referring to a just and upright group from among the People of the Book. This group included 'Abd Allāh b. Salām and his companions; Buḥayra the monk and his companions; the Negus, the king of Abyssinia; and Salmān al-Fārisī and his companions.[84] In comparison with the list of "moderate Jews and Christians" provided by Muqātil, this list includes Buḥayra and the Negus, who are not known to have converted to Islam (although some have speculated that the Negus had secretly accepted Islam). In this possibly quite early exegesis (if its attribution to Ibn 'Abbās is accepted), *umma*

**83** Muqātil, *Tafsīr*, 1:491.
**84** *Tanwīr al-miqbās*, 128.

*muqtaṣida* includes Christians who are popularly known to have been exceptionally well disposed towards Islam, some of whom had actively aided Muslims in their time of dire need, as the Negus did, and who recognized their scriptural kinship to Muslims without converting, like Buḥayra.

Aṭ-Ṭabarī understands *umma muqtaṣida* to refer to those People of the Book who are "moderate in their speech regarding Jesus, son of Mary, speaking the truth about him that he is the Messenger of God and His word which He cast into Mary and a spirit from Him," and not exceeding the bounds by saying that he was the son of God nor being remiss in saying that he lacked divine guidance. The rest of the Jews and Christians, and they are in the majority, err in not believing in the prophetic mission of Muḥammad and in claiming that the Messiah was the son of God in the case of Christians and in rejecting both Jesus and Muḥammad in the case of Jews."[85]

As he is wont to do, aṭ-Ṭabarī provides attestations for these exegetical understandings. Thus, according to one chain of transmission, the late first/seventh century exegete Mujāhid is quoted as glossing *umma muqtaṣida* as "those who had submitted (*muslima*) from among the People of the Book." Here submission however does not mean specifically accepting Islam as one's religion but rather submitting to God.[86]

A Companion report (that is, a report going back to an associate of Muḥammad only, not to the Prophet himself) from Qatāda explains "a moderate community" as referring to those from among the People of the Book who "abide by His book and His command," while the rest, the majority, who do not are criticized in the Qur'ān for their wrong-doing. A very early exegete as-Suddī (d. 745/128) is quoted by aṭ-Ṭabarī as equating "a moderate community" with "a believing (*mu'mina*) community." Ibn Zayd, another early authority, says that *umma muqtaṣida* referred to people who were known for their obedience to God (*ahl ṭa'āt allāh*), "and these are the People of the Book."[87] Finally, ar-Rabī' b. Anas is cited as saying that *umma muqtaṣida* referred broadly to "those who are neither harsh nor excessive in their religion."[88] These specific glosses going back to early authorities, as recorded by aṭ-Ṭabarī, recognize and praise moderation among observant Jews and Christians who are true to their own scripture and laws and who are thus obedient to God.

---

**85** Aṭ-Ṭabarī, *Tafsīr*, 4:645–646.

**86** Ibid., 4:646.

**87** Ibid.

**88** Ibid.

In his exegesis of Qur'ān 5:66, Fakhr ad-Dīn ar-Rāzī defines *al-iqtiṣād*, which is related to the adjective *muqtaṣida*, as "moderation" or "judicious balance" (*al-i'tidāl*) in one's deeds that avoids both excess (*ghulūw*) and a falling short of something (*taqsir*). As regards the term *al-umma al-muqtaṣida*, ar-Rāzī points to two schools of thought on this issue. One of them regards only those who believed from among the People of the Book, such as 'Abd Allāh b. Salām from among the Jews and the Negus[89] from among the Christians, as belonging to the *umma muqtaṣida*. The other school, however, was of the opinion that *umma muqtaṣida* referred to practicing Jews and Christians who are just (*'udūlan*) and upright in their religion and are not exceedingly stubborn nor harsh in their behavior. Ar-Rāzī points out that praise for upright scriptuaries is found elsewhere in the Qur'ān, as in 3:75, which states, "There are those among the People of the Book who, if you were to give them a coin for safekeeping, they would return it to you."[90] Jews and Christians are thus equally capable of being just and honest and such a trustworthy contingent among them also deserves the epithet *al-muqtaṣida*, according to this school of thought.

In his brief commentary on the meaning of *al-muqtaṣida*, al-Qurṭubī (d. 1273/671) echoes the views of many of his predecessors. Like ar-Rāzī, he too identifies two strands of thinking on this issue. One, to which al-Qurṭubī himself subscribes, was of the opinion that this phrase refers to "believers" (*al-mu'minūn*) such as the Negus, Salmān al-Fārisī, and 'Abd Allāh b. Salām for "they were temperate (*iqtaṣadū*) and only said in regard to Jesus and Muḥammad, upon them be blessings and peace, what was appropriate of them." Others have understood this phrase to refer to those "who did not believe (*lam yu'minū*) but who did not cause any harm nor did they jeer [sc. at Muslims] – and God knows best." Al-Qurṭubī recognizes as well the application of the principle of *iqtiṣād* primarily in the realm of deeds in addition to theological tenets. *Al-iqtiṣād*, he says, refers to balanced and purposeful judiciousness (*al-i'tidāl*) in one's actions, since *iqtiṣād* is derived from *qaṣad* ("purpose").[91]

In the nineteenth century, Muḥammad 'Abduh echoes many of his pre-modern predecessors in his understanding of *umma muqtaṣida*. He says that the phrase refers to a "contingent of people who are moderate and upright in matters of religion" (*jamā'a mu'tadila fī amr ad-dīn*), who are neither extreme nor deficient in the practice of their faith. Some believed that this moderate contingent referred to upright (*'udūl*) Jews and Christians while others thought that it refer-

---

**89** Here, the Negus is clearly assumed to have formally accepted Islam.

**90** Ar-Rāzī, *Tafsīr*, 4:399.

**91** Al-Qurṭubī, *Jāmi'*, 6:228.

red to those from among the People of the Book who had embraced Islam (*aslamū*). ʿAbduh disagrees with the latter interpretation and understands this verse to affirm that no community or nation has ever lacked a righteous contingent of people who strive to better and elevate their community. Nations are headed for disaster on account of the larger numbers of people who resort to wrong-doing and wreak havoc on earth and the paucity of those who do good. From among this contingent of upright people from various communities who hasten to do good and effect reform, continues ʿAbduh, arise prophets and sages who revive religion at different times in history.[92] ʿAbduh thus does not think that righteousness is confined to the Muslim community alone and that moderateness is an attribute that is a monopoly of the Muslims.[93]

There is also a significant cluster of verses (Qurʾān 3:113–115) which similarly indicates divine approbation for righteous scriptuaries within the Abrahamic tradition:

> They are not [all] the same; among the People of the Book is a community standing [in obedience], reciting the verses of God during periods of the night and prostrating [in prayer]. They believe in God and the Last Day, and they enjoin what is right and forbid what is wrong and hasten to [do] good deeds. And they are an upright community (*umma qāʾima*). And whatever good they do – never will it be removed from them. And God is Knowing of the righteous.

Once again, a diachronic survey of exegetical works discussing this cluster of verses reveals a range of inclusivist and exclusivist views that often reflected the varying historical circumstances of the commentators themselves. The following provides a synopsis of such views.

The earliest exegete in our survey Mujāhid b. Jabr equates *umma qāʾima* with a "just" (*ʿādila*) community and imputes no confessional meaning to the term. This is further corroborated by aṭ-Ṭabarī who preserves this early non-sectarian understanding of the term attributed to Mujāhid. Aṭ-Ṭabarī also refers to the eighth/second century exegete as-Suddī who understood "upright" to mean "obedient" and lists the names of the Successors Qatāda b. Diʿāma and Rabīʿa b. Anas, who are on record as having understood *umma qāʾima* to be a community firmly based upon the book of God and the commandments that it prescribes. These broad glosses indicate that there were early authorities through

**92** Riḍā, *Tafsīr*, 6:381.
**93** See further Afsaruddin, Asma, "The Hermeneutics of Inter-Faith Relations. Retrieving Moderation and Pluralism as Universal Principles in Qurʾanic Exegeses," *Journal of Religious Ethics* 37 (2009), 331–54.

the second, eighth century who maintained that *umma qāʾima* was the description of a righteous contingent of people within Jewish and Christian communities who were distinguished by their sincere faith, prayerfulness, and good deeds.[94] Aṭ-Ṭabarī's own preference for the view that *umma qāʾima* can only refer to Muslims is reflective of an exclusivist tendency that had begun to take hold of Muslim theologians by his time in the late ninth/third century.

In the late twelth/sixth century, ar-Rāzī helpfully preserves the tension between two schools of thought: the first represented by Sufyān ath-Thawrī (ca. 716–778/97–161) and ʿAṭāʾ b. Abī Rabāḥ who recognized piety and righteousness in worshipful Jews and Christians and who further displayed good will toward Muslims. The second was represented by ʿAbd Allāh b. Masʿūd and al-Qaffāl who understood *umma qāʾima* to be a specific reference to a pious contingent of worshippers who pray the night prayer and can therefore only be Muslims (who are regarded as having an exclusive monopoly on prayer at night).[95] Ar-Rāzī's preference for the latter school of thought is telling and reflective of fraught Muslim relations with non-Muslims during the Seljuq period.

In his irenic and inclusive reading of these critical phrases, ʿAbduh in the late nineteenth century however resurrects some of the earliest non-confessional interpretive strands preserved in the commentaries of aṭ-Ṭabarī, ar-Rāzī, and others and goes against the pre-modern exegetical grain through his cogent arguments against the sectarianism displayed by most of his predecessors.[96] It is clear that the idea of the possibility of salvation for practitioners of other monotheistic faiths became quite a threatening idea for most of our pre-modern exegetes. As ʿAbduh notes in his commentary, many pre-modern Muslim commentators for various socio-historical reasons, were unwilling to recognize genuine righteousness in those belonging to other religious traditions, and progressively crafted a more exclusivist theology. Fraught relations with the Byzantines during the Umayyad period and continuing through the Abbasid period, the growing influence of *dhimmī* populations in the urban areas of the Islamic world from the ninth/third century onward; the onset of the Crusades, followed by the Spanish Reconquista and the Mongol attacks from the twelfth/sixth century onward clearly must have left their mark on how Muslims envisioned their relations with non-Muslims in these specific historical contexts. Despite European colonization of his own country, ʿAbduh is however clearly secure in his faith and religious practices to continue to recognize the soteriological potential in Christi-

**94** Aṭ-Ṭabarī, *Tafsīr*, 3:397–406.
**95** Ar-Rāzī, *Tafsīr*, 3:331–332.
**96** Riḍā, *Tafsīr al-Qurʾān*, 4:59.

anity and Judaism, based on what he clearly understands the Qur'ān to be espousing. The possibility of genuine religious pluralism was rather slim in the pre-modern world with its severely demarcated political realms and sectarian identities, and it remains a fraught and debated concept in our own times. ʿAbduh was without doubt much ahead of his time in his embrace of this concept (within an Abrahamic milieu), a concept he saw as naturally emerging through a faithful and holistic reading of the Qur'ān.[97]

## 10 Revelation as Affirmation of Monotheism as Common Ground between Jews, Christians, and Muslims

The following verse (Qur'ān 3:64) has received considerable attention in recent times, the reasons for which will be explained below. Like Qur'ān 29:46, it is also concerned primarily with Muslim relations with Jews and Christians. The verse states,

> Say, O People of the Book, let us come to a common word (*kalimat sawā'*) between us and you that we will not worship but the one God nor ascribe any partner to Him or that any of us should take others as lords besides the one God. If they should turn their backs, say: "Bear witness that we submit to God (*muslimūn*)."

In his brief commentary on this verse, the early Umayyad exegete Muqātil b. Sulaymān glosses the phrase *kalimat sawā'* as "a just word" agreed upon sincerely by Muslims and the People of the Book that they will worship the one God alone and not ascribe partners to him. If they should turn away at that, it means that they have disavowed monotheism; Muslims are instructed in any case to assert that they have submitted to God. However, Muqātil goes on to assert that Qur'ān 6:107 should be regarded as abrogated by Qur'ān 9:5.[98]

Aṭ-Ṭabarī notes that some earlier exegetes believed that the People of the Book mentioned in this verse was an exclusive reference to the Jews of Medina while others thought that it referred specifically to the Christian delegation consisting of about 60 men from Najrān who met with Muḥammad in 631 CE. As an

97 See further my article "The 'Upright Community'. Interpreting the Righteousness and Salvation of the People of the Book in the Qur'ān," in: Josef Meri (ed.), *Jewish-Muslim Relations in Past and Present. A Kaleidoscopic View*, 48–69, Leiden: Brill, 2017.

98 Muqātil, *Tafsīr*, 1:281.

aside, it should be mentioned that according to our sources, the Christians of Najrān were received kindly by the Prophet and allowed to pray in the mosque at Medina over the protests of some. They also concluded a pact with Muḥammad, according to which they were granted full protection of their churches and their possessions in return for the payment of a tribute.[99]

Aṭ-Ṭabarī's own understanding is that the verse refers to both Jews and Christians who are summoned by the Qur'ān to "a word of justice between us and you." The "word of justice" indicates the common belief in the unity of God and "repudiating all other beings as objects of worship except Him." The phrase "that any of us should take others as lords besides the one God" is understood to mean that one should not obey any human in matters which contravene God's commandments nor exalt one another by prostrating before another as one prostrates before God. If they should fail to affirm that, the believers (*al-mu'minūn*) should assert that they are Muslims; that is, that they have surrendered to God.[100]

Az-Zamakhsharī in the twelfth century similarly points to the different interpretations of the People of the Book, variously understood to be a reference to the Christians from Najrān, the Jews of Medina, or to both communities. The Arabic word "*sawā'* refers to what is [deemed] upright by us and you, regarding which the Qur'ān, the Torah, and the Gospel do not differ." The "word" or "statement" is elaborated upon by the verse itself, explains Az-Zamakhsharī: "that we worship none but God and not ascribe partners to Him and that none of us should take others as lords besides the one God." If the People of the Book disregard this summons, he continues, then Muslims are free to assert that only they have truly submitted to God.[101]

Considerable agreement can therefore be noted among pre-modern exegetes until the twelfth century regarding the meaning of *kalimat sawā'* as a "just/equitable statement" that underscores the shared monotheism of Jews, Christians, and Muslims. The verse is further understood to contain an exhortation to the People of the Book to affirm this basic monotheism which characterizes them and to assert, alongside Muslims, that they will continue to believe in the absolute unity of God by refusing to ascribe any partners to Him.

In comparison with this standard commentary on Qur'ān 3:64, ar-Rāzī in the late twelfth century offers us a somewhat refreshingly new reading of this important verse. In summary, he understands this verse to be concerned specifically with the Christians of Najrān, like a number of exegetes before him. Ar-Rāzī com-

**99** See, for example, Lings, Martin, *Muḥammad. His Life Based on the Earliest Sources*, Cambridge, Eng.: Islamic Texts Society, 1995, 302.
**100** Aṭ-Ṭabarī, *Tafsīr*, 3:300–302.
**101** Az-Zamakhsharī, *Kashshāf*, 1:567.

ments that the revelation of this verse occurred after the Prophet had engaged in a vigorous debate with these Christians and had apparently frightened them to a certain extent with the fervor of his arguments and his call for "mutual imprecation" (*al-mubāhala*).[102] Ar-Rāzī comments that it is as if God was saying to Muḥammad in this verse, "Give up this manner of speaking and adopt another which the sound intellect and upright disposition recognizes as speech founded upon fairness and justice (*al-inṣāf*)." Accordingly, the Prophet abandoned disputation with the Christians of Najrān and instead, as the verse exhorted him, summoned them to arrive at a common word or statement based upon fairness between them with no preference shown towards anyone at the expense of the other. The statement is, as given in the verse "that we worship none but God and we do not ascribe partners to Him."[103]

The conciliatory nature of this verse directed towards the Christians of Najrān is indicated by the Arabic appellation *ahl al-kitāb* ("People of the Book") for them, says ar-Rāzī. He says that this is so because it is the best of appellations and the most perfect of titles, for it indicates that the Christians of Najrān were "worthy [*ahlan*] of the Book of God." Its equivalents are the titles conferred upon those who have memorized the Qur'ān, such as in the address, "O the bearer of the Book of God" (*yā ḥāmil kitāb allāh*) and upon the exegete of the Qur'ān, "O commentator upon the Speech of God" (*yā mufassir kalām allāh*). Such sobriquets coined in conjunction with "the Book [of God]" (*al-kitāb/kitāb allāh*) are intended to honor those who are so addressed and to cultivate their good will, and to persuade people to abandon the path of disputation and obstinacy and embark instead on a quest for fairness and just relationships.[104]

The phrase *kalimat sawā'* is further understood by ar-Rāzī to refer to "a word which embodies fairness or equality between us," and no one is accorded any preference. He explains the Arabic word *sawā'* as occurs in the verse as specifically referring to "justice and fairness" (*al-ʿadl wa-l-inṣāf*). Fairness (*al-inṣāf*) furthermore implies equality, says ar-Rāzī, because it implies equal sharing (*niṣf*) and thus avoiding oppressing oneself and others, which involves getting more than your equal share. *Kalima* refers therefore to a word that is just, upright, and egalitarian. The word held in common between Muslims and Christians is a reference to that "we will worship no one but God nor ascribe any partner to Him and not take each other as lords other than God." Ar-Rāzī then goes on to document what he describes as the erroneous beliefs of Christians, partic-

**102** For a quick overview of this event, see the article "Mubāhala" by Werner Schmucker in the *Encyclopaedia of Islam*, second edition, vol. 7 Leiden: Brill, 1991, which centers on Qur'ān 3:61.
**103** Ar-Rāzī, *Tafsīr*, 3:251.
**104** Ibid., 3:252.

ularly their trinitarian conception of God and their tendency to exalt and obey their priests uncritically, which, according to him, seriously undermines their adherence to the "common word." Despite this critique of specific Christian tenets and practices, ar-Rāzī's commentary is remarkable nevertheless for its emphasis on establishing common ground between Muslims and Christians on the basis of Qur'ān 3:64 and for its insistence that such common ground is best established by approaching one another with civility, good will, and respect, forsaking the desire to vanquish the other through harsh or clever arguments.[105]

After him, Ibn Kathīr[106] and the nineteenth century reformer Muḥammad ʿAbduh[107] replicated much of what is stated by ar-Rāzī in their own commentaries on this verse, indicating that ar-Rāzī's views emphasizing respectful and kindly inter-faith dialogue between Muslims and the People of the Book were widely accepted and continued to resonate in diverse locales, even through the fraught Mamluk period marked by the Mongol invasions and the period of European colonization through the early twentieth century.

In a number of academic and popular venues today, a new hermeneutics of interfaith relations that draws upon past exegeses of the Qur'ān often to recast them in a new light is becoming quite evident. According to this modern hermeneutic trend, many verses in the Qur'ān that have a bearing on interfaith relations can be read with fresh eyes today in the context of our own socio-historical circumstances, while yet remaining faithful to their actual wording and semantic landscape. A case in point is provided by the reinterpretation of the Qur'ānic phrase *kalimat sawā'* in Qur'ān 3:64 offered in what has now become known as "the Common Word" statement issued by 138 Muslim scholars and clerics in 2007. The 138 Muslim scholars and leaders who represented the original signatories were deliberately selected to represent all major schools of law and theology within Islam: Sunnī, Shīʿī, including Jaʿfarī (Imāmī or Twelver Shīʿī), Zaydī, and Ismāʿīlī, as well as Ibāḍī (the later peaceful incarnation of the seventh century dissident faction, the Khawārij).[108] The Common Word statement was addressed to Christian religious leaders and communities representing various denominations (with the exclusion initially of the evangelical Protestants) in 2007 and has received considerable attention in religious circles worldwide for drawing attention to the common theological ground between Muslims and Christians. Among the first Christian leaders to respond enthusiastically and in great

---

**105** Ibid., 3:252–53.
**106** Ibn Kathīr, *Tafsīr*, 1:351.
**107** Riḍā, *Tafsīr*, 3:268–71.
**108** For a recent study of the Ibāḍīs, see Hoffman, Valerie J., *The Essentials of Ibadi Islam*, Syracuse/New York: Syracuse University Press, 2012.

detail to this overture was the Reverend Dr. Rowan Williams, Archbishop of Canterbury at the time. The Archbishop in a follow-up official statement released July 14, 2008, described *A Common Word Between Us and You* as "a powerful call to dialogue and collaboration between Christians and Muslims", and that he and his co-religionists "are committed to reflecting and working together, with you and all our human neighbours, with a view both to practical action and service and to a long term dedication to all that will lead to a true common good for human beings before God."[109]

The Common Word statement followed an earlier communiqué issued by Muslim leaders titled "An Open Letter to the Pope," which was generated in response to Pope Benedict's controversial Regensburg Speech in 2006. The 2006 letter provided a response to the Pope's unfortunate and rather inscrutable allegation that Islam was incapable of developing a rational approach to its tenets because of the emphasis on submission to a transcendent God, as opposed to the Christian Trinitarian and immanenist doctrine which allowed humans to draw near to God and therefore presumably predisposed them to rationality. The Pontiff also further intimated that Islam had spread through violence which would then appear to further corroborate the irrationality at its core; such assumed irrationality would foreclose the possibility of having a genuine dialogue with Muslims.[110]

The Common Word statement challenged these rather insular perspectives and stressed instead the two commandments of the love of God and love of the neighbor as providing the basis for meaningful theological engagement to emerge between Christians and Muslims. This common ground does not elide essential theological differences that do exist between the two faith communities but rather accepts these differences as part of a broader ethic of respectful dialogue and peaceful co-existence.

The title *A Common Word Between You and Us* given to the statement reflects a contemporary translation of the Arabic phrase *kalimat sawāʾ* in Qurʾān 3:64, whose pre-modern interpretations we discussed above. The phrase in turn was further amplified by the Muslim signatories to refer to "love of God and love of neighbor" as the commandment held in common with Christians. The introductory paragraph to the Common Word statement reads as follows:

---

**109** This statement and responses from other Christian leaders and scholars are available at http://www.acommonword.com/category/site/christian-responses/ (last accessed Nov 4, 2019).
**110** The full transcript of his address given at the University of Regensburg, Germany, September 12, 2006 is available at https://epub.uni-regensburg.de/406/1/Papstredeneu.pdf (last accessed Nov 4, 2019).

> Muslims and Christians together make up well over half of the world's population. Without peace and justice between these two religious communities, there can be no meaningful peace in the world. The future of the world depends on peace between Muslims and Christians.
>
> The basis for this peace and understanding already exists. It is part of the very foundational principles of both faiths: love of the One God, and love of the neighbour. These principles are found over and over again in the sacred texts of Islam and Christianity. The Unity of God, the necessity of love for Him, and the necessity of love of the neighbour is thus the common ground between Islam and Christianity.[111]

As we recall, all the exegetes we surveyed earlier with regard to the phrase *kalimat sawāʾ* are in agreement that it is primarily and broadly a reference to "a word of justice;" a locution which in itself is open to interpretation. Justice is variously interpreted as "sincerity" by Muqatil, as "upright" and an assertion of the oneness of God by aṭ-Ṭabarī and Az-Zamakhsharī ; as "fair" and "equitable" by ar-Rāzī, Ibn Kathīr, and Muḥammad ʿAbduh. With interpretive creativity, the signatories to the Common Word statement may be regarded as having distilled these various significations of justice into the pithy commandment "Love God and your neighbor." What after all could be more upright, sincere, just, and common than this commandment which resonates immediately with Abrahamic communities, and reaching even further, with all religious and ethical people? Such interpretive discernment in the context of dialogue is born of deep reflection on the whys and wherefores of inter-faith encounters and existential necessity.

The Common Word statement ultimately appeals to the central role that revelation plays in Christian-Muslim relations, for the common ground that it seeks is believed to be grounded in a higher authority that transcends the human propensity to be fractious and self-aggrandizing.[112]

---

**111** The full text is available at http://www.acommonword.com/the-acw-document/ (last accessed Nov 4, 2019).

**112** In the wake of its proclamation in 2007, the Common Word statement has led to three high-level meetings between Muslim and Christian religious leaders, academics and inter-faith activists. The first was held at the Yale Divinity School in July, 2008, where Muslim and primarily Protestant theologians discussed at length the two themes of the Common Word statement. A highly significant letter which articulated a very favorable response to the statement following this meeting was signed by three hundred prominent Protestant theologians and scholars and subsequently published in the *New York Times*. The second meeting was hosted by the University of Cambridge in October, 2008 which culminated in a meeting with the Archbishop of Canterbury in London. The third high-level meeting took place at the Vatican in Rome on November 4–6, 2008 between 60 Muslim and Catholic scholars and religious leaders, which was constituted as the first Seminar of the Catholic-Muslim Forum that continues till today. Since 2008, sev-

## 11 Conclusion

Revelation is a powerful key concept within Islam that underscores the centrality of divine communication with humankind through special emissaries. Revelation provides divine guidance to constantly-erring human beings who however can restore their rightful relationship with their Creator through a covenantal relationship based on gratitude and devotion to him as commanded by Scripture. Revelation conveys God's message, unchanging at its core, to humans who are consequently required to reflect on it, interpret it and implement it in their lives and communities. Revelation is a manifestation of God's limitless justice and mercy towards humankind; for it is through his self-disclosure and proclamation of his design that humanity is prodded to reach its fullest potential on earth. Revelation is multivalent – encoded in scripture, its text can be read and reread, parsed and re-parsed in changing contexts by the reader.

Revelation is about choices to be made by humans in relation to their Creator. Although free to choose between belief and unbelief, good and evil, revelation reminds that these choices have consequences, both in this world and the next. Revelation can foment dissension when later revelations are understood to supersede or abrogate the prior ones and/or when revelation is understood to confer a privileged status on the recipient community to the exclusion of all others. The tension between inclusivism and exclusivism remains palpable to our day and represents an intractable problem that is perhaps not about to dissipate soon.

In the contemporary period, scholars and practitioners from the Abrahamic communities are however increasingly making the case that revelation is a divine gift that is meant to bring us together rather than divide. Rereading of revealed scripture through such a lens can reveal more common ground than not. The Common Word initiative represents one of the most significant and noteworthy rereadings of scripture in recent times that has generated considerable good will and reciprocity on the part of Christian scholars to whom it was directed by Muslim theologians and can be regarded as a beacon of hope – however fragile – in our very fractious times.

Ultimately therefore, revelation may be regarded as a divine phenomenon that is meant to bring us together, for revelation underscores our common hu-

eral follow-up meetings have taken place at Georgetown University in Washington DC, as well as spin-off meetings at Oxford University, Heythrop College in London and, most recently, at Mater Dei University in Dublin, Ireland (2013).

manity and the dignity that has been afforded us by God, especially as recipients of his communication.

# Bibliography

Abbott, Nabia, *Studies in Arabic Literary Papyri. Historical Texts*, Chicago: University of Chicago Press, 1957.

ʿAbduh, Muḥammad, *The Theology of Unity*, trans. Ishaq Musaʾad and Kenneth Cragg, London: George Allen and Unwin Ltd., 1966.

Abū Ḥanīfa, *al-Fiqh al-Akbar*, 4; www.mailofislam.com/uploads/Al-Fiqh_Al-Akbar.pdf (last accessed Nov 4, 2019).

*A Common Word Between Us and You*, http://www.acommonword.com/the-acw-document/; (last accessed Nov 4, 2019).

Afsaruddin, Asma, *Contemporary Issues in Islam*, Edinburgh: Edinburgh University Press, 2015.

Afsaruddin, Asma, "The Excellences of the Qurʾān. Textual Sacrality and the Organization of Early Islamic Society," *Journal of the American Oriental Society* 122:1 (2002), 1–24.

Afsaruddin, Asma, *Excellence and Precedence, Islamic Discourse on Legitimate Leadership*, Leiden: E. J. Brill, 2002.

Afsaruddin, Asma, "The 'Upright Community.' Interpreting the Righteousness and Salvation of the People of the Book in the Qurʾān," in: Josef Meri (ed.), *Jewish-Muslim Relations in Past and Present. A Kaleidoscopic View*, 48–69, Leiden: Brill, 2017.

Ayoub, Mahmoud, "History of the Qurʾan and the Qurʾan in History," *The Muslim World* (2014), 429–441.

Al-Aʿẓamī, Muḥammad Muṣṭafā, *The History of the Qurʾanic Text, From Revelation to Compilation*, London: UK Islamic Academy, 2003.

Al-Baʿalbakkī, Fakhr ad-Dīn, *Mukhtaṣar Tibyān*, Ms. Leiden University Library, OR 1525.

Al-Bāqillānī, *Iʿjāz al-Qurʾān*, I.D. A. (ed.) Haydar, Beirut, n.d.

Benedikt XVI., *Glaube, Vernunft und Universität. Erinnerungen und Reflexionen*, https://epub.uni-regensburg.de/406/1/Papstredeneu.pdf (last accessed Nov 4, 2019).

Blois, F.C. De, "Zindīḳ," in: P. Bearman et al. (eds), *Encyclopaedia of Islam, Second Edition*, http://referenceworks.brillonline.com/entries/encyclopaedia-of-islam-2/zindik-COM_1389?s.num=1&s.au=Blois%2C+F.C.+De (accessed Nov 4, 2019).

Al-Bukhārī, *Ṣaḥīḥ*, Qāsim ash-Shammāʿī ar-Rifāʿī (ed.), Beirut: Dār al-qalam, n.d.

Al-Ghazali, *The Jewels of the Qurʾan. Al-Ghazali's Theory*, trans. Muhammad Abu al-Quasem, Kuala Lumpur: University of Malaya Press, 1977.

Graham, William A., *Beyond the Written Word, Oral Aspects of Scripture in the History of Religion*, Cambridge, Eng.: Cambridge University Press, 1993.

Graham, William A., "The Qurʾan as Spoken Word. An Islamic Contribution to the Understanding of Scripture," in: Richard Martin (ed.), *Approaches to Islam in Religious Studies*, 23–40, Tucson: University of Arizona Press, 1985.

Griffith, Sidney, "Habib b. Khidma Abu Raʾitah, a Christian *mutakallim* of the First Abbasid Century," *Oriens Christianus* 64 (1980), 161–201.

Havemann, Axel/Johansen, Baber (eds), *Gegenwart als Geschichte. Islamwissenschaftliche Studien*, Leiden: Brill, 1988.

Hoffman, Valerie, *The Essentials of Ibāḍī Islam*, Syracuse/New York: Syracuse University Press, 2012.

Ibn ʿAbbās (attributed), *Tanwīr al-miqbās min tafsīr Ibn ʿAbbās*. Beirut: Dār al-Kutub al-ʿilmiyya, 1992.

Ibn al-Jawzī, *Kitāb al-mawḍū'āt*, ed. ʿAbd ar-Raḥmān Muḥammad ʿUthmān, Medina, 1966–68.

Ibn Kathīr, Ismāʿīl b. ʿUmar, *Tafsīr al-qurʾān al-ʿazīm*, Beirut: Dār al-Jīl, 1990.

Al-Jurjānī, *Dalāʾil al-Qurʾān*, 9, trans. Margaret Larkin, "The Inimitability of the Qurʾan. Two Perspectives," *Religion and Literature* 20/1 (1988), 31–47.

Al-Khaṭīb al-Baghdādī, *Taqyīd al-ʿilm*, Yūsuf al-ʿIshsh (ed.), Beirut, Dār iḥyāʾ as-sunna an-nabawiyya, 1974.

Lings, Martin, *Muḥammad. His Life Based on the Earliest Sources*, Cambridge, Eng.: Islamic Texts Society, 1995.

Messick, Brinkley, *The Calligraphic State. Textual Domination and History in a Muslim Society*, Berkeley: University of California Press, 1993.

Muqātil b. Sulaymān, *Tafsīr Muqātil b. Sulaymān*, ʿAbd Allāh Maḥmūd Shiḥāta (ed.), Beirut: Muʾassasat at-Taʾrīkh al-ʿArabī, 2002.

An-Nasafī, "Sea of Discourse", in: F. E. Peters (ed.), *A Reader on Classical Islam*, 173, Princeton: Princeton University Press, 1994.

Nasr, Seyyed Hossein et al. (eds), *The Study Qurʾan. A New Translation and Commentary*, New York: HarperOne, 2015.

Al-Qurṭubī, *al-Jāmiʿ li-aḥkām al-Qurʾān*, ʻAbd al-Razzāq al-Mahdī (ed.), Beirut: Dār al-kitāb al-ʻarabī, 2001

Ar-Rāzī, Fakhr ad-Dīn, *at-Tafsīr al-kabīr*, Beirut: Dār iḥyāʾ at-turāth al-ʿarabī, 1999.

Riḍā, Rashīd, *Tafsīr al-qurʾān al-ḥakīm*, Beirut: Dār al-Kutub al-ʿilmiyya, 1999.

Sachedina, Abdulaziz, *The Islamic Roots of Democratic Pluralism*, Oxford: Oxford University Press, 2001.

Salem, Elie Adib, *Political Theory and Institutions of the Khawārij*, Baltimore, MD: Johns Hopkins Univ. Press, 1956.

Schmucker, Werner, "Mubāhala," in: *Encyclopaedia of Islam*, second edition, vol. 7, Leiden: Brill, 1991, 276–77.

Sezgin, Fuat, *Geschichte des Arabischen Schrifttums*, Leiden: E.J. Brill, 1967.

As-Suyūṭī, *al-Itqān fī ʿulūm al-qurʾān*, Beirut: Dār ibn Kathīr, 1993.

As-Suyūṭī, *al-Laʾālī ʾl-maṣnūʿa fī l-aḥādīth al-mawḍūʿa*, Beirut, n.d.

Aṭ-Ṭabarī, Muḥammad b. Jarīr, *Tafsīr aṭ-Ṭabarī*, Beirut: Dār al-Kutub al-ʿilmiyya, 1997.

Vasalou, Sophia, "The Miraculous Eloquence of the Qurʾan: General Trajectories and Individual Approaches," *Journal of Qurʾanic Studies* 4 (2002), 23–53.

Watt, W. Montgomery, *Islamic Political Thought*, Edinburgh: Edinburgh University Press, 1968.

Watt, Montgomery W., *The Formative Period of Islamic Thought*, Edinburgh: Edinburgh University Press, 1973.

Az-Zamakhsharī, *al-Kashshāf an Ḥaqāʾiq ghawāmid at-tanzīl wa ʿuyūn al-aqāwīl fī wujūh at-taʾwīl*, ʿĀdil Aḥmad ʿAbd al-Mawjūd and ʿAlī Muḥammad Muʿawwad (eds), Riyadh: Maktabat al-ʿUbaykān, 1998.

Az-Zarkashi, *al-Burhān fī ʿulūm al-Qurʾān*, ed. M.A. F. Ibrahim, Dar Ihya al-Kutub al-ʿArabiyya, 1957–9.

## Suggestions for Further Reading

Arberry, A.J., *Revelation and Reason in Islam*, New York: Routledge, 2008.
Al-Ghazali, *The Principles of the Creed. Book 2 of the Revival of the Religious Sciences*, trans. Khalid Williams, Louisville, KY: Fons Vitae, 2016
Izutsu, Toshihiko, *God and Man in the Qur'ān. Semantics of the Qur'ānic Weltanschauung*, Tokyo: Keio Institute of Cultural Studies, 1964.
Lings, Martin, *Muhammad. His Life Based on the Earliest Sources*, Cambridge, UK: Islamic Texts Society, 1995.
Marshall, David (ed.), *Communicating the Word. Revelation, Translation, and Interpretation in Christianity and Islam*, Washington D.C.: Georgetown University Press, 2011
Michot, Yahya, "Revelation," in: Tim Winter (ed.), *The Cambridge Companion to Classical Islamic Theology*, 181–96, Cambridge: Cambridge University Press, 2008.
Rahman, Fazlur, *Islam*, Chicago: University of Chicago Press, 1979.
Rahman, Fazlur, *Major Themes of the Qur'an*, Minneapolis: Biblioteca Islamica, 1980.
Reinhart, Kevin A., *Before Revelation. The Boundaries of Muslim Moral Thought*, New York: State University of New York Press, 1995.
Tilman, Nagel, *The History of Islamic Thought from Muhammad to the Present*, Princeton: Markus Wiener Publishers, 2009.

Georges Tamer, Katja Thörner and Bertram Schmitz

# Epilogue

## 1 Introduction

Judaism, Christianity and Islam are considered as revelation-based religions: Each one of them emerged out of an event of revelation. All three traditions are centered around texts believed to be products of divine revelation. Even in Christianity, which is based on the incarnation of Jesus Christ, he is held to be the Logos, the revealed Word of God. Besides their belief in the One God as the Creator and the Judge of the Last Judgement, the other fundamental matter of faith that is common between the three religions is their belief in revelation as the cornerstone on which they developed. Without this original act of divine communication none of them would have existed. The very foundational moment of revelation lasts as long as the religion based on it; it is an essential, identity-establishing factor which keeps the religious community alive. Therefore, the community endeavors in the liturgy and other rites to keep the event of revelation activated in its life through perpetual interpretation, representation and recalling. Furthermore, revelation entails normative dimensions which are particularly preserved in the exegetical and legal corpus of each one of these religions. However, do Judaism, Christianity and Islam share the same concept of revelation? How is revelation conceptualized in each one of these religions? Do these conceptions bear similar features as well as differences?

In the following, we will give a concise summary of the concept of revelation in Judaism, Christianity and Islam before we point out clearly, at the end, the points they share and those they differ in.

## 2 The Concept of Revelation from a Jewish Perspective

Revelation is certainly a core principle of Judaism, though one with many aspects, meaning much more than just the revelation of a text. Primarily, revelation is an ongoing process of God's interaction with his creation, uncovering and exploring higher steps and levels of existence. This interpretation includes struggles and uplifting experiences which are laid down in the great narratives of the Hebrew Bible. The culmination is the "Giving of the Torah" on Mount Sinai, with the proclamation of the Ten Commandments; but God does not

https://doi.org/10.1515/9783110476057-005

cease to uphold the discourse with his people. Prophets were sent; and even after the end of the prophetic era, the rabbis were eager to accept and acquire the prophets' former role.

From a linguistic point of view, it has to be stated that Hebrew does not know a direct translation of the term "revelation". In the Hebrew Bible we find a range of verbs – from the verb *g-l-h*, meaning "to uncover" or "to reveal", through *r-ʾa-h*, meaning "to see" to *y-d-ʿa*, meaning "to know" – which represent different approaches to the concept. All these slightly different forms of the concept of revelation are needed in equal amount in order to understand what Judaism means when it speaks about revelation. Revelation here has a sense of unveiling, as well as a visual aspect, which all together lead to an understanding and acceptance of the content of the revelation.

Within this scheme, the Torah stands exclusive. In contrast to the other books of the Hebrew Bible, the Torah is more than just a revealed text; she guarantees continuity and an ongoing revelation for all generations to come. The "Giving of the Torah" is a central act, not just a revelation of God's will, but also the designation of Israel as God's chosen people. By accepting the "Tablets of Stone", Israel voluntarily binds itself to God, like a bride to her bridegroom.

The "Giving of the Torah" was a visible and audible event; the rabbis strongly debated on whether it was in itself a natural event or a supernatural one, surpassing the human capability of understanding. Moreover, it is a matter of discussion if the double revelation – of both a written and an oral Torah – on Mount Sinai contained all and everything and remained a single event, or if God, whose voice "did not cease" (Deut. 5:22), still reveals himself. Jewish thought is not dogmatic about this question. If the double revelation is considered to be a single event, even the prophets are part of it and the temporal dimension completely fades in the assumption that all the generations that follow have been literally "there", together with their ancestors and all Jews at Mount Sinai to experience the "Giving of the Torah."

Another focal point of interest is the content of this revelation and its authority. Two tablets of stone containing the commandments seem to be undoubtable; but the Torah is thought of in such a way that it already contains all its future interpretations and therefore all the sacred texts rabbinic Judaism knows until today. Again, the idea of both a written and an oral Torah remains crucial.

In classical rabbinic understanding, the discussions of the rabbis in Mishna and Talmud are also revealed by God himself. There is a famous story in the Talmud in which Moses wanted to know how the history of the Jewish people will continue. Rabbi Akiba was shown to him teaching in a rabbinic way that was even difficult to understand for Moses himself. At the end of the lesson Moses asked Rabbi Akiba about the fundament of his teaching. He answered: It was given to Moses! According to the rabbinic interpretation it seems to mean, that all the discussions in the Talmud are already included in the Sinai revelation, even the names of the rabbis are mentioned who have different positions. The word of God was once given to the rabbis in ancient times and the "law" itself will not be changed by God evermore, but because it was given to the scholars, they have the responsibility to explain it – and this explanation is also part of the continuous revelation. Therefore, the law was and is fixed and is not fixed at the same time, because God is eternal but nevertheless he is a living God. In this sense, a modern Jewish understanding can argue (in opposition to the orthodox understanding) that the core of law is fixed, but nevertheless it was formed in an ongoing process starting in the Bible itself, continuing in Mishna, Talmud, Responses, Shulchan Aruch and so on, and all this is influenced by God himself on the basis of his revelation.

The Jewish group of the Karaites (Qaraites) has opposed this position from the beginning of the time of the Pharisees and the authority of the rabbis until now. The word "Qaraites" has in the original Arabic the same root as "Qur'ān". Both only accept the written revelation as "word of God" and not any oral tradition given to the Jews.

It is also interesting to see from *whence* the revelation came. Here, Sinai seems to be a cypher, a non-place in a no-man's land, which signifies the condition of the hearts and minds of those who receive the divine revelation. In this, the universal approach of the Torah is again underlined, for it was not given in a specific country which belongs to a specific nation, but in no-man's land so that every nation would have been able to accept it. Accepting the Torah is – according to a *midrash* – more or less an act of free will. In this sense, Sinai in general, and Mount Sinai in particular, are together more than just the place of origin of the Torah. As it is a divine gift, the Torah's roots are to be traced in heaven. Its message is a divine one and, therefore, its origin is God himself; Moses was merely the medium, for he could not possibly bear all the superior knowledge the Torah contains. This leads to a fascinating picture in Jewish thought: As the Torah was sent down from heaven for humanity to accept, it no longer actually *is* in heaven and therefore is now delivered to the hands of humanity. Here, on earth, it is subject to interpretation and to the laws and customs of the rabbis, even to democratic forms of decision making which, in a famous story, even don't allow God himself to surpass the commandments he has once given.

Following the idea of a "revealed" religion throughout the ages, a strong criticism of this idea occurs in the Age of Enlightenment, with its core shift towards reason as an independent source of knowledge. For many leading thinkers of the Enlightenment, Judaism became the archetype of a gloomy, irrational religion, dependent on supernatural theophanies which supersede human understanding and demand obedience even against the *ratio*. Many Jewish thinkers, most influential among them are the *Haskala*-thinkers like Moses Mendelssohn, searched for an answer and a solution to this challenge and tension. Here we encounter Judaism at the crossroads, finding – or, for others, losing – a new relationship with the *Halakha*, and the idea of what it means to be a Jew.

Timeless conceptions such as revelation only *seem* to be abstract. They manifest themselves concrete when they begin to touch the daily life of the individual believer. Modernity forces Jews to rethink the place of revelation, of the Torah, in their lives, and to have a chance to challenge this new alienation threatened by the Enlightenment. Starting with Franz Rosenzweig's, Hermann Cohen's and others' suggestions to reduce religion to a system of ethics, Martin Buber shifted the focus towards the individual encounter of God and humanity in a dialogical procedure, and towards a somewhat universalized revelation. Communication as such remains the overall basic meaning, Judaism being as flexible and dynamic as it was and is. The paradox of the relation between revelation and reason may remain unsolved; however, for all Jews, the Torah offers a means of orientation and a home, that connects the believer to a personal and yet timeless understanding and experience of revelation. This may include a universal approach across the boundaries of religions, yet this universal approach must recognize the limits of both human reasoning and religion to provide answers – for the ever-changing thoughts of humans eventually fail in this task.

## 3 The Concept of Revelation from a Christian Perspective

As we have seen above, the Hebrew Scripture does not have a concept of revelation as such. There are various ways to express the procedure of divine communication in Hebrew and the meaning oscillates between unveiling, knowing, communicating or simply speaking, respectively hearing and answering. God himself speaks in the first person; humanity hears and is addressed in the second person. God acts and reveals himself or his message in diverse forms. That definitely distinguishes him from the silent idols of the gentiles. Divine revelation is an encounter with the godhead, direct and foundational for the eschatological and salvific relationship between the creator and the creature. God proclaims his glory, his rule over Israel and his provision for the days to come.

For Christianity, God's ultimate revelation occurs in Jesus Christ. The New Testament uses a quite similar vocabulary to the Hebrew Scriptures when talking about revelation, with the twist that Jesus is the incarnated word of God; all revelatory events of the past point to him as the fulfilment of the divine promises. With him, his words and acts, the Kingdom of Heaven is already established. He is the self-disclosure of God; knowledge about the Father is hence only possible through the Son. The help of the Holy Spirit secures this communication, even from Christ's leaving the world until the day of judgement. Thus, there is a line, stemming from the creation, extending over to the prophets and leading to Jesus Christ, the fulfilment, who with his resurrection raises humankind and the whole creation from the boundaries of death, moving them towards freedom in the eternal life of God.

From a historical point of view, antiquity saw the contention between Greek philosophy and Christian thought. This caused not only troubles between the different schools of thought, but also within Christianity itself, through the rise of heresies. All these intellectual endeavors finally reach a concept of revelation with God as the creator, redeemer and consummator of the world, and establish the possibility of living a Christian life in the light of revelation. By drawing a line from Philo to Justin Martyr and his famous *Dialogue with the Jew Trypho*, we see Christ becoming the Logos incarnate, which poses a threat to ancient philosophy with its sharp distinction between the material and the spiritual world. Furthermore, Christianity had to be aware of the dangers of, on the one side, including gnostic depictions of a creed degrading the flesh and, on the other, losing its connection with the Hebrew Bible. Revelation had to be assured, from the beginning until the end of the world that has to be redeemed, not superseded. Revelation grants the possibility of reuniting the created world, which is of divine origin, with the Holy Scriptures as an extension of the incarnation.

In the medieval period, theologians were mainly concerned with the harmonization of transcendent and supernatural revelation with human reason. For Anselm of Canterbury, finding God was the fulfilment of the human essence, the need and desire for it was but darkened by sin. The soul yearns for God, and performing the deeds and acts grounded in revelation means the establishment of this message in the created world. The orientation of the human being towards God is also a central teaching of Thomas Aquinas, who distinguished the mere immanent philosophy from its outdoing in theology. In a threefold picture, he developed a system of revelation before the law, under the law (which is Judaism), and finally its fulfilment under grace, which is Jesus Christ. Understanding these realities is itself a gift of grace, where natural reason cannot follow.

The rise of the Lutheran Reformation brought forth a new approach to revelation. The guiding idea was no longer reason, but justice. How can humanity be just and justified before God? Humanity has the Gospel as a sign of revelation, which changed the divine reality of the relation between humanity and God in a fundamental way; a person is able to fulfil what God wants him or her to do, because he or she stands in God's grace which is given by Jesus Christ. But he or she always fails to fulfil what God wants him or her to do. Faith is the redeeming factor; however, the Holy Spirit, not humanity, evokes faith. Scripture becomes anew the focus of knowledge about God's self-disclosure; it becomes central as the means of God's teaching about himself. The Council of Trent formulated a decisive answer, holding the church to be the bearer of tradition and successor of the apostles, and thus to have the authority of teaching and preserving the continuity of revelation.

Throughout the Age of Enlightenment, reason triumphed over supernatural revelation and its inbreeding authority. According to the teaching of "natural religion", reason is capable of recognizing revelation within immanent nature; divine revelation was, at the time, forced to be in accordance with reason. Revealed religion seemed to be inferior and history no longer the place to encounter divine manifestations of God's will. Revelation had to justify itself against reason. Of course, every movement keeps in itself its own backlash, and so it is not surprising that the theology of the 19th century, especially within German romanticism and idealism, sharply criticized the Enlightenment's cult of reason. Hegel and Schelling held revealed religion for the only true religion and brought history back into the idea of revelation. This formed the background of the lively debates on revelation from the second half of the 19th into the 20th century. With the First Vatican Council, Catholicism not only formulated a strong condemnation of modern "errors" and a confirmation of the church's authority, but also shaped a passage in between the extremes of rationalism, on the one side, and fideism on the other. According to Karl Rahner, who was a key thinker of the Second Vatican Council, every human being is capable of and longing for transcendence, a longing which is fulfilled in Jesus Christ. Protestantism, on the other hand, explored the relation between the Law and the Gospel, and the nature of revelation. Karl Barth strongly condemned the idea of natural religion and identified God with his revelation. Rudolf Bultmann "demythologized" the New Testament in order to underline its existential meaning, and Wolfhart Pannenberg identified Jesus' resurrection as the anticipation of the end of history and the ultimate self-revelation. Following an elaborated model developed by Eilert Herms, revelation consists of content, an author, a recipient and a particular situation that confronts the recipient in the totality of his or her embodied existence and requires a reaction.

# 4 The Concept of Revelation from an Islamic Perspective

In the Qur'ān, the Arabic terms *waḥī* and *tanzīl* are used to signify verbal revelation sent down from above. Their origin in the foundational text of Islam and their different interpretations throughout the history of Islamic thought depict revelation as a means of God's indirect communication with his creation. Revelation is thus seen as an invitation to, and not an imposition of, faith.

It is important to keep in mind that the Qur'ān was originally revealed as a recitation; its orality is fundamental for understanding its conception of revelation. The tension between the recited and the written text reflects a society in transition, and a translation of power to an elite of scholars mastering the written text. However, not only a tension between the spoken and the written word can be outlined in this context, but also the question arising as to whether all parts of the Qur'ān are of the same quality. The text as a whole is deemed to be of inimitable beauty, in a rich Arabic language. This linguistic beauty is seen as a stunning proof of the Qur'ān's divine provenance and the perfection of God's speech. No human being seemed to be able to imitate but one verse in such mastery as provided in the Qur'ān. Muḥammad is said to be unlettered, which should underline the miraculous nature of the perfect composition of the scripture. Even modern thinkers still see the uniqueness of the text as a proof of its divine nature.

Such a text must have had, at least according to several scholars, not just a divine origin, but also a primordial existence. Quite similar to the pre-existent Torah, the Qur'ān has a celestial archetype, the "Preserved Tablet". In a process of revelation, the content of this tablet was conveyed to the archangel Gabriel, who later revealed it to Muḥammad in gradual portions over a period of twenty-two years.

The Qur'ānic revelation is held to be a concluding offering in a long line of God's speaking to prophets, from Adam to Muḥammad. Therefore, this revelation is a sign of mercy, a message of both hope and fear; for the expected blessings of paradise as well as the sufferings of hell are all transmitted within its content. Revelation becomes, thus, a sign of both God's mercy and justice.

A broad discussion arose concerning the question of whether Prophet Muḥammad was sent to all humans or just to the believers. God's imposition of mercy upon himself and upon his apostle is clearly articulated in the Qur'ānic revelation and invites humanity to find hope in this aspect of divine self-disclosure. Thus, in a broader sense, revelation can be seen as a message of hope and guidance to all humanity, proclaimed by several prophets throughout history, who all are equal and not responsible for all the quarrels that occurred after their proclamations. Despite all human misinterpretations, the revealed Qur'ān is seen as a clear, guiding message, which nevertheless needs the use of reason and human understanding to teach the believers what is right and what is wrong, what is licit and what is illicit. Over all, the triumph of good over evil remains central in the message. Especially in times of despair, the Qur'ānic revelation assures the believers that things shall turn out well, be it in their earthly life or in the world to come. If humankind should forget, the revealed Qur'ān is a distinct and continuous reminder. Being a believer in God or not, a person has a natural sense, called *fiṭra*, which instinctively brings him or her to God and serves as a moral compass, because also this "natural sense" is given to him or her by God himself. The natural desire to worship God is, therefore, inbred in humankind; revelation, prophets and even the Qur'ān just remind the human being of his or her natural disposition towards his or her creator. The concept of the "*umma muqtaṣida*" (*balanced community*), which consists of non-Muslims and even Jews and Christians as "People of the book", implicates the question: Are "moderate and upright" persons, who are not Muslims, but are loyal and faithful believers, addressees of the Qur'ānic revelation? The discussion between inclusivists and exclusivists throughout history provides stunning evidence of a tradition of tolerance besides the storms of the centuries.

Summarizing all these approaches to revelation in Islamic thought, one can clearly recognize that revelation is conceived of as constant communication between the creator and the creation; it is both a gift and a task to bear. As God's invitation to his creatures, it is not a concept that leads to division, but to unity.

# 5 Common Features and Differences

On a basic level, revelation is a *one way* discourse between God and humanity; this fundamental assumption can be found in the three religions we encounter in this volume. By means of revelation, the creator, the transcendent God of Judaism, Christianity and Islam, communicates with his creatures and reveals to them his intention that is not visible in creation by itself.

It can be considered as a special feature shared by all three monotheistic religions that God's self-disclosure is a verbal one. God speaks to the human beings; he dictates words and enters the world as the "Word" or "Logos". In contrast to mere signs which can be interpreted in one way or another, by means of revelation through words God communicates with humanity in the same way as human beings communicate with each other, and thus grants them the ability to understand him rightly. A common language, on the basis of a shared rationality, is the fundament of successful verbal communication. Therefore, God deliberately chooses a clearly understandable form of self-communication as it is stated in the Qur'ān 43:3: "We have made it a Qur'ān in Arabic, that ye may be able to understand (and learn wisdom)."[1]

However, this verse indicates at once some problematic features of verbal revelation, which the adherents of the three religions have to deal with. Firstly, human languages are numerous. The belief of a religious community that God's revelation occurred in its language is usually associated with collective pride and complacency against other communities and languages. As far as revelation in Judaism is understood as a special word to the Israelites, it is obvious that God spoke to them in their language, which later became their holy language. Being a part of the Hellenistic Empire, the question arose whether or not the common language of the ancient world of that time, Greek, could be the adequate language of their respective revelation, like in Alexandria. This was also the understanding of the most important ancient Jewish Philosopher, Philo. But then the Christians had taken over that universal *lingua franca* for their universal message because their revelation was person-focused and not scripture-focused. Therefore, the Jews chose to write again only in Hebrew due to the specific nature of the revelation they received. A third way was taken by the Muslims: They elevated – up to the present day – their specific language, Arabic, the language of their religion in their area, to the universal language of their revelation and made all believers learn it.

Secondly, the revealed texts are not easy to understand even for those who are experts in the language in which the texts are revealed. Therefore, although it is *possible* to understand God's message, it is far from guaranteed that everybody is able to understand and even accept it. All three religions agree that it is God's will that human beings are free to listen to his message and to accept or reject it. But at the same time, all three religions include those who believe that no one can choose his or her religion by his or her own free will, because it is God himself who causes any person to believe or not. This is what the Jewish philosopher Emmanuel Levinas calls the pre-decision by God. Nevertheless, there is one important difference in the general self-understanding of these three religions. A born Jew is a Jew, independent of the fact whether he or she believes in the revelation. Even if he or she does not know anything about the revelation – like some of the post-Soviet Jews – he or she is considered and accepted as a Jew. This is normally not possible in Islam which requires the confession of the *Shahāda*, which articulates the belief in revelation, as an indispensable con-

1 The translation of Yusuf Ali.

dition to become a Muslim. Christianity requires the baptism of the person who believes in the revelation of Jesus as the Christ. However, there are quite different opinions – even within the same tradition – concerning the principles which should lead the reader of revealed scriptures to come to valid conclusions.

There is one more specific moment seen in Christianity which is not found in the other two religions, Judaism and Islam: As far as Jesus is seen as Christ and, consequently, God revealed himself in Jesus Christ, this revelation is not only a given word which can be accepted or not, but this revelation itself has worked and changed creation. The "Word" has done something. It has healed the sick, had impact on relations and society, and it has sacrificed itself. According to Christian understanding, the broken relationships were generally repaired by the redemptory work accomplished in the revelation of Jesus as the Christ, as the Son of God. In this sense, the revelation was not only "given", but as it is understood as salvation, it has transformed through Christ's existence and his achievements the fallen creation into a new creation which is *potentially* reconciled with God, even if it is *actually* not yet reconciled. This is the meaning of the words "it is ... and is not yet" in the parables given in the Gospels. For Judaism and Islam this kind of transformation is not necessary because, according to their theology, the creation has not fallen in an absolute sense; therefore, God did not need to change his relation to his creation by his self-revelation.

Through the Sinai revelation, God's relation to his people received a firm foundation in the covenant. Through the revelation of the Qurʾān, the eternal *umm al-kitāb* – the Original Heavenly Book, so to say – was given in a perfect form. However, the creation and God's relation to the creation was not changed from a fallen to a reconciled state. As far as a Jewish or Islamic understanding is mostly focused on revelation as "verbal word", it makes it difficult from that perspective to see in which way Christianity understands revelation as a person (who is the son of God and one person of the Divine Trinity), and to understand his salvific deeds, which totally changed the situation of humanity in the eyes of God.

At this point, a fundamental misunderstanding occurs sometimes among the three religions. This explains why it seems that the Gospel as "*evangelion*" (in Arabic: "*injīl*") is not understood in Islam as the story of Jesus and his deeds. In the Qurʾān, as well as in common Islamic understanding, the words spoken by Jesus are understood in the same way as the words of the other prophets in Judaism and Islam are understood.

In all three traditions, there is a tension between a more rigid and a more progressive pattern of revelation. On the one hand, there are in Judaism, Christianity and Islam central events that form the core of revelation: The Giving of the Torah on Mount Sinai, the incarnation of God's word in Jesus Christ and the revelation of the Qur'ān to the prophet Muḥammad. These initial events lie at the heart of each one of the three religions. All of them share the assumption that God revealed himself even before these events, and that the communication between him and humankind does not end with them. Although the divine message is completely incorporated in this initial revelation, the process of revelation continues, as there is need to receive the revelation, preserve it and hand it down to the following generations. A striking image of this inseparable unity of the message and the process of apprehension, interpretation and delivering the message to posterity is the idea of the double revelation of both a written Torah and a verbal Torah in Judaism. In Christianity, it is the sending of the Holy Spirit, which makes sure that the original message is preserved in the Scriptures of the New Testament, in the souls of the believers and, from a Catholic and an Orthodox point of view, also in the church and her doctrines. In Islam, the mentioned unity can be found in an elaborated system of different methods and practices, which work like checks and balances to make sure that the Qur'ān can be understood properly if one seeks to discover its whole message.

Although each one of the three religions focuses differently on the written text, it is obvious that in none of these three sometimes so-called "religions of the book" is revelation all about the text. What is striking in Christianity – where the core of revelation lies in the incarnation, that is, in a human person and not a text – is also important with respect to the concept of revelation in Judaism and Islam. Although revelation in both of them is verbal (written and oral), it is not exhausted in the text. It is God's self-disclosure and ongoing process of communication to human beings, based on a shared Logos.

The idea of a common Logos beyond the mere text forms the common ground on which interfaith dialogue might be established. Revelation forms a constitutive moment in the act of accepting a religion in multitudinous and variant shapes and ways. Focusing on revelation as it is conceived of in all three traditions, one can find some crucial overlapping features and continuities. The beginning of the Gospel of John where Jesus is introduced as God's word is clearly related to the beginning of the creation account in the Pentateuch. The Ten Words or Commandments given on Mount Sinai are not denied or abrogated by Christianity; according to Matthew 5:12, Jesus came to fulfil and not to destroy the Law. In a similar way, a number of Qur'ānic verses underline the shared monotheism between Jews, Christians and Muslims, whereby the oneness of God defines the red line that should not be crossed, lest one is to become a non-believer. Here, of course, the question about the treatment of the Christian Trinity arises and it has been dealt with quite differently among Muslim scholars. Nevertheless, modern authors underline a common ground for an interfaith dialogue between Jews, Muslims and Christians.

In this sense, the concept of revelation can endorse interreligious understanding. For a believer, the experience and recognition of revelation can constitute a positive attitude towards the other's revelation, since we know that we are not the authors, but the recipients of the truth. The foundation of being able to tolerate and recognize the recipient of a different faith tradition is not relativism and does not mean giving up one's own belief; on the contrary it is faith itself. To speak with Abraham Heschel: "The first and most important *prerequisite of interfaith is faith.*"[2]

Nonetheless, it cannot be ignored that the concept of revelation in Judaism, Christianity and Islam has some crucial, different features with respect to the medium, the addressees, duration, and so on. Finally, yet importantly, one cannot speak about revelation without considering the content of revelation, which can hardly be named the same. Even the most central elements of revelation in Judaism, Christianity and Islam – like the Giving of the Torah to Moses, the idea of God's incarnation in Jesus Christ or the idea that the prophet Muḥammad received the Qur'ān by reciting the words of Gabriel – cannot be proven from outside or demonstrated by reasonable thinking. Particularly in the Age of Enlightenment, these elements were seen to be opposed to reason and branded to be mere superstition. Even today, we can see efforts to expel these elements and transform revelation-based religions merely to a mind-set based on the common ground of reason.

---

**2** Heschel, Abraham Joshua, "No Religion is an Island," *Union Seminary Quarterly Review*, 21, no. 2 (1966), 117–134, (123).

# List of Contributors

**Asma Afsaruddin** is Professor of Near Eastern Languages and Cultures in the Hamilton Lugar School of Global and International Studies at Indiana University, Bloomington. She received her doctorate in Arabic and Islamic Studies from Johns Hopkins University in Baltimore, Maryland. She is the author and editor of eight books, including *Jihad. What Everyone Needs to Know*, forthcoming; the award-winning *Striving in the Path of God. Jihad and Martyrdom in Islamic Thought*, 2013, which is being translated into Bahasa Indonesian; and *The First Muslims. History and Memory*, 2008, which has been translated into Turkish and Bahasa Malay. Her fields of specialization include pre-modern and modern Islamic religious and political thought, Qur'ān and ḥadīth, and Islamic intellectual history.

**Frederek Musall** studied Jewish Studies, Islamic Studies, Semitic Philology, and Comparative Study of Religion in Heidelberg and Jerusalem. In 2005 he completed his interdisciplinary Ph.D. thesis on the medieval Jewish thinkers Moses Maimonides and Hasday Crescas. Afterwards he taught at the universities of Basel, Graz and Halle-Wittenberg.
Since 2009 he is chair for Jewish Philosophy and Intellectual History at the Heidelberg Center for Jewish Studies and program director of the international M.A. program "Jewish Civilizations" in cooperation with Paideia – The European Institute for Jewish Studies in Stockholm. He is currently Interim Rector of the Heidelberg Center for Jewish Studies.
His research interests are Jewish philosophical, theological and mystical thought (particularly in relation to Islamic-Arabic intellectual traditions); political thought and traditions in Judaism; history of Jews in the Muslim world; Sefardic history; Jewish identity; Jewish pop-culture; Visual Culture Studies; sociology of knowledge; methodology in Jewish Studies.

**Christoph Schwöbel** is Professor of Systematic Theology at The School of Divinity at University of St Andrews in Scotland, UK. He studied theology and philosophy at the Kirchliche Hochschule Bethel and the University of Marburg. He received his Dr. theol. in 1978 and completed his habilitation in 1990.
1986 Lecturer in Systematic Theology and Director of the Research Institute in Systematic Theology, King's College London; 1993 Chair in Systematic Theology, University of Kiel; 1999 Chair in Dogmatics and Director of the Institute for Ecumenical Studies, University of Heidelberg; 2004 Chair in Systematic Theology and Philosophy of Religion, Director of the Institute for Hermeneutic and Inter-Cultural Dialogue, University of Tübingen. Since 2018 he holds the Chair in Divinity (est. 1643) at The School of Divinity at University of St Andrews, Scotland, UK
Publications: *God, Action and Revelation*, 1992; *Gott in Beziehung*, 2003; *Christlicher Glaube im Pluralismus*, 2004; *Gott im Gespräch*, 2011.

**Bertram Schmitz** is Professor for Comparative Religion at Friedrich Schiller University of Jena. His theological doctorate (1990) was on Paul Tillich and Karl Jaspers, his seccond Ph.D. (1994) on the term of religion in a multicultural context, the habilitation (2003) on the process of transformation of the israelitic tempel ritual of Yom Kippur into the Christian celebration of eucharist. His further publications are on the relation of Judaism, Christianity and

Islam, Paul and the Qurʾān and an interreligious analysis of the second sura of the Qurʾān. His recent interest is on religion und art, and in human body in religion and art.

**Georges Tamer** holds the Chair of Oriental Philology and Islamic Studies and is founding director of the Research Unit "Key Concept in Interreligious Discourses" and speaker of the Centre for Euro-Oriental Studies at the Friedrich-Alexander-University of Erlangen-Nuremberg. He received his Ph.D. in Philosophy from the Free University Berlin in 2000 and completed his habilitation in Islamic Studies in Erlangen in 2007. His research focuses on QurÞānic hermeneutics, philosophy in the Islamic world, Arabic literature and interreligious discourses. His Publications include: *Zeit und Gott. Hellenistische Zeitvorstellungen in der altarabischen Dichtung und im Koran*, 2008, and the edited volumes *Islam and Rationality. The Impact of al-Ghazālī*, 2015 and *Hermeneutical Crossroads. Understanding Scripture in Judaism, Christianity and Islam in the Pre-Modern Orient*, 2017.

**Katja Thörner** is research assistant in the Research Unit "Key Concept in Interreligious Discourses" at the Friedrich-Alexander-University of Erlangen-Nuremberg. She studied Philosophy and German Literature in Trier, Würzburg and Berlin and received her Ph.D. in Philosophy at the Munich School of Philosophy in 2010. She is author of *William James' Konzept eines vernünftigen Glaubens auf der Basis religiöser Erfahrung*, 2011 and published with Martin Turner, *Religion, Konfessionslosigkeit und Atheismus*, 2016 and in collaboration with Trutz Rendtorff, *Ernst Troeltsch: Schriften zur Religionswissenschaft und Ethik (1903–1912)*, 2014. Her research focuses on the philosophy of religion, theories of interreligious dialogue and comparative studies of concepts of the hereafter in Islam and Christianity.

# Index of Persons



https://doi.org/10.1515/9783110476057-007

# Index of Subjects



https://doi.org/10.1515/9783110476057-008